Urban Life and Urban Landscape Series
Zane L. Miller and Henry D. Shapiro, General Editors

SUBURB

❧ in the City

Chestnut Hill, Philadelphia, 1850–1990

David R. Contosta

OHIO STATE UNIVERSITY PRESS

Columbus

Published with the support of the Chestnut Hill Historical Society.

Library of Congress Cataloging-in-Publication Data
Contosta, David R.
    Suburb in the city : Chestnut Hill, Philadelphia, 1850–1990 /
David R. Contosta.
        p.   cm. — (Urban life and urban landscape series)
    Includes bibliographical references and index.
    ISBN 0–8142–0580–1 (alk. paper). — ISBN 0–8142–0581–X (pbk. :
alk. paper)
    1. Chestnut Hill (Philadelphia, Pa.) — History.   2. Philadelphia
(Pa.) — History.   I. Title.   II. Series.
F158.68.C45C66   1992
974.8'11 — dc20   92–9820
                                                                          CIP

The paper in this book meets the guidelines for permanence and durability of the
Committee on Production Guidelines for Book Longevity of the Council on Library
Resources.

9   8   7   6   5   4

For Mary and Mary

Contents

Illustrations

Maps

Acknowledgments

I am indebted to the dozens of individuals who granted me interviews over a period of some five years. These interviewees, several of whom have since died, ranged in age from their early fifties to their late nineties, the oldest subject having been born in January 1888. These men and women also came from a variety of backgrounds and represented every part of the community. Some of the interviews were lengthy, tape-recorded exchanges, undertaken as part of the Chestnut Hill Historical Society's oral history project; others were much briefer and conducted by telephone. I list all those who gave interviews in alphabetical order:

Sr. Consuelo Maria (Elizabeth T.) Aherne, S.S.J., E. Digby Baltzell, James Bond, Mary Wickham Porcher Bond, Alfred Clay Borie, Emily Revinus Bregy, Sr. Margaret Rose (Margaret Mary) Brown, S.S.J., The Rev. John F. Casey, O.S.A., Audry K. Chancellor, Thomas Williams Clark, Edward Biddle Clay, Mary Joe Concannon, Dorothy M. Corn, Matilda Borda Cross, Margaret Harris Dale, Sr. Mary Julia (Mary Theresa) Daly, S.S.J., Sara Dick, Henry Disston II, Mary Clay Disston, Walter T. Dwyer, Jr., William L. Dwyer, Anna M. Earle, Anthony Filippi, William "Bill" Foulk, William G. Foulke, Louisa L. W. Foulke, Cornelia Dodge Fraley, Joseph Galante, Edmund B. Gilchrist, Jr., William E. Gillies, Bertha Smythe Graham, Shirley Hanson, John McArthur Harris, Jr., Josephine Wayne Hatfield, George L. "Ted" Helmetag, Quita Woodward Horan, Nancy Hubby, Oscar E. Jansson, Morton

Jenks, Marie Reinhart Jones, Dudley J. King, James N. Kise, Sallie
Smith Kise, Margaret Why Kimes, Charles H. Landreth, Margaret
Jane Lawless, John Brock "Jack" Lear, W. Thacher Longstreth,
Alma Lorenzon, John Lukacs, Louise S. Magarity, Anna Nicoletti
Mastroni, John L. McClenehan, Joseph M. McLaughlin, Russell L.
Medinger, Lorraine Lukens Minott, Helen Moak, Daniel Pierson
Nelson, The Rev. Scott T. O'Brien, Hank O'Donnell, Henry T.
O'Donnell, Jane Jordan O'Neill, Frederick Peck, Georgia Perkins,
G. Holmes Perkins, Eleanor E. Potter, Philip Price, Sr., Mary
"Polly" Lear Randall, Barbara Clayton Rex, Maria Madeleine Ro-
mano, Sante Romano, Ruth R. Russell, Ernesto D. Santa Maria, Jo-
sephine Swope Santa Maria, Eli Schmidt, Frederick Schnaible, Mary
Jane Shelly, Eleanor Houston Smith, Christine Smith, Hugh Smith,
Elizabeth F. Spangler, Virginia Wetherill Stout, Joseph Penning-
ton Straus, Josephine Vecchione, Francis Vecchione, Michael Von
Moschzisker, Elizabeth Colt Walker, Henry Wells, Lloyd P. Wells,
Elizabeth West, Helen Howe West, Vivian White, Edwin Wolf, 2nd,
Edward F. R. Wood, Charles Woodward, Elizabeth Gadsden Wood-
ward, Stanley Woodward, Sr.

Several individuals and institutions provided photographs and
other illustrations for the book. These are Architectural Archives of
the University of Pennsylvania, Mary Wickham Porcher Bond,
Chestnut Hill College Archives, Chestnut Hill Community Center,
Chestnut Hill Historical Society, *Chestnut Hill Local,* Environmental
Research Group, Francis James Dallett, Germantown Historical So-
ciety, Print Department of the Library Company of Philadelphia,
Photo-Journalism Collection of the Temple University Library, the
Pennsylvania Genealogical Society, and St. Martin-in-the-Fields
Church.

A number of individuals assisted me with my research. Among
these are Lizabeth M. Holloway, archivist and librarian, and James
M. Duffin, assistant librarian, of the Germantown Historical Society;
Kathryn G. Shaifer, executive director of the Chestnut Hill Historical
Society; Marie Jones, editor, and Katie Worrall, assistant editor, of
the *Chestnut Hill Local*; Kenneth Finkel and Susan Oyama of the Print
Department of the Library Company of Philadelphia; Helen Hayes,
director of the Chestnut Hill College Library; Sr. Grace Margaret,

S.S.J., archivist of Chestnut Hill College; Francis James Dallett, historian and genealogist; Julia Converse, director of the Architectural Archives of the University of Pennsylvania; Mark Frazier Lloyd, director of the University of Pennsylvania Archives; the staff of the Urban Archives of Temple University; the staff of the (Hagley) Elutherian Mills Library; the staff of the Philadelphia Free Library; Mary "Liz" Lewis, manager of the Chestnut Hill Community Center; and Walter Moleski, executive director of Environmental Research Group. I especially want to thank the Germantown Historical Society for allowing me to use its incomparable collection on Chestnut Hill. Without these materials this study would have been difficult if not impossible to undertake. I must also thank Joseph Pennington Straus, president emeritus of the Chestnut Hill Historical Society; and Peter M. Saylor, current president of the Chestnut Hill Historical Society, for their support and encouragement.

Historian and friend John Lukacs read the entire manuscript and made a number of helpful suggestions. Francis James Dallett also read the manuscript and provided welcome criticisms. Mary Corbin Sies of the University of Maryland, who is a suburban historian and who knows a great deal about Chestnut Hill through her own researches, was extraordinarily helpful to me during the final revisions of the manuscript. The co-editors of this series, Zane Miller and Henry D. Shapiro, were excellent critics whose suggestions complemented each other and strengthened the manuscript in many ways. Alex Holzman, assistant director at the Ohio State University Press, has been an inspiring editor from beginning to end. I also wish to thank assistant editor Lynne M. Bonenberger and the copyeditor, Anita Samen.

The *Pennsylvania Magazine of History and Biography* granted permission to use segments from my article "Suburban Quasi-Government in Chestnut Hill, Philadelphia," which appeared in the issue of July 1992. In the process of publishing this article, *Pennsylvania Magazine* editor Randall Miller assisted in my understanding of community organizations in Chestnut Hill, as well as elsewhere in the United States.

Once again I want to thank my wife, Mary, for her loving companionship and support.

INTRODUCTION

In 1854 the city and county of Philadelphia were merged by an act of the state legislature. With a stroke of the pen the old city of Philadelphia, which had occupied only two square miles of land between the Delaware and Schuykill rivers, became a giant of some 129 square miles. It was the largest annexation to date in the United States, and it ensured that Philadelphia would remain one of the most important cities in North America for years to come. In the process of this massive consolidation, dozens of villages and other small settlements were swept into the City of Brotherly Love.

On the edge of this newly consolidated city, some ten miles northwest of downtown, lay the village of Chestnut Hill. For a century or more it had served the needs of surrounding farms and mills, as well as of travelers and teamsters passing through on their way to the city below. Because Chestnut Hill lay at one of the highest points in Philadelphia County (and then in the consolidated city), it had also attracted summer people for several decades, prosperous men and women who wanted to escape the sultry heat of Philadelphia streets. This summer trade received a boost with the arrival of train service to Germantown, some five miles to the southeast, in 1832. The train also brought a few suburban commuters to Chestnut Hill, who took advantage of a stagecoach line and later of an omnibus service to the railroad depot in Germantown. Then in 1854, the same year as the city/county consolidation, Chestnut Hill received its own rail link to downtown Philadelphia.

1

With the railroad came a burst of suburban development in Chestnut Hill. Within twenty years Victorian villas had arisen on the slopes around the railroad station in an area now known as North Chestnut Hill. In 1884 an immensely wealthy entrepreneur named Henry Howard Houston brought a second commuter line into the west side of the Hill. This was a spur of the Pennsylvania Railroad, around which Houston created a planned suburb called Wissahickon Heights, in reference to the adjacent Wissahickon Creek. In the early twentieth century his son-in-law George Woodward extended this suburban development and changed its name to St. Martin's, after St. Martin-in-the-Fields Episcopal Church, which Houston had built in 1889.

The emergence of these commuter suburbs within Chestnut Hill did not obliterate the earlier village. Rather, the new suburbanites coexisted with local craftsmen and shopkeepers, whose numbers were actually augmented by new arrivals in their trades, who were intent on making a living by serving the Hill's prosperous suburban residents. The suburbanites also brought numerous domestic servants with them, contributing yet another element to the population. Chestnut Hill thus remained a heterogeneous community made up of distinct neighborhoods that overlapped or intersected at certain points.

However varied its population may have been, Chestnut Hill has been essentially suburban in nature for much of its existence. Even before the city/county consolidation in the middle of the nineteenth century, the community's well-being had depended upon its proximity to Philadelphia. Commuters in later generations were likewise attracted by the Hill's convenient access by rail to jobs downtown. In this respect, the question of whether Chestnut Hill was legally a part of the city was not of controlling importance, for the Hill was essentially suburban—both before and after the consolidation. As such, Chestnut Hill displayed the most salient characteristics of the American suburb: a low density of housing and population combined with an economic dependence upon the city.

Yet as a suburb within the city limits, Chestnut Hill and other communities like it, such as Germantown and West Philadelphia, faced conditions that politically independent suburbs outside the city have escaped. Above all, Chestnut Hill has not been able to exercise official government at the local level to provide utilities, build and maintain public works (including schools), and control the development of real estate. Despite this impediment, Chestnut Hill has remained a successful suburb in the city for nearly a century and a half.

There are several factors, both natural and human, that account for Chestnut Hill's survival as a suburban community. One of these is its favored location. Poised on the edge of the city and located a full ten miles from downtown, the Hill was insulated from development on its borders for several generations. It was not until the early twentieth century that substantial building took place directly to the south, in the Mount Airy section of Philadelphia, and it was not until after World War II that land beyond the city limits in Montgomery County was transformed into automobile suburbs for the baby-boom generation.

Adding to Chestnut Hill's isolation is the deep Wissahickon gorge, which flows along its west side, providing a physical as well as visual boundary between the Hill and the Roxborough section of Philadelphia to the west. Over the years residents of Chestnut Hill have worked to preserve this natural divide through supporting its acquisition by Philadelphia's Fairmount Park system, donating parcels of land to the park, blocking automobile traffic in the valley, and opposing development projects along its edges.

Chestnut Hill's physical elevation has likewise reinforced a feeling of separation from the rest of the city. From their homes on the heights, residents could survey the city below or gaze out on the rolling hills to the north and west in Montgomery County.

A sense of the past has also helped to maintain a feeling of separation, as residents remember the old village in various ways. Several dozen eighteenth-century structures, constructed of stone in an unsophisticated vernacular style, survive as solid reminders of the Hill's village past. A campaign in the 1950s to restore the commercial district along colonial lines, however inaccurate and misconceived, only reinforced these memories. Associations with the American Revolution, although much romanticized, heightened the sense of historical identity: both American and British forces had marched back and forth through Chestnut Hill just before and during the British occupation of Philadelphia. Since its founding in 1967, the Chestnut Hill Historical Society also has raised an awareness of local history through campaigns to save and restore older buildings and a variety of other projects.

Chestnut Hill's historical society is only one of many civic organizations that local residents have created to deal with being a suburb in the city. In addition to exerting pressure on city authorities to deliver more and better services, these organizations have raised their own funds and have launched their own programs to improve life in Chestnut Hill. Residents also have used these organizations to monitor land use, direct landscaping projects, and curb commercial development.

This active civic life originated during the preconsolidation period, i.e., before 1854, when local residents banded together to create churches, schools, cemeteries, and fire companies. During the late nineteenth and early twentieth centuries, two improvement associations provided direction for the Hill. After World War II, the Chestnut Hill Community Association emerged as the chief instrument of civic life. Out of this association has come a system of unofficial government that Chestnut Hill residents proudly refer to as their quasi government.

Although prosperous residents of the Hill have always been in the minority, comprising no more than 40 percent of the population at any time, they have dominated the community's civic life. These residents have used their managerial skills, as well as their social and political connections throughout the city, state, and nation, to obtain favors and appropriations from governmental authorities. They have employed these same connections and skills to found and lead Chestnut Hill's civic organizations. This abundance of talent also has enabled residents to persist in their civic efforts; despite flagging energies at various periods, Chestnut Hill's community organizations have lasted longer and accomplished far more than their counterparts in other sections of Philadelphia. Although these civic organizations have sometimes worked for the good of the entire city, most of their efforts have focused more narrowly on maintaining the quality of life in Chestnut Hill, as defined by its most prosperous inhabitants.

Although they had their roots in the late nineteenth century, the Hill's civic organizations have always reflected many characteristics of the Progressive Era. Like the progressive reformers in the early twentieth century, they have emphasized nonpartisanship, expert leadership, and essentially private solutions to local problems. The persistence of these civic groups provides an intriguing glimpse into the survival of progressive ideas well after the Progressive Era supposedly ended with the American entrance into World War I. It also lends strength to the argument that most progressive reformers were members of the middle and upper classes who often were more interested in promoting their own welfare than in launching sweeping reforms throughout American society.

However narrow in focus their community organizations have been, Chestnut Hill residents also have identified themselves with the city at large. Only in the city could they earn incomes that allowed commutation back and forth from spacious suburban homes in Chestnut Hill. Only in the city could they visit art galleries, attend the opera and symphony orchestra, and sit on the boards of prestigious cultural and philanthropic societies. Chestnut Hill residents wanted to enjoy the best of both worlds: the riches of the city, and the peaceful, semirural surroundings of the suburb. Thus, like most suburbanites until recent decades, they maintained a dual identity — one urban and the other suburban. It was a selective identity, however, which sought the wealth and culture of the city but wanted to escape the worst of its squalor and crime through the evening train ride back to Chestnut Hill.

Complicating this dual identity have been internal divisions on the Hill itself. In their drive for attractive homes, creature comforts, and social ease, Chestnut Hill's more prosperous suburbanites have created a world of their own. By living in North Chestnut Hill or the West Side, and by establishing a series of exclusive associations, they have had little or no social contact with the shopkeepers, craftsmen, and other members of the local working class, who traditionally have lived in the central and eastern sections of the community. At the same time, the local working class has been divided by religious and ethnic differences that persist even as the twentieth century comes to a close.

Until World War II these dualities and divisions created few difficulties for prosperous suburban residents of Chestnut Hill. So long as Philadelphia flourished economically, and so long as Chestnut Hill itself was surrounded by other attractive suburbs or undeveloped lands, the two worlds of city and suburb could coexist without undue effort or thought. But by the 1950s, the newer automobile suburbs to the north and east of Chestnut Hill, with their convenient shopping centers, began to challenge the Hill's commercial district. At the same time, the proliferation of automobiles had ended Hillers' dependence upon the commuter train, which had one main destination — the railroad station downtown. With automobiles, Chestnut Hill residents could work and shop just as easily outside city boundaries as within them.

Meanwhile, Mount Airy and Germantown to the south began to experience serious decline, with decaying properties, rising crime rates, and increasing racial tensions. Despairing over such conditions, some Chestnut Hillers proposed to secede from the city altogether. Although this movement failed, civic organizations in Chestnut Hill had to work harder than ever to fend off these threats, both real and imagined. Complicating this task were the social divisions within Chestnut Hill itself, which mitigated community consensus and made quasi government more difficult.

A study of how Chestnut Hill has evolved as a suburb in the city should help to illuminate the long and often troubled relationships between American cities and their suburbs. It is important to remember, however, that attitudes toward suburbs have changed over the decades. Commentators on the American family during the middle of the nineteenth century, for example, saw the suburb as an ideal site for a proper Christian home, removed from the ugliness and immorality of urban life. By the end of the century, some students of the city believed that trolleys and railroads would allow nearly all urban residents to live in suburban communities — however humble — and thus alleviate the overcrowding and other dangers of large cities. In the early twentieth century, some reformers refined this concept by talking about an "organic city," where a variety of neighborhoods, including suburbs, each played a distinct but healthy role in the city's life. Only in the post–World War II period, when older cities began to lose population and to decay in various ways, did large numbers of opinion makers begin to castigate suburbanites and blame a multitude of urban ills on the suburbs. It is thus essential not to judge the early suburbanization of Chestnut Hill entirely from the perspectives of later generations.

With such reservations in mind, much can be learned from studying Chestnut Hill. Because it has existed as a suburban community inside municipal limits, its relationship to the city has been even more revealing than that of suburbs outside the city, which have had far more freedom to ignore their urban neighbors. Yet like Chestnut Hill in recent decades, these more independent suburbs are slowly learning that their welfare depends upon the health of the entire region, including its urban core.

The author hopes that this study will appeal to enlightened general readers in both cities and suburbs, who are struggling to understand how their communities have evolved and where they might be headed. At the same time, the author has tried to address the growing number of urban and suburban historians who, like men and women outside the profession, seek answers to one of the greatest problems of American life — the problem of cities and suburbs. For as the twentieth century comes to an end, approximately 80 percent of Americans live in urban areas, and about half of these dwell in suburbs of one kind or another. To understand the country's cities and suburbs is to understand the essence of American life.

1

BEFORE SUBURBIA

The Gateway Village

The completion of Chestnut Hill's first railroad in 1854 marked its beginnings as a flourishing commuter suburb in Philadelphia. But for decades before, Chestnut Hill had been molded by a welter of forces and events that would affect its suburban development. It was during this early period that Chestnut Hill developed a community of economic interests, that its first churches and schools were erected, that its two main streets were laid out, that it forged a tradition of local associations, and that its village identity emerged. The memories of this early period, before Chestnut Hill's annexation by the city in the mid-nineteenth century, helped to give residents a sense of autonomy within the larger municipality. During its decades as a gateway village, Chestnut Hill had formed important economic bonds with Philadelphia. By the time that annexation took place, Chestnut Hill had already developed a sense of local identity that mitigated its growing dependence on the city below.

Yet before any of these forces emerged, there was the land and its abundant resources. A range of forested hills passed through the future site of Chestnut Hill, reaching a peak near the spot where two Indian trails and later two highways would converge to form a fork in the road. Not far beneath the soil was layer upon layer of stone, a sparkling gray, blue, and brown mica-schist that would prove an excellent building material and provide jobs to masons and quarriers. Below these slopes to the north and east, there were huge beds of limestone that over the years would yield lime for the soil, mortar for building houses and barns, and the impetus for laying out several roads that made their way up from the pits and lime kilns into Chestnut Hill. In the valleys surrounding the hill, there were thousands of acres of rich soil, waiting only for the axe and plow in order to grow an abundance of fruits and grains.

It is impossible to say exactly when a portion of this landscape became the village of Chestnut Hill. In 1683 the land formed part of the 5,700 acres that William Penn sold to two German/Dutch interests, the Frankfurt Company and the Crefeld purchasers, which both engaged Francis Daniel Pastorius as their agent. The 5,700-acre tract was named German Township because of the predominance of German-speaking residents during the first decades.

The settlers divided the land into four segments: Germantown proper, in the southernmost portion, and three other villages northwest of Germantown (i.e., the township contained the village of Germantown and the three other settlements). Moving from south to north, these outlying settlements were Kriesheim (later spelled Cresheim), Sommerhausen, and Crefeld. Kriesheim, the original home of an early contingent of settlers, eventually became the neighborhood of Mount Airy. Sommerhausen and Crefeld, named, respectively, for the birthplace of Pastorius and the hometown of the first group of immigrants, combined to become Chestnut Hill. Sommerhausen extended from the present Mermaid Lane to Chestnut Hill Avenue, and Crefeld from there to the present city limits at Northwestern Avenue.[1]

Because the modern boundary of Philadelphia corresponds with the northern limits of Crefeld, there has been little dispute about the upper border of Chestnut Hill. For many years the southern boundary of Sommerhausen (at Mermaid Lane) was considered to be the lower limit of Chestnut Hill, but the creation of park land a little further south along Cresheim Creek has led many twentieth-century residents to view the creek as Chestnut Hill's southern extremity. During the early nineteenth century some residents even considered Allen's Lane, several blocks south of the creek in the present Mount Airy, as their lower boundary. (Mount Airy would develop as a fashionable railroad suburb much like Chestnut Hill, with its western portion containing large, architect-designed houses similar to those on Chestnut Hill's West Side, and its eastern segment comprising smaller dwellings, much like Chestnut Hill's East Side.) But in the 1980s, when the Chestnut Hill Historical Society successfully petitioned to have the entire community designated as a historic district, it adopted the Cresheim Creek border. It seems likely that this division will be accepted into the foreseeable future, in part for convenience and in part because of perceived urban decay in Mount Airy.[2]

A logical eastern boundary for Chestnut Hill is Stenton Avenue, which separates Philadelphia from Springfield Township in Montgomery County. Lying directly across this line is the community of Wyndmoor (formerly Springfield Village), whose demographic contours are similar to Chestnut Hill's. Until the mid-twentieth century, inhabitants of Wyndmoor frequently listed their addresses as Chestnut Hill, and even now Wyndmoor residents have Philadelphia post office addresses, sharing Chestnut Hill's 19118 zip code. Yet for the purposes of this study, the author will follow the decision of the Chestnut Hill Historical Society in accepting Stenton Avenue as the community's eastern limit.[3] By contrast, there has been little problem over the decades in regarding the rocky Wissahickon gorge as the Hill's western border. Within these somewhat irregular boundaries, Chestnut Hill occupies an area of 2,200 acres — or 3.4 square miles.

It is unclear just when and why the name Chestnut Hill replaced the earlier Sommerhausen and Crefeld. The earliest written mention

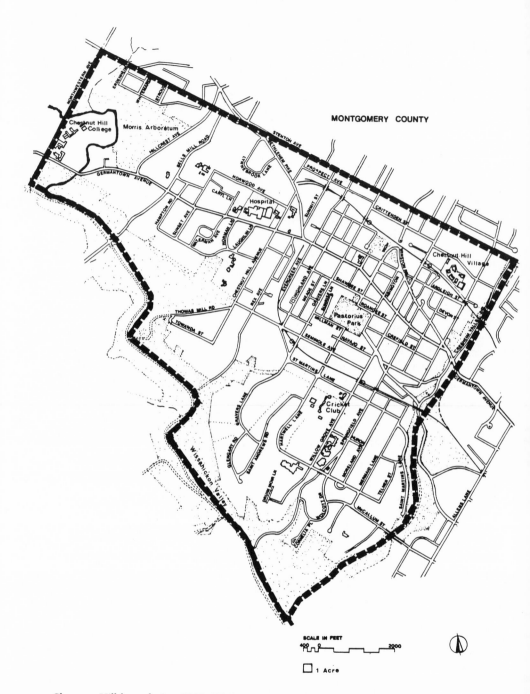

Chestnut Hill boundaries, 1990. ERG.

of the name occurs in a deed from 1711, but it could have been in use for some years before that date. "Chestnut" may refer to an abundance of chestnut trees in the vicinity, but because there were no more of them there than elsewhere in the region, such an explanation remains conjectural. The word "hill," on the other hand, was obvious and appropriate: The land occupied by Chestnut Hill rises steeply from 294 feet above sea level at its southern boundaries around Mermaid Lane to 446 feet at Summit Street, and then descends to 152 feet on its northern limits at Northwestern Avenue.[4]

It is equally difficult to determine just when Chestnut Hill emerged as a settlement. Because Germantown's leaders forbade residents to build on outlying properties before they had erected structures along the main road in Germantown itself, very few people lived in Chestnut Hill during the first two or three generations.[5] In 1710, for example, Quakers to the north in Plymouth Meeting complained about having to travel through "the wilds of [upper] Germantown" on their way to Philadelphia.[6] Twenty years later there were only two dozen landowners and renters in all of Chestnut Hill. Understandably, it was often known as the "back part" of Germantown. Not until the 1740s and 1750s did Chestnut Hill begin to grow appreciably, benefiting from the heavy immigration into Pennsylvania during the middle of the eighteenth century, and from the growth of German Township as a whole. By 1800 the population of Chestnut Hill had reached about 600, and by 1850 it had risen to around 1,000.[7]

Physically, early Chestnut Hill might be described as a strip village, with its houses, shops, and stores strung out along the main road (later Germantown Avenue), no real cross streets, and few structures built beyond the central thoroughfare. This same pattern existed throughout German Township (which continued to comprise the village of Germantown, Chestnut Hill, and several other small settlements). This arrangement of plots arose from a decision by Germantown founder Francis Daniel Pastorius to divide the land into long strips, with a minimum frontage of 125 feet, that ran back in either direction from the main road. Larger parcels lying beyond these long, narrow lots were also assigned to the first settlers. This arrangement, so familiar in Pastorius's native Germany, allowed each

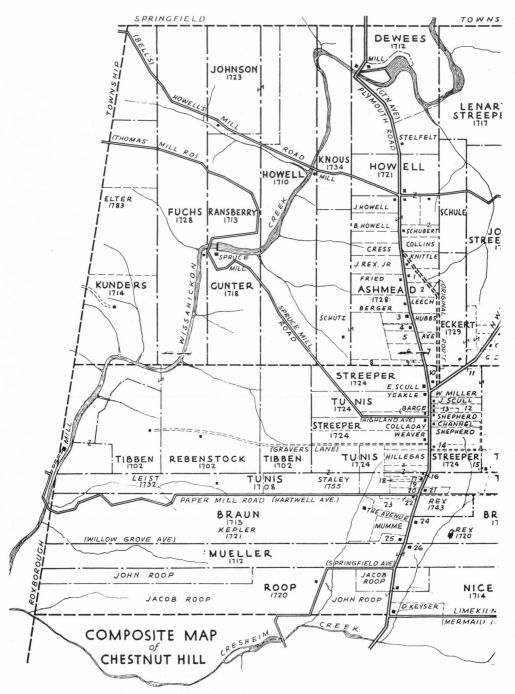

Landholdings in Chestnut Hill, colonial period. Note the narrow strips running back in both directions from the main road (Germantown Ave.). Roach, "Back Part of Germantown."

8031 Germantown Ave. Erected in 1762 and somewhat altered over the years, this structure gives an idea of the size and scale of buildings along Germantown Ave. in the latter half of the eighteenth century. The edifice originally housed Abraham Rex's "great store." CHHS.

landowner to build a house on the main road. Some of these were farmhouses, but from the beginning merchants and craftsmen erected shops and dwellings along the thoroughfare. Although they made their livings from handicrafts, they and their families typically used the large lots behind their dwellings to plant vegetable gardens, to cultivate fruit trees, and even to raise a few pigs, cows, or chickens.[8]

By the early nineteenth century one- and two-story stone or wooden structures lined both sides of Chestnut Hill's main street. These were simple in design, executed in the plain vernacular style of the day, with unadorned facades and small-paned sash windows

Germantown Ave. as it crossed the Cresheim Creek bridge in 1884. Even at this date, Chestnut Hill's main street was often a muddy and deeply rutted road. The old Mermaid Hotel can be seen at right center. Photo by George Bacon Wood. LCP.

punctuating both the first and second stories. Most of them were built with pent roofs, shingled eaves that hung down over the first story in order to throw rain water away from the walls and foundations.

The main road itself was an expanse of mud or ice during much of the year, becoming a long carpet of dust in the warmer months. In all seasons its surface was deeply rutted and covered with bone-jarring potholes. Despite its deplorable condition, this road was an economic lifeline for Chestnut Hill, Germantown, and the other settlements along its route. Originally it had been an Indian trail that followed the contours of the land. European settlers widened it to make a narrow cart road. Later it became a wagon route and was known for years as the Plymouth Road, after its northern terminus at the Quaker settlement in Plymouth Meeting. In 1801 a private turnpike company obtained a charter to extend the road further north and west to Perkiomen, and still later to Reading, Pennsylvania. Depending on its destination, residents knew it as either the Perkiomen

Toll gate on the Bethlehem Turnpike at the point where it crossed Stenton Ave., as it appeared around 1900. CHHS.

or Reading Turnpike. In the twentieth century, it has been known as Germantown Avenue within Philadelphia, and as Germantown Pike (State Route 422) outside the city.

Branching off from the main route at the very top of Chestnut Hill, and thus forming a fork in the road by the mid-eighteenth century, was another important highway. The owners of lime kilns in nearby Whitemarsh Township, who needed a way to transport their bulky product to Philadelphia, opened it in 1703. A century later, in 1804, a turnpike company acquired the route, extending it to Springhouse and eventually to Bethlehem, Pennsylvania. Although the turnpike company has long been defunct, the label Bethlehem Pike survives, and is the official name of this still-busy thoroughfare.[9]

For three centuries these two routes have served Chestnut Hill. Even in the late twentieth century, they provide the only direct roadways through the center of the community. During the early decades, these roads allowed Chestnut Hill to function as a what might be called a "gateway village." Like Charlestown and Cambridge outside

Boston, and similar fringe communities near Baltimore and New York, Chestnut Hill sat astride a main road (in this case two of them) that ran into the city and allowed the village to serve as commercial gateway to the metropolis beyond.[10]

By the late eighteenth century, this commercial gateway opened into the largest city in British North America and, after independence, in the entire United States. Not until 1820, following completion of the Erie Canal, would New York City overtake Philadelphia as the largest city in the country. Philadelphia would then hold second place until the very end of the nineteenth century.

Philadelphia's growth and prosperity stemmed initially from William Penn's welcome to settlers from all over Europe, regardless of their religious or national backgrounds, and from the cheap land prices that he offered to prospective immigrants. But it was Philadelphia's prime location that ensured its continued success: the city lay about midway between New England and the South, and was thus in a good position to undertake a lucrative coastal trade in both directions. Its sheltered seaport at the head of Delaware Bay also offered an excellent harbor to ships from all over the world. Spreading out north, west, and south of the city were thousands of acres of rich land that soon became the bread basket of the American colonies, and a source of trade and wealth to Philadelphia merchants in the grain and shipping businesses.

Philadelphia's wealth was invested in further business ventures, as well as in paved and illuminated streets, elegant homes and churches, and handsomely crafted furniture, portraits, and silverware. Leading citizens also created schools, libraries, and other such institutions, including North America's first hospital (the Pennsylvania Hospital) and North America's first learned society (the American Philosophical Society). Because of its central location, Philadelphia hosted the First and Second Continental Congresses and witnessed the signing of the Declaration of Independence. Its convenient location also recommended it as the nation's capital during much of the American Revolution and again between 1790 and 1800.

Chestnut Hill thus flourished on the fringes of a prosperous and growing city. The gateway village was a suburb in the most literal

Yeakel General Store, c. 1870, which stood inside the forks of Germantown Ave. and Bethlehem Pike. Although not a "great store," this establishment served the needs of local residents and neighboring farms. This was later the site of the Maple Lawn Inn (nicknamed the Dust Pan) and still later of two successive Gulf Oil stations. GHS.

meaning of the term: A settlement located near the city with which it had strong economic ties. Indeed, its reputation as a processing center for raw products, such as leather and grain, accorded well with pre-nineteenth-century definitions of the suburb — as an often unsavory place where such obnoxious trades as tanning were carried on — before the railroad permitted suburbs to become attractive residential communities.[11]

During Chestnut Hill's gateway village period (c. 1740–1850), nearby farmers brought their produce into the village to be sold at one of the "great stores," so called because of their relative size and importance, thus avoiding the extra ten-mile trip into Philadelphia. In the very early period it was farm women who commonly made this journey into the Hill. The roads were often so impassable for wheeled vehicles that they brought their produce in on horseback, loading it into side "panniers and hampers." In Chestnut Hill they exchanged their wares in the stores for such items as "salt, fish, plaster of Paris [for the soil], clover and grass seed, groceries and dry goods." Philadelphia merchants periodically came up from the city to buy the vegetables, fruits, and cured meats that farm women had exchanged in the stores. The most prosperous of these establishments in the 1760s belonged to Abraham Rex. His two-and-one-half-story stone building still stands as part of 8031–8033 Germantown Avenue. Once the turnpike companies had made the main roads more passable, local farmers hauled their produce all the way to Philadelphia themselves and the great stores in Chestnut Hill disappeared.[12]

Fortunately, the new turnpikes stimulated an already existing trade for innkeepers in Chestnut Hill. Over these improved roads came teamsters driving heavy wagons filled with grain, hay, and other farm products destined for city markets. They, as well as passengers on stagecoaches traveling to and from the city, often interrupted their trip at Chestnut Hill for a meal or an overnight stay.

The first regular stage line through the Hill was begun in 1763 by George Kline of neighboring Flourtown. It ran from Philadelphia to Bethlehem once a week and, by the end of the century, every day. The opening of the Reading and Bethlehem turnpikes soon after 1800 stimulated stage traffic, and by 1820 there were six stage lines passing along the streets of Chestnut Hill. One of them, owned by Jacob Peters, used the Bethlehem Pike to reach Montrose, Pennsylvania, and from there travelers could go on to Buffalo and Montreal. Vacationers heading for the Poconos or the Delaware Water Gap also took stage lines that passed through Chestnut Hill.[13]

Catering to this traffic were the local innkeepers. The cruder establishments, known as wagon stands, served passing teamsters, many of whom slept on bags of hay thrown down on the barroom floor. The better houses refused to admit these drivers and sought business from passing stage travelers. Among these was an inn (now demolished) just opposite the forks of the two pikes, owned by Edward Scull and later by Henry Antes. Another flourishing establishment, a long stone structure built about 1790, was Henry Cress's hotel at the northeast corner of Germantown and Highland avenues,

Mermaid Hotel (Inn), built c. 1795 at the southeast corner of Germantown Ave. and Mermaid Lane. The original building has been demolished and replaced by an early twentieth-century structure. Photo by G. W. Williams, c. 1895. LCP.

which now houses Robertson's Flowers. During the yellow fever epidemic of 1793, it attracted prosperous Philadelphians fleeing the deadly disease.[14] According to local tradition, it was these unlikely guests at Cress's and other inns on the Hill who alerted well-to-do Philadelphians to the pleasant summer breezes of Chestnut Hill and surrounding communities, and that launched the Hill's nineteenth-century reputation as a summer retreat.[15]

Also depending on Chestnut Hill's road system were a series of mills along the Wissahickon and Cresheim creeks on the western and southern boundaries of the village. Grain from the fertile farmlands surrounding the Hill was hauled down into the Wissahickon valley along especially built mill roads, some of which, like Bell's Mill Road, still exist and, widened and paved, carry traffic. Still other mill roads or their extensions have been given modern street names. Among these are Henkel's Mill Road (now Springfield Avenue) and Spruce's Mill Road (a former segment of the present Highland Avenue).[16]

Robert's (or Townsend's) Mill in Germantown, a grist
mill begun in the late seventeenth century, and which
was similar to many of the mills along the Wissahickon
and Cresheim creeks in Chestnut Hill. GHS.

Beginning in the middle of the eighteenth century, Chestnut Hill's
grist mills ground out tons of flour for Philadelphia exporters. One
of these belonged to Joseph Paul. His and other mills along the Wissahickon were so busy that it was not uncommon, according to local
historian John J. Macfarlane, to see "on various mill roads a long
line of teams carrying flour to the city."[17]

Equally important were a series of paper mills along the Wissahickon. Among these was the second paper mill in North America,
established in Chestnut Hill about 1708 by William Dewees. Now
demolished, it stood on a property near Germantown and Northwestern avenues that forms part of the Chestnut Hill College
Campus. (The first such mill had been established downstream in

Germantown by William Rittenhouse in 1690.) Paper making continued to be an important industry in the area until the Fairmount Park Commission acquired properties on both sides of the creek in the 1860s, shut down the mills, and eventually destroyed them. The largest paper manufactory along the Wissahickon was opened in 1858 by Edward Megargee, who used pure spring water to produce a paper of unusual whiteness. There was also a calico mill on the creek, established by Issachar Thorp in 1836 and located just above the bridge at Thorp's (later Bell's) Mill Road.[18]

The same roads that served Chestnut Hill's mills, inns, and stores were also major routes used by both American and British forces during the Revolution. In 1777 and 1778, when the British attacked and then occupied Philadelphia, the residents of Chestnut Hill on several occasions found themselves in the path of large armies. On 8 August 1777, nearly 11,000 men from General George Washington's Continental army marched through Chestnut Hill on their way from the falls of the Schuykill near Germantown to Whitemarsh Township and points further north. On 26 September, a large column of British troops passed through the Hill en route to Germantown. Following Washington's defeat at the Battle of Germantown on 4 October, colonial soldiers streamed through Chestnut Hill in retreat, pursued for a time by the British. During the night of 22 October, Washington himself led part of his army through Chestnut Hill on his way back to Germantown, where he failed to locate the enemy. Early December found the British in Chestnut Hill once more, with about 12,000 men. Taking the home of Mathias Busch (no longer standing) at the forks of Germantown and Bethlehem pikes as their headquarters, the army spent 5 and 6 December on the Hill. The British reportedly plundered a number of houses, setting several of them on fire.

For several months thereafter only small contingents from both sides passed through the Hill. Then on 20 May 1778, about 2,000 British troops appeared and spent several hours at the forks before returning south. On 18 July the British evacuated Philadelphia altogether, ending any further danger to Chestnut Hill. Some ninety men from Chestnut Hill also served in the militia during the War for Independence, although it seems that many of them did only token

A romantic view of the American Revolution that appeared in John J. Macfarlane's *Early History of Chestnut
Hill,* opposite p. 33.

service during the conflict. In any case, the village's unwanted participation in the Revolution had no lasting effects, except to give future residents a feeling that they and their community were somehow
connected to a distant and romantic past.[19]

Two or three centuries later, it is difficult to determine just what
sort of communal identity the residents of early Chestnut Hill may
have felt. Although later generations have wanted to see the old gateway village as a closely knit community of German settlers who had
imported ancient folkways to the Hill, such a picture appears to be
false. As in Germantown itself, from the beginning there was a mix-
ture of nationalities, despite a majority of German-speaking inhabitants in the early decades. Unlike many later immigrants to the

United States, early residents in the area appeared to take little interest in what was happening back in Europe — or with family and friends whom they had left behind — probably because of the virtual impossibility of returning to their homelands. There was also a great deal of intermarriage of German- and English-speaking residents throughout German Township. Neither strong ethnic loyalty nor serious ethnic divisions seem to have played a significant role in early Chestnut Hill.[20]

Religion also failed to provide a sense of community in the early generations. Close to half the families in the township did not go to any church at all, and the great majority of those who did attend religious services were Lutherans and German Reformed.[21] Because of its sparse population and lack of churches, it is likely that the number of churchgoers in Chestnut Hill was even smaller than in Germantown proper. In 1710 a group of local men, all with German or Dutch surnames, established the Whitemarsh Reformed Church in Chestnut Hill. It met in the two-story house of mill owner William Dewees, a structure (now demolished) that stood on Germantown Avenue opposite the present Chestnut Hill College grounds. The congregation broke apart, however, following Dewees's death in 1745. For the next eighty years, anyone from Chestnut Hill who wanted to attend church services had a choice of the Reformed congregation in Germantown or St. Peter's Lutheran a mile or so north at Barren Hill. There was also an Anglican parish at St. Thomas, Whitemarsh, which probably had little appeal to Chestnut Hill's nominal Lutheran and German Reformed population.[22]

Although itinerant preachers held services in the open air on occasion, Chestnut Hill did not enjoy any permanent church building until 1822, when a Scotch Presbyterian farmer named John Magoffin raised enough money to build the Union Chapel. Built on land donated by fellow farmer Abraham Heydrick, the edifice held about 150 people and stood at the northwest corner of what became Shawnee Street and West Gravers Lane. The chapel was open to all Protestant faiths and, lacking any permanent clergy on the Hill, Magoffin himself often led services by reading from a printed sermon.[23]

In time the different denominations using the Union Chapel

Chestnut Hill Baptist Church, built in 1835 at the southeast fork of Germantown
Ave. and Bethlehem Pike. The structure has since been altered and enlarged.
Harris Collection, CHHS.

formed their own congregations and erected separate churches. The
earliest to do so were the Baptists, who built a small edifice in 1835
at the corner of Germantown Avenue and Bethlehem Pike. Although
rebuilt and enlarged several times, the church stands at the original
location and is the oldest religious structure on the Hill. The Methodists also built a small chapel in 1845 (later replaced) just north of
the intersection of Germantown Avenue and Chestnut Hill Avenue.[24]
But unlike the established churches of Europe, where the local
church of an established religion was often a focus of community life,
these small Chestnut Hill churches did not become major meeting
places or sources of community identity for local residents. This was
likewise true of the churches in Germantown.[25]

Chestnut Hillers also failed to forge a sense of community through
a stable population. For as Stephanie Grauman Wolf's study of migration in and out of German Township in the eighteenth century

shows, there was a considerable turnover of people in the area. Examinations of land tenure in Chestnut Hill by Hannah Benner Roach demonstrate the same pattern. What both studies reveal is that individuals and families came and left Chestnut Hill primarily because they wanted to improve themselves materially. In the last analysis, it was the opportunity to acquire and speculate in land, to own or work in a mill, or to set up as a craftsman or storekeeper that attracted the great majority of people to Chestnut Hill in the presuburban period. Similarly, it was a degree of success in these endeavors that kept some of them on the Hill.[26] This should not be surprising in a country that has always attracted the vast majority of its immigrants for economic reasons — however much this fact may contradict the long-held but erroneous view that most people came to the United States for religious and political freedom.

Philadelphia's *City Directory* for 1855, the first to include Chestnut Hill, offers some helpful insights into the variety of economic activity in the village just as it was entering its transition to a railroad suburb. That directory listed 255 householders on the Hill.[27] The total population, including children and other dependents, was of course larger than this, probably 1,000 to 1,200 persons at the time. In any case, the listed occupations indicate that Chestnut Hill was still essentially a gateway village. It is clear from the addresses that most of the population remained clustered along the two gateway pikes.

A numerical analysis of occupations in 1855 shows that the great majority of residents were laborers, skilled craftsmen, or local storekeepers. Forty men were listed as laborers, meaning that they did not possess any particular skills and depended on physical strength to make a living. Although some of them may have worked on farms, it is likely that most found jobs in the local mills.

Just over 100 residents worked in skilled crafts or trades. Among these were twelve butchers, whose number suggests that farmers in the area were still having their cattle slaughtered on the Hill. The livelihoods of some sixteen shoemakers were also linked to cattle raising in the area. Other artisans supported themselves by serving the daily needs of the local population. In numerical order these were: carpenter (21); blacksmith (5); painter (5); weaver (4); stonecutter

(4); mason (4); tailor (3); cooper (or barrel maker) (3); coachbuilder (2); cabinetmaker (2); seamstress (2); wheelwright (1); contractor (1); printer (1); pump maker (1); slate roofer (1); and brickmaker (1). The number of carpenters (21) seems unusually large, but it is consistent with numerous carpenters in Germantown. In both places the mills, which were largely made of wood, probably required the services of many carpenters to build and maintain them.[28]

Several other categories of skilled workers were more obviously associated with the mills. There were five millers, three dyers, one color maker, one cloth lapper, one calico printer, one calico finisher, and one grindstone manufacturer. Three carpet weavers also appeared in the directory, but it is unclear whether they worked as hand weavers or were associated with one of the mills. In all probability, it was the latter.

Some thirty residents made their livings from a variety of commercial activities, nearly all of them located along the present Germantown Avenue, then known as Main Road Pike. There were six hotel proprietors, four grocers, two shopkeepers (the nature of whose business was not revealed), a victualer (or food wholesaler), the owner of an oyster house, the owner of a feed store, a milliner, nine men who simply listed themselves as dealers, and a man who put himself down as a trader.

Others who served local needs for goods and services were the owner of a stagecoach line; the proprietor of a livery stable; a postmaster, who doubled as a tollgate keeper; a driver; a teamster; two nurses; two gardeners; and three carters (or haulers). There was also a lone mariner, whose residence in a community so far from the sea, or even from Philadelphia's port, is a mystery.

The professions were represented on the Hill by five men claiming to be physicians, two clergymen, and four educators. There was an overlap in these last two categories, because the Reverend Roger Owen was also the headmaster of the newly formed Chestnut Hill Academy (a short-lived institution that apparently is not related to the present academy of the same name). Included also in the directory were ten "gentlewomen," probably widowed or unmarried women who had sufficient property or income to live without working, and five "gentlemen," who seem to have inherited wealth or were retired from active work.

Besides these listings, some forty residents described themselves as farmers. According to the property tax lists for 1854, only seventeen of them owned over ten acres of land. Conspicuously absent in the directory were the occupations of lawyer, banker, broker, insurance underwriter, and corporate executive — all of which would be very common in Chestnut Hill once it had become a commuter suburb.

However, the *City Directory*, tax lists, and other sources indicate that there was another small but significant element in the local population. This might be called the gentlemen farmers, who owned large estates on the Hill. From the beginning of colonial Pennsylvania, wealthy men had bought country estates, in imitation of their counterparts in Great Britain. Some occupied these seats all year, whereas others spent only summers in the country. Among the gentlemen farmers in Chestnut Hill were Samuel Hildeburn, who was a shipping merchant in Philadelphia and owned seventy-one acres of land west of Germantown Avenue. There was also Joseph Middleton, who was president of the Wissahickon Turnpike Company and in all probability the possessor of inherited wealth. Middleton owned a total of 66.5 acres, including a tract at the corner of Germantown and Northwestern avenues on the future site of Chestnut Hill College. Just above the main road he built an attractive brick residence and called it Monticello in honor of Thomas Jefferson, whom he greatly admired. The house still stands, but it has been absorbed into a later structure and is no longer recognizable.[29]

The most impressive of all these establishments was Union Place, the property of Owen Sheridan, a long-time director of the Germantown National Bank. With 220 acres located near the present Highland railroad station, Sheridan was the richest man in the area; his property was valued for tax purposes in 1854 at $19,450. A description of his holdings in the *Germantown Telegraph* for 2 July 1845 leaves no doubt that Sheridan's property was impressive:

> The farm is about three-fourths of a mile south of the main street of Chestnut Hill. . . . It is most beautiful, romantic, and if we may so express ourselves,

Joseph Middleton's Monticello, built c. 1850 near the northeast corner of Germantown and Northwestern avenues. The house is now surrounded and completely obscured by a larger structure that serves as the mother house of the Sisters of St. Joseph. GHS.

sequestered tract of land, highly improved with superior mansion, tenant houses, barns, etc., and produces probably equal to any farm of its size, or as much per acre as the best managed plantations in the country.[30]

For some residents, Chestnut Hill was thus an attractive locale for a country seat. For humbler citizens, the Hill was a good place to make a living. Both sorts of people were free to pursue their own economic self-interest, without — especially after the American Revolution — undue interference from government, tradition, or neighbors. In this sense, too, the Hill was far different from the old European village, where individuals were restrained in many ways by custom and belief. Yet like other villages and towns in America, Chestnut Hill was not large enough to create a community in which a formalized local government and highly structured organizations provided a means of cooperation. Thus Chestnut Hillers and their counterparts throughout the country formed small associations to satisfy their public needs.[31] This was a habit that struck Alexis de Tocqueville forcefully during his visit to the United States, and about which he remarked in his classic *Democracy in America*:

Owen Sheridan's residence at Union Grove, which stood on or near the present Tohopeka Court on East Highland Ave. Photo c. 1870. LCP.

> Americans of all ages, all conditions, and all dispositions, constantly form as-
> sociations. . . . The Americans make associations to give entertainments, to
> found seminaries, to build inns, to construct churches, to diffuse books, to
> send missionaries to the antipodes; they found in this manner hospitals, pris-
> ons, and schools.[32]

Although Tocqueville discovered this practice to be widespread, political conditions in colonial (and later) Pennsylvania may have made it especially necessary. For the Quakers, who founded and dominated eastern Pennsylvania politically, disliked powerful government at any level. Unlike the Puritans of New England, they did not believe in governments led by members of a divinely appointed elite. With their insistence on the equality of all human beings, the Quakers preferred local governments based on community consensus, a method that they also used for governing their religious bodies. Nor did the Quakers in Pennsylvania create powerful town governments, like those in New England, with wide grants of authority. Instead the Quakers located political authority at the county level, with little or no official power going to the towns and villages themselves, very few of which were incorporated in any case. Even these county governments in Pennsylvania were confined to minimal functions, such as collecting modest taxes, caring meagerly for the poor, punishing criminals, recording property transactions, and maintaining courts for civil suits.[33]

The political experiences of both Germantown and Chestnut Hill illustrate how this system operated. From 1683 to 1691, the German Quakers and Pietists who lived in Germantown formed a loose community order under the leadership of Francis Daniel Pastorius, who was the land agent and legal representative of the Frankfurt Company. This company had been established by a group of investors in Frankfurt, Germany, who purchased land in Pennsylvania but never came to occupy it, thus forfeiting the property. Pastorius had also agreed, after arriving in Philadelphia, to represent a group of immigrants from Crefeld, Germany.

Under Pastorius's guidance, in 1689 Germantown obtained a borough charter from William Penn that was approved in England two years later. From 1691 until 1707, when the charter was rescinded, Germantown enjoyed its own government, complete with bailiff (or mayor), recorder, clerk, treasurer, sheriff, coroner, constable, and general court. However, it often was difficult to find men willing to fill these positions, as many objected that office holding violated their religious beliefs. There also were disputes over jurisdiction between Germantown officials and Philadelphia County. Thus in 1707 colonial officials closed the Germantown general court and effectively ended the community's existence as an independent borough.[34]

Unlike neighboring Germantown, Chestnut Hill was never an incorporated borough, though it seems to have been under the jurisdiction of Germantown until 1707. Between that time and its annexation by Philadelphia in 1854, Chestnut Hill was an unincorporated village within Philadelphia County. With a system of such weak local government, Chestnut Hillers had no choice but to form local associations to secure schools, cemeteries, or other public amenities. In New England, by contrast, the towns were required by law to found churches, schools, and other such institutions.

The creation of a semipublic school in Chestnut Hill offers a good example of how civic-minded residents, bereft of compelling political forces, functioned as an unofficial board of education. During the earliest days, schools on the Hill were opened sporadically by self-appointed teachers who offered classes to those who wished to attend and could afford the modest fees. One such school was opened by Robert Loller in 1771 near the site of the present railroad station at Bethlehem Pike and Chestnut Hill Avenue.[35] In 1794 his schoolhouse (no longer standing) and land were acquired by a board of trustees, who established a neighborhood school. Reflecting their decision to admit children from adjoining parts of Montgomery County, they called their institution the Harmony School. This board of trustees, and others like it at the time, did not act under an official corporate charter, but existed legally under common-law provisions for holding property in trust. The school was semipublic in nature, in that it was seen as a service to the community and was open to anyone in the area who could pay the modest tuition. In 1841, soon after the establishment of a public educational system in Pennsylvania, the Harmony trustees sold their property to the new school system.[36]

Another group of local trustees organized and superintended Chestnut Hill's Union Burying Ground. The name signified that it was open to all religious faiths, which in fact meant that it was available to all Protestants, because at the time there were few if any Roman Catholics and no known Jews in Chestnut Hill. Approximately 150 residents, representing virtually every household on the Hill, donated money for the burial ground and elected a three-member board of trustees. The trustees purchased one and a quarter acres between West Gravers Lane and Meade Street at a point where Millman Street intersects Gravers Lane. Thus, the site was near the Union Chapel, where funerals might take place. All contributors and their descendants could use the cemetery free of charge. Noncontributors and nonresidents, the latter defined as anyone who lived south of Allen's Lane, would pay one dollar per grave site. In 1869, the trustees voted to charge contributors and their descendants one dollar and others two dollars. This surcharge for outsiders did not appear to arise from any social animosity, but rather from fears, groundless as it turned out, that the cemetery would fill up too quickly, as did the burial grounds in Germantown, if it were too open to nonresidents.

The establishment of cemeteries by both the Baptist and Methodist congregations caused Chestnut Hillers to abandon the Union Burying Ground for the most part. The organization of a Chestnut Hill Cemetery Company in 1855, with grounds at the intersection of Rex Avenue and Thomas Mill Road, also may have failed because of the two church graveyards. By the early twentieth century, the Union grounds had become an overgrown, weed-infested lot. In 1913 the title was obtained by Dr. George Woodward, who removed and reinterred the bodies in another cemetery (unknown to the author) as part of his real estate development in the neighborhood.[37]

Local residents likewise joined together to provide their own fire company in the early nineteenth century. In 1815 they organized the Chestnut Hill Company, changing its name to the Congress Company in 1835. Like volunteer fire brigades throughout the region, the local company was as much a fraternal club as a public service. It held frequent meetings, dances, fairs, and other fund-raising events. After the consolidated city/county government took over fire fighting on the Hill in 1871, the Congress Company lingered on for many years as a social club.[38]

It is not surprising that such initiatives occurred during Chestnut Hill's early decades. What is impressive is that they would continue and increase after the city/county consolidation of 1854, when the city of Philadelphia was supposed to provide necessary public services. In the latter half of the twentieth century, such local organizations would become the basis for a sophisticated system of quasi government in Chestnut Hill (see chapter 8).

By the middle 1850s, Chestnut Hill was thus a flourishing gateway village, with a sense of its own past, a reputation for economic opportunity, and a habit of creating local associations to meet specific community needs. It had also experienced a growing economic dependency on Philadelphia's expanding markets and population. Even before the arrival of suburban commuters, Chestnut Hillers had experienced both local and urban ties. Over the next several decades these connections would develop into a powerful sense of dual identity between suburb and city.

2

NORTH CHESTNUT HILL

The Romantic Suburb

In the mid-1850s a number of forces converged, both locally and in the world beyond, to encourage a portion of Chestnut Hill to develop as a suburban community of the romantic mid-nineteenth century. These included the arrival of a commuter railroad, religious and associationalist concepts of architecture and the home, and a burgeoning industrial growth—all somewhat contradictory characteristics of the late romantic period in Europe and America. In the United States particularly these forces encouraged many prosperous citizens to abandon the congestion, noise, and disease of city streets for the more relaxed and healthful air of nearby villages.

Because many of the men, in particular, maintained strong ties to their businesses, professions, clubs, and cultural organizations in the city, they enjoyed the best of both worlds — urban and suburban. In Chestnut Hill, they created a suburb in the city that allowed them to identify with both Philadelphia and their suburban homes. Even those who did not commute daily began to experience something of this dual identity after Chestnut Hill became an official part of Philadelphia in 1854.[1]

The wealthy new suburbanites congregated in certain sections of the Hill, where they built expensive, architect-designed houses that less prosperous residents of the community could never hope to afford. Soon after arriving, they began to create a set of religious, social, educational, and cultural institutions that made life in the suburb more convenient and that set them off from the remainder of the local population. Thus, in addition to separating themselves residentially from the rest of the city, they also sought to isolate themselves from less favored sections of Chestnut Hill. This contributed greatly to the fragmentation of Chestnut Hill, and to the city of Philadelphia as a whole.[2]

The initial suburban development in Chestnut Hill, later called North Chestnut Hill, would coexist for several decades with the gateway village, whose characteristics disappeared only gradually. The community thus remained home to dozens of shopkeepers and artisans, older residents as well as newcomers, who found the Hill a good place to make a living. Still others found the village an excellent real estate investment.

Coming to the Hill at the same time as the suburbanites were scores of domestic servants, adding yet another element to the population. Perhaps half of these were Irish men and women who formed the Hill's first Roman Catholic population and found themselves quite unwelcome. Their socially prominent employers were likely to be Episcopalians, who provided the basis for yet another (and highly prestigious) denomination on the Hill. (See also chapters 5 and 6.)

The coexistence of these groups resulted in new social layers and communal identities. For instance, the presence of prosperous newcomers on the Hill led citizens throughout the Philadelphia area to begin viewing Chestnut Hill as an upper-class suburban community (despite the existence of many working-class families), instead of as a rural village on the metropolitan fringe. Chestnut Hill thus remained a collection of localities and interests that were established at different times and that overlapped at certain points.

Among the factors that led to Chestnut Hill's emergence as a nineteenth-century suburb were the rapid industrialization and accompanying population growth of Philadelphia. In 1850 the city's sheltered seaport at the head of Delaware Bay was second (after 1820) only to New York in the value of goods moving across its docks. Philadelphia's vast agricultural hinterland continued to pour grains, dried fruits, cured meats, and other produce into the port city for sale up and down the Atlantic coast, and even in Europe. Since the 1820s, Philadelphia had also been the major distribution center for anthracite (hard coal), brought down from the mines above Reading, first by canals and then on the Philadelphia and Reading Railroad, which was chartered by the state legislature in 1833.[3]

Having witnessed the great success of the Reading, the legislature incorporated an even more important railroad in 1846. This was soon called the Pennsylvania Railroad, and would forge its rails across the mountains to Pittsburgh by 1854 and eventually link Philadelphia to Chicago, St. Louis, Kansas City, and points further west. The Pennsylvania, with its headquarters and principal terminus in Philadelphia, became the most important railroad in America, as well as the country's largest corporation.[4]

With all its advantages in transportation, in addition to its nearby large sources of coal (the essential fuel for industry and railroads in the nineteenth century), Philadelphia would come to be known as the "workshop of the world." By 1850 it led the nation in the production of textiles, machine tools, and railroad locomotives, and supported a flourishing ship-building industry. Not surprisingly, the population of Philadelphia City and County soared between 1840 and 1850, from 285,748 to 408,672. Nearly 30 percent of these were foreign-born, the largest group of recent arrivals having fled the devastating potato famine in Ireland.[5]

As might be expected, there were great extremes in living standards among Philadelphians in the middle of the nineteenth century. In 1845 the city contained an estimated ten millionaires, along with

234 men who were worth $100,000 or more. At the other end of the scale, unskilled factory operatives earned only seventy-eight cents per day in 1854, and carpenters earned about ten dollars for a sixty-hour week. Many of the poorest residents of the city lived in South Philadelphia, where dozens were forced into begging and prostitution in order to support themselves.[6]

Like other cities with densely packed slums, Philadelphia's mortality rate began to rise alarmingly at midcentury, with epidemics of cholera, smallpox, and typhoid fever visiting the metropolis every few years. Accompanying such health problems were increasing levels of crime and violence. Much of this violence was aimed at racial or religious groups. Philadelphia blacks, who numbered about 20,000 in the late 1840s, were frequent targets of mob violence. But the worst such incident was directed against Roman Catholics in the late spring and summer of 1844. Several Catholic churches and schools were burned, and 5,000 state militiamen had to be called in to quell the rioting. Before the smoke had cleared, fifteen people were killed and over fifty were seriously injured.[7]

These anti-Catholic riots provided the final impetus for a long-considered consolidation of Philadelphia City and County. Under a consolidated system, proponents argued, the city could create a large enough police force to contend with most instances of mob violence, in addition to having the jurisdiction to pursue criminals, who often escaped punishment by fleeing into the surrounding Philadelphia County. Civic leaders also believed that the larger, consolidated tax base would provide greater funds for desperately needed municipal improvements and services, as well as put an end to the wasteful duplication of multiple taxation districts. There were elements of competition and pride behind the idea, too. The consolidation would make Philadelphia the largest city in the United States in land area, and it would ensure that the city would remain the nation's second-largest municipality in population, after New York, well into the foreseeable future. Thus, in early 1854, the Pennsylvania state legislature passed an act that combined the city of Philadelphia, which was only about two square miles before the merger, with surrounding Philadelphia County. The result was an enormous expanse of 129 square

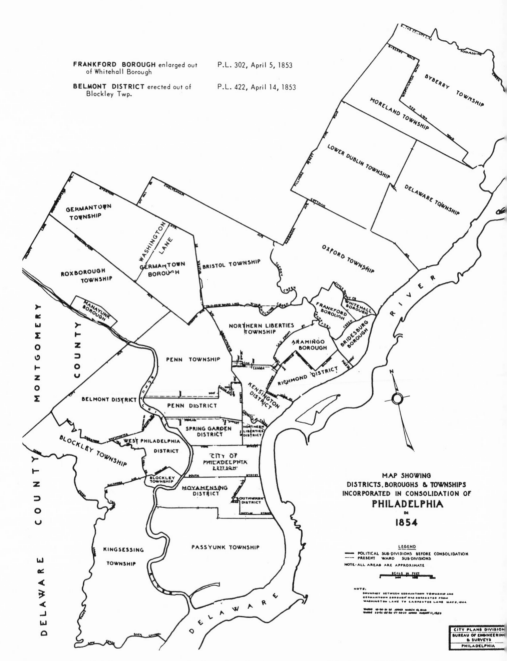

FRANKFORD BOROUGH enlarged out of Whitehall Borough — P.L. 302, April 5, 1853

BELMONT DISTRICT erected out of Blockley Twp. — P.L. 422, April 14, 1853

MAP SHOWING
DISTRICTS, BOROUGHS & TOWNSHIPS
INCORPORATED IN CONSOLIDATION OF
PHILADELPHIA
IN
1854

LEGEND
— POLITICAL SUB-DIVISIONS BEFORE CONSOLIDATION
--- PRESENT WARD SUBDIVISIONS
NOTE - ALL AREAS ARE APPROXIMATE

SCALE IN FEET

Philadelphia County just before the city/county consolidation of 1854, showing major subdivisions. Philadelphia Bureau of Surveys.

miles (including Germantown and Chestnut Hill) within the consolidated area.[8]

Many residents of Chestnut Hill, and of German Township at large, were dubious about the idea of a city/county consolidation. Some feared that it would result in higher taxes, whereas others suspected that their communities would lose a sense of local identity. An emotional editorial on 12 February 1851 in the *Germantown Telegraph,* a weekly newspaper that served the township, summed up such feelings:

> From every quarter of the county, we hear but one sentiment relative to the villainous scheme to unite the rural parts of the county with the city. Meetings are being held, and remonstrances are being signed, representing this scheme in its true light, to the legislature. We have no doubt these representations will be heeded, being, as we are, well assured that this body will never inflict such a gross wrong upon a portion of their constituents who happen to reside within a certain distance of the city of Philadelphia.[9]

Urban businessmen and professionals, in contrast, tended to favor the scheme, believing that it would help to restore order, stimulate economic growth in general, and provide new opportunities for speculation in real estate. Because the question was entirely under the jurisdiction of the state legislature, with no provision for local referenda, there was little that residents of the township could do. However, the act became more palatable after the city agreed to assume the debts of the subdivisions within the county, and to assess farmland within the county at lower rates than developed properties. It was also comforting for many of those who contemplated a move from downtown up to Germantown or Chestnut Hill to know that they could continue to vote in municipal elections, now that both communities were part of the city.[10]

Although the city/county consolidation helped the municipality to cope better with certain situations, such as fire fighting and law enforcement, numerous members of Philadelphia's middle and upper classes despaired over continuing urban problems. For them the dirty and noisy streets, the rising crime rates, and the ever-present threat of epidemic disease made the central parts of the city appear an increasingly undesirable place in which to live.

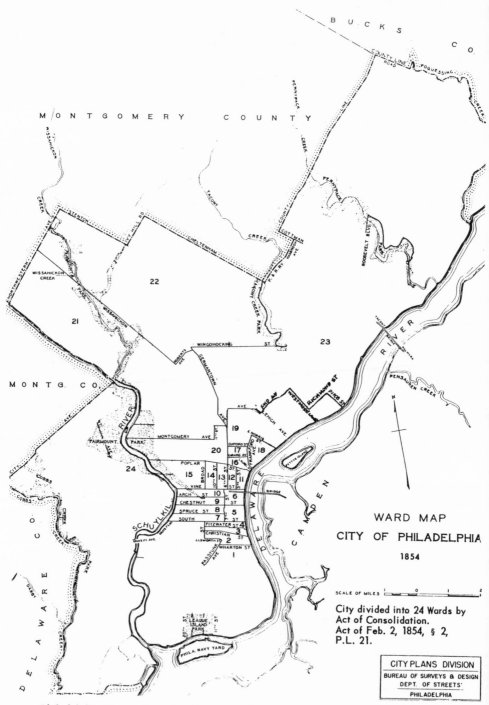

Philadelphia County just after the city/county consolidation of 1854, showing ward divisions. Philadelphia Bureau of Surveys.

In addition to these more practical objections to urban life, more educated Philadelphians had begun to shun the city on philosophical, aesthetic, and religious grounds. Sharing the main tenets of romanticism, they believed that a regular exposure to nature was essential to physical, emotional, and spiritual health. Yet it was not a wild or untamed nature that attracted them, but one that humans had curbed to some degree — or even "improved." They were likely to find such surroundings on the urban fringe, in such gateway villages as Chestnut Hill.

Many clergymen, in addition to the authors of books on domestic life, encouraged the move to the suburbs. Influenced by the romantic/transcendental views of the day, they believed that nature was an emanation of the divine. God was ever-present in nature and observable in its overwhelming beauty; frequent exposure to nature could thus draw the individual closer to God. Religious spokesmen also believed that it was easier to establish and maintain a proper Christian home in the suburbs, where children in particular would not be exposed to urban vices. These same preceptors held that women were especially receptive to the spiritual healing and moral lessons of nature. Their prescription for an ideal Christian setting thus comprised an attractively appointed home in a semirural setting, presided over by a loving wife and mother who was insulated from the hard and often immoral world of work in the city.[11]

It is impossible to tell how many individuals in Chestnut Hill were consciously motivated by romantic/transcendental concepts of nature. Editorials in the *Germantown Telegraph* embraced such concepts as early as 1852. Looking forward to the building of a railroad into Chestnut Hill, the writer proposed that it would "open a vast field for cottages for at least a mile on both sides of [the route], presenting some of the handsomest sights in the country. . . ."[12] Just a year before, the same newspaper had linked the fresh air and natural beauty available in Germantown and Chestnut Hill with increased health and morality: "A clean, fresh-aired, sweet, cheerful, and well-situated house," the writer extolled, "exercises a moral as well as a physical influence over its inmates, and makes the members of the family peaceful and considerate of the feelings and happiness of others. . . ."[13]

Romantic illustration of Wissahickon Creek, mid-
nineteenth-century. Artist unknown. GHS.

Three decades later, the Reverend S. F. Hotchkin was moved to even
greater eloquence in his history of Chestnut Hill. Contemplating the
rolling countryside as it appeared from one of the larger houses on
the northeast side, he wrote:

> The magnificent and varied scenery which meets the eye at this point, . . . and
> indeed throughout the Hill, should move a thankful and devout mind to
> praise God who piled up the hills and hollowed out the valleys, which in their
> light and shade, under sun and shower, covered with green grass, or shining
> with a pure snow mantle, draw exclamations of delight and wonder by their
> exceeding beauty.[14]

The most rapturous descriptions were reserved for the wild and
romantic Wissahickon Creek, with its sparkling waters, jutting cliffs,
and shifting patterns of light and shadow. Local lore was already full
of stories about noble Indians, bottomless pools, and star-crossed lov-

Indian Rock Bridge over Wissahickon Creek, c. 1900. CHHS.

ers who had jumped to their deaths from the rocky heights. Poets tried to capture its beauty in verse. Even John Greenleaf Whittier succumbed to the beauties of the creek during a visit to Philadelphia:

> And when the miracle of autumn came,
> And all the woods with many-colored flame
> Of splendor, making summer's greenness tame,
>
> Burned, unconsumed, a voice without a sound
> Spake to him from each kindled bush around,
> And made the strange new landscape holy ground![15]

Another famous visitor to the Wissahickon was Edgar Allan Poe, who made extended visits to a friend at East Falls on the Schuykill River. From there Poe often walked up the Wissahickon Creek. Inspired by its haunting sights, he published a sketch in 1844 entitled "Morning on the Wissahickon."[16] In one long paragraph he summed up the whole transcendental love affair that drew so many visitors to its banks:

Not long ago I visited the stream . . . , and spent the better part of a sultry
day in floating in a skiff upon its bosom. The heat gradually overcame me,
and, resigning myself to the influence of the scenes, I sank into half a slum-
ber, during which my imagination reveled in visions of the Wissahiccon [*sic.*]
of ancient days — of the "good old days" when the demon of the Engine was
not, when pic-nics were undreamed of, when "water privileges" were neither
bought nor sold, and when the red man trod alone, with the elk, upon the
ridges that now towered above. . . .[17]

Such romantic enticements to suburban living were reinforced by
an earlier tradition of building country houses on the outskirts of cities like Philadelphia. During the eighteenth century, wealthy Philadelphians attempted to imitate their English counterparts by owning
houses in both the city and countryside, the latter serving as retreats
during the hot summer months. Germantown became a favored site
for such houses, including Grumblethorpe, built in 1744 by John
Wister, and the spectacular Cliveden, erected in the 1760s by
Benjamin Chew, who was later chief justice of Pennsylvania. Even
President George Washington and his cabinet found refuge in Germantown during the deadly yellow fever epidemic of 1793. Washington stayed at what has come to be called the Deshler-Morris
House (the main portion erected in 1772), and liked it so well that
he returned the next summer with his wife, Martha, and her grandchildren.[18]

It was the railroad that allowed prosperous Philadelphians to
spend more time at these country retreats, as well as in newer suburban residences. Ironically, these very railroads became one of the
great despoilers of the romantic landscape that suburban dwellers so
admired. Thus, from the very beginning, suburbanites lived contradictory and even compromising lives as they sought to escape from
the ugly and artificial scenes that they were creating in their very own
banks, businesses, and law offices. It was a contradiction that few
suburbanites — or their descendants — would either recognize or
admit.

Prospects for this escape into the suburban fringe opened in the
early 1830s, when a group of Germantown entrepreneurs built the
Philadelphia, Germantown, and Norristown Railroad, with the first

Locomotive "Old Ironsides" and coaches of the Philadelphia, Germantown, and Norristown Railroad, as they appeared when the road opened in 1832. GHS.

trains arriving in Germantown in late 1832. In addition to stimulating commerce and manufacturing in the area, it made Germantown into Philadelphia's first true railroad suburb, and one of the earliest such suburbs in the United States. Later this pioneering line became part of the Reading Railroad system.[19]

Anxious to share in Germantown's good fortune, residents of Chestnut Hill welcomed the establishment in 1833 of regular stage-coach service from the Germantown depot (at Germantown Avenue and Price Street) to various points on the Hill. At first the fare was twenty-five cents, but a year later it was reduced to eighteen and three-quarters cents in order to attract more riders.[20] Yet even the lower price was beyond the reach of workers, who generally earned less than a dollar a day at the time. Only wealthier men could afford to commute in this way.

By 1851 there was also Jacob Peters's horse-drawn omnibus ser-vice, which ran hourly between Philadelphia, Germantown, and Chestnut Hill.[21] In 1859 it was superseded by the horsecars of the Germantown Passenger Railroad. These were multipassenger vehi-cles that ran along iron rails. The fare from Chestnut Hill to down-town was seven cents. The horsecars were slow and stopped fre-

Horsecar of the Chelten Ave. line. Similar to the horsecars used in Chestnut Hill.
Photo c. 1890. GHS.

quently to allow passengers to get on and off. Like the electrified
trolleys that replaced them between 1894 and 1896, they were most
useful for short distances along the main arteries into the city. They
also had the virtue of being comparatively cheap and, like the trolleys,
were favored by less prosperous residents. Yet a one-way fare of even
seven cents meant that a worker could not afford a round-trip commute from Chestnut Hill to more industrial areas of Philadelphia.
Thus low wages and relatively expensive transportation ensured that
Chestnut Hill would attract commuters mainly of upper-middle- and
upper-class backgrounds.[22]

The establishment of a railroad to Germantown, with stage and
then omnibus connections to Chestnut Hill, resulted in a few well-
to-do suburban commuters living on the Hill as early as the 1840s.
Among these was Jesse Kneedler, who owned a successful dry-goods
company downtown on Market Street. During the winter the Kneed-
lers lived in town on Washington Square, but each spring they returned to their property (still standing) at 8864 Germantown Avenue

Early electrified trolley car. The words "Roxborough" and "Chestnut Hill" appear on the side of the car. Photo c. 1890s. CHHS.

in Chestnut Hill. Rather than taking one of the public conveyances, Kneedler was driven each morning in his own carriage down to Germantown, where he caught the train to his office in the city. His habit of spending his winters downtown, where he could enjoy the social season and avoid difficult carriage rides along icy, muddy, or snow-covered roads, was shared by other early suburban residents of the Hill and would persist into the late nineteenth and early twentieth centuries. Kneedler himself would settle permanently in Chestnut Hill by the 1880s. He and his descendants played an active role in the community's civic life for several generations.[23]

The necessity in the 1840s of commuting in a horse-drawn vehicle to the train station in Germantown stood in the way of extensive suburban development in Chestnut Hill. Thus, in the spring of 1848 a committee of local men obtained an act of incorporation from the state legislature that would allow them to raise funds and build a railroad from Chestnut Hill to Germantown. Two years passed, however, before the group held a public meeting at Chestnut Hill's Eagle Hotel (the former Cress Hotel, which now houses Robertson's Flowers) on 1 August 1850 to discuss the venture and to encourage residents to buy stock in the project. In March 1851 they held another public meeting at the home of William Stallman, owner of the local stage-coach line, where citizens were again urged to invest.[24]

A month after this meeting, the *Germantown Telegraph*, which always went out of its way to boost local ventures, reiterated the call to buy stock in the new transportation project, going so far as to say that investing in the railroad was a moral and civic duty. "Those who feel an interest in the road," the newspaper proclaimed, "will not only have to subscribe liberally themselves, but each man must consider himself a 'committee of vigilance' to procure subscriptions from others who may not come forward voluntarily for that purpose."[25] In April 1852, the newspaper was still urging local residents to do their duty by purchasing stock, this time citing the profit motive. According to the writer, a particular property had just sold for "*three times* [italics original] the amount it would have commanded three or four years ago, and 33 percent more than it was offered for only one year ago."[26]

Such economic considerations were not lost on the railroad's first board of managers, elected in early 1852, who hoped to make a profit themselves on the line, now known officially as the Chestnut Hill Railroad. These were Coffin Colket, who was elected president of the company, John Hildeburn, Cephas G. Childs, George W. Carpenter, Samuel S. Richie, Augustus L. Roumfort, Clayton T. Platt, James Smith, and H. K. Smith. Colket was a Philadelphia merchant and entrepreneur, with offices at 312 North 7th Street. Carpenter had made a fortune in the drug business and lived in a huge Greek Revival mansion (now demolished) in Mount Airy known as Phil-Ellena. Roumfort also lived in Mount Airy and had been the head of Mount Airy College, a well-known military school of the day situated on the grounds of the present Lutheran Theological Seminary at Allen's Lane and Germantown Avenue. Because the rail line would also connect Mount Airy to Germantown and central Philadelphia, both Carpenter and Roumfort stood to benefit directly from it. At least three

Gravers Lane Station of the Reading (Chestnut Hill-East) line. The station was designed by Frank Furness and built in 1883. Photo from early twentieth century. *Local.*

of the other directors were pioneer suburbanites in Chestnut Hill: Hildeburn, a commercial merchant; Platt, who was also a merchant; and Childs, a well-known lithographer and publisher. Richie was a highly successful chandler. The backgrounds of James Smith and H. K. Smith remain obscure.[27]

In April 1852 the board engaged the firm of Sidney and Neff to undertake the construction from Chestnut Hill to Germantown. The railroad officially opened on 3 July 1854, with its terminus at Bethlehem Pike and Chestnut Hill Avenue on the site now occupied by the station of the Southeast Pennsylvania Transportation Authority's (SEPTA) Chestnut Hill-East line. A modest wooden structure served as the first depot. There originally were four trains daily, each way. The earliest left Philadelphia for Germantown and Chestnut Hill at 6:00 A.M., while the first train from Chestnut Hill departed for the city at 7:40. The last trips of the day were at 6:00 P.M. from the city, and at 7:40 P.M. from Chestnut Hill. The one-way fare was twenty cents — again more than members of the working class could afford on a daily basis. Riders had to change trains at Germantown, where an engine pushed the cars up to Chestnut Hill. Returning trains took advantage of gravity, coasting all the way back to Germantown. Besides carrying passengers, the railroad provided freight service to and from the Hill.[28]

By any measure the Chestnut Hill Railroad proved an instant success. In January 1855, after just six months of operation, the board of managers declared a 3 percent dividend. The managers were also delighted to report that the total number of passengers for 1855 stood at an impressive 85,295.[29] This flourishing line would remain an independent corporation until it was leased to the Philadelphia and Reading Railroad in November 1870. The Reading then erected a new two-story stone station in 1872. On the second floor was a large meeting room that was used for several decades by many civic groups on the Hill. This structure (now demolished) and the smaller one that preceded it were the first unofficial community centers in Chestnut Hill.[30]

The Chestnut Hill Railroad would not only prosper for many years, but it, and the Pennsylvania line built later on the West Side of the Hill, also would prove an excellent vehicle for creating and maintaining a semirural suburb for the upper-middle- and upper-class commuter. The round-trip fare of thirty-five to forty cents made rail commutation much too expensive for the average worker, who counted himself fortunate to make a dollar a day; only prosperous Philadelphians could even consider a daily trip by rail. The railroad also meant that land lying more than a half mile away on either side of the tracks would likely remain open and undeveloped, because most commuters did not want to walk more than several hundred yards to the station twice each day. Later the automobile would open adjoining tracts of land for development, and in the process change many older suburbs by obliterating the semirural atmosphere that had made them so attractive. In Chestnut Hill, both human and natural factors (to be discussed later) would mitigate many effects of the automobile age for several decades after its arrival.[31]

The railroad would also encourage a dual identity with both city and suburb. The Chestnut Hill Railroad and all subsequent railroads in the Philadelphia area, like those in other metropolitan areas, had their main terminals downtown. By the end of the nineteenth century, these rail lines were like the spokes of a wheel, leading thousands of people in and out of the urban hub on a daily basis. In addition to male commuters, riders included women on shopping trips or on visits to clubs, theaters, and other cultural attractions. Both men and women traveled downtown to see doctors and dentists, and some children commuted to schools in the city. Until the advent of the automobile, all roads literally led to the city.

It was during the first stages of this railroad age that the earliest suburban development in North Chestnut Hill emerged. Even as the Chestnut Hill Railroad was nearing completion, several enterprising men had already taken the first steps toward developing the valuable land surrounding it. Among these early real estate entrepreneurs was a prosperous Philadelphia lawyer named Samuel Austin. He purchased 5.75 acres of land immediately southeast of Bethlehem Pike that in the early nineteenth century had been part of the Levi Rex farm. He then widened a small wagon road through the property to fifty feet and extended it down to Stenton Avenue. Because the new thoroughfare began at the highest elevation in Chestnut Hill, Austin named it Summit Street. It commanded a superb view (then unobstructed by buildings and trees) of the rolling Whitemarsh Valley below, and thus offered an ideal site for the romantic suburb.[32]

Unlike Henry Howard Houston's project several decades later on the West Side of Chestnut Hill, Austin did not develop Summit Street as an integral unit. He probably lacked the funds, and he followed the practice of Germantown developers, who for several decades had been buying up long strips of farmland off the main road, cutting new streets down the middle of them, and selling rectangular lots on either side.[33] It was thus individual purchasers, some of whom bought several lots for their own speculative purposes, who built dwellings along either side of Summit Street. The street was almost completely developed by the Centennial year of 1876, with approximately twenty dwellings on its two-block length.[34]

In this era before zoning laws, Austin and other developers were almost completely free to do what they wanted. They hired their own surveyors, laid out and paved streets themselves, and subdivided the

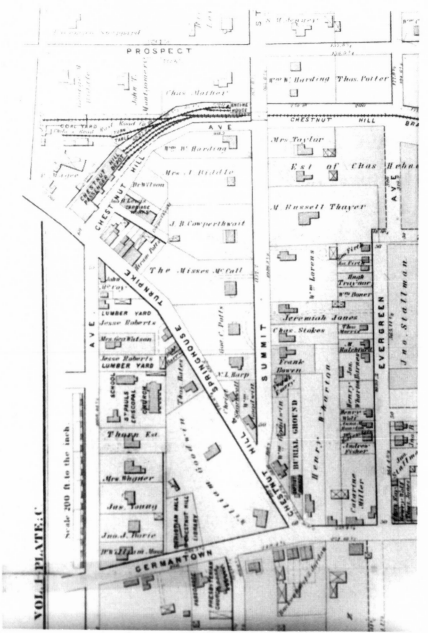

North Chestnut Hill as it appeared in the *Philadelphia Atlas* (or plat map) of 1876.

properties into whatever lot sizes they chose. Their general practice
was to deed streets and other rights-of-way to the city. The sale of
individual lots was recorded by the registrar of deeds, whose office
also drew diagrams of the lots onto plat maps. Because the city of
Philadelphia forbade the construction of wood-frame houses as a fire
precaution, developers had to build with either brick or stone. This
requirement reinforced the traditional use of stone in Chestnut Hill
and resulted in a pleasing uniformity of color and texture, despite
different architectural styles. It was up to the developer or the individual property owner to arrange with private companies to provide
gas and other utilities. Once the city took over water and sewage
systems, an agreement had to be made with municipal authorities to
extend these services to new developments.[35]

Many of the houses built on Summit Street started out as second
residences. Their owners maintained townhouses in the city and re-
treated to Chestnut Hill in the summer to escape the heat, and sometimes in the winter to enjoy sledding, skating, and other cold-weather
sports "in the country."[36] Such dwellings were transitions between
the older tradition of building a country house and the emerging custom of living in a suburban residence to which one commuted in all
seasons.

Whether or not they were year-round residents, those who settled
with their families on Summit Street were men of some wealth whose
principal place of business was in the city. Among these early residents were the bookseller and merchant William Goodwin; landscape gardener James Gleason; conveyancer (or real estate agent)
Charles C. Longstreth; merchant Daniel C. E. Brady; lumber merchant John Naglee; attorney and Common Please Judge Martin
Russell Thayer; publisher George B. Cowperthwait; marble importer
Charles Heebner; *Philadelphia Inquirer* publisher William Harding;
carriage maker George Watson; drug manufacturer Spencer Janney;
Adams Express executive Edward S. Stanford; rope manufacturer
George Weaver; merchant Norman L. Hart; Nicholas Biddle's
daughter Anne Biddle; and attorney Samuel Austin himself.[37]

Most of the Summit Street houses were executed in the Italian
palazzo style that was then popular in the eastern United States. Ar-

Italianate house at 100 Summit St., c. 1860. Photo by author, 1991.

chitectural writers such as Alexander Jackson Downing and Philadelphia's own Samuel Sloan insisted that this style was well suited to
suburbs. Based loosely on villas in the countryside around Florence
and other northern Italian towns, it was urbane enough for metropolitan commuters, and less organic and therefore less rural in its
associations than the Gothic Revival cottage. The Italianate villa,
with its reminders of a distant time and place, also appealed to the
romantic imagination.[38] The most spectacular of these villas on Summit Street is the stuccoed stone residence (number 100) built between
1855 and 1861 by carriage maker George Watson at the southeast
corner of Prospect Avenue. Still standing in 1991, it features prominent brackets, overhanging eaves, a third-floor balcony, and a huge
campanile-style tower on the east side. Smaller and more domestic in
feeling is 17 Summit Street, built about 1861 by merchant Norman
L. Hart. This stone structure, also still standing, has deeply hooded
dormer windows, a wooden front porch with graceful rounded arches
filled with fretwork designs, and a square tower on the west side that
was demolished in 1948. Around the spacious front yard there is a

Gothic Revival house at 52 Summit St. (1874–76).
Photo by author, 1991.

cast-iron ornamental fence that sets the property off from the street while at the same time inviting entry through the gate.[39]

The other houses on Summit Street were in the Gothic Revival, Mansard, or early Tudor Revival styles. Although writers of architectural treatises proposed that Gothic motifs were most suited to rural cottages, more subdued Gothic designs did appear in suburbs during the post–Civil War period. Characterized by steeply pitched gables and fretwork carpentry, such houses were associated with medieval churches and thus thought to be appropriate for the proper Christian home. Numbers 52 and 54 Summit Street still provide excellent examples of this style. Both of these stone houses contain high, peaked gables and pointed windows. Bordering the roof gables of number 52 are wide barge boards, their centers ornamented with cutout quatrefoil patterns.[40]

Having been built on farmland, Summit Street was treeless at first. But by the end of the nineteenth century, a canopy of trees reached from one side of the street to the other. The wide front lawns also were filled with trees and shrubs. Stepping onto Summit Street from near the busy intersection of Germantown Avenue and Bethlehem Pike still gives the walker a sense of moving into a green and sheltered world that is far removed from the workaday life of the city below.

The only rival to Summit Street in North Chestnut Hill was the Norwood Avenue development undertaken a block or so away by Charles Taylor, a successful Philadelphia grain merchant. Taylor had come to Chestnut Hill in 1849 and was one of its suburban pioneers. Over a period of several years he accumulated about forty acres of land. On it he built a spacious house called Norwood (now demolished), described by a contemporary writer as being in the English cottage style. In 1860 he opened his land for development by running a road, now Norwood Avenue, through the property, extending from Chestnut Hill Avenue on the south to Sunset Avenue on the northern end of the tract.[41]

Unlike Austin on Summit Street, Taylor built at least four houses himself and offered them for sale. He sold the other parcels of land to individuals, who then built their own dwellings. Among the residents of Norwood Avenue were Colonel George H. North, a banker and broker; Charles B. Dunn, another successful banker; Arthur Howe, a prosperous leather merchant; Edward S. Buckley, an iron plate manufacturer; Morris S. Waln, a commercial merchant; and William Disston, whose family-owned saw manufacturing works (Henry Disston and Sons) in the Tacony section of Philadelphia had become one of the most spectacularly successful industries in the United States. Various members of the Disston family would live in Chestnut Hill over the decades and help to form the inner core of its upper class.[42]

The houses on Norwood Avenue were just as impressive as those

Residence of Col. George H. North (demolished), northwest corner, Norwood and Chestnut Hill avenues. Drawing from Hotchkin, *Ancient and Modern*, opposite p. 452.

on Summit Street and were likewise executed in Italianate, Gothic Revival, Mansard, and early Tudor Revival styles. Framing the entrance to Norwood Avenue, on the Chestnut Hill Avenue end, were two corner houses, both built fairly close to the street. But as one moved down Norwood Avenue, the houses were set back much further, giving the avenue the appearance of a rural lane, without either sidewalks or curbings. A leafy arcade formed from parallel rows of elms invited entry to the road, which led downhill towards a thickly wooded ravine and creek, one of the small rivulets that project like long jagged fingers into many areas of Chestnut Hill. Unlike Summit Street, Norwood Avenue and its residences have undergone serious degradation, with several dwellings, including those on the corners at Chestnut Hill Avenue, having been demolished by institutions in the neighborhood (see chapter 9).

In addition to the Norwood Avenue and Summit Street residences, there were large, attractive houses on several other streets in North Chestnut Hill that extended north and east from the railroad station, where residents enjoyed the best views in the area. These

Looking north on Norwood Ave., 1898. GHS.

included Chestnut Hill Avenue, Germantown Avenue (north of Rex Avenue), Stenton and Prospect avenues, the far east end of Gravers Lane, Crittenden Street, and the eastern extremities of Willow Grove Avenue.

One of the largest and most impressive residences on these streets stood at the northeast corner of Stenton Avenue and Summit Street. Called The Evergreens, its owner was Thomas Potter, who had made a fortune in the manufacture of oilcloth and later in life became president of the City National Bank of Philadelphia. The now demolished house was in the Italianate style, a massive three-story edifice with a square cupola rising from the center of its hipped roof.[43] In 1883 Potter's son Charles located himself in a house at the northeast corner

Thomas Potter. CHHS.

of Prospect and Evergreen avenues. Named The Anglecot[t], the
dwelling was designed by the well-known Philadelphia architect Wilson Eyre, Jr. It remains one of the most artful examples of the shingle
style in America.[44]

Just two blocks away, at the northeast corner of Stenton Avenue
and Gravers Lane, was the Patterson compound, containing two
Queen Anne houses (the present numbers 493 and 495) built between
1876 and 1885 and owned by Christopher Stuart Patterson. His father, Joseph Patterson, Sr., had been president of the Western National Bank, and at his death in 1887 he left an estate worth the then
handsome sum of $600,000.[45] One block west of the Patterson dwell-
ings, and on the other side of Gravers Lane, was the attractive Gravers Lane station of the Reading Railroad (1883), designed by
Philadelphia's renowned Frank Furness in his own unique style.[46]

By the middle 1880s, the developed portions of North Chestnut
Hill extended from approximately Rex Avenue on the south to Sunset
Avenue on the north. The western boundaries reached a block or so
beyond Germantown Avenue, and on the east they ranged just be-

Wyncliffe (1875–76). Now part of Temple University's Sugarloaf Conference Center. CHHS.

yond Stenton Avenue into Wyndmoor in Springfield Township. There was also a southern "dogleg" between Stenton Avenue and the Chestnut Hill (Reading) Railroad tracks that ran down to Willow Grove Avenue.

The land north of Sunset Avenue was much farther from the railroad station, was generally quite hilly, and was accordingly cheaper than the real estate further south. This land remained in large parcels best suited for larger estates, like that of Joseph Middleton at Germantown and Northwestern avenues. Another formidable estate in this area was Wyncliffe, a large Gothic Revival dwelling built in 1875–1876 at the northwest corner of Germantown Avenue and Bell's Mill Road that is today part of the Sugarloaf Conference Center of Temple University. The ample size of such estates made them prime candidates for institutional use at a later date. Examples are the Morris Arboretum at Germantown and Hillcrest avenues; the Woodmere Art Gallery, on the northeast corner of Germantown Avenue and Bell's Mill Road; the Chestnut Hill Hospital, between Norwood and Germantown avenues; and Chestnut Hill College at Germantown and Northwestern avenues.[47]

The location of the Chestnut Hill Railroad also determined that tracts just south and west of the rail line, which did not enjoy views of the Whitemarsh Valley, would become sites of small dwellings for craftsmen, shopkeepers, and certain domestic servants. Known for many years now as the East Side, this portion of Chestnut Hill is characterized by small single dwellings, semidetached "twins," and row houses, many built in red brick. Yet these residences, too, were generally set back from the street by at least twenty-five feet, providing room for trees, small lawns, and flower gardens, thereby giving something of a suburban flavor to these otherwise urban-style units. (See also chapters 5 and 6.)

It was these less prosperous residents of the East Side, who did not commute and who lived in Chestnut Hill all year around, who identified themselves most closely with the Hill. Their wealthier male neighbors in North Chestnut Hill, on the other hand, had to divide their time and energies between their homes on the Hill and their various business, cultural, and social activities downtown. Several residents of North Chestnut Hill illustrate this phenomenon well. Publisher Cephas Childs, for example, was secretary of the Philadelphia Board of Trade and a director of the Pennsylvania Academy of Fine Arts. Owen Sheridan belonged to a number of Philadelphia clubs, including the prestigious Farmer's Club of Pennsylvania (an organization strictly for gentlemen farmers) and the elite First Troop, Philadelphia City Cavalry. He also owned a house in the city, where he lived during various times of the year. Banker Charles B. Dunn listed the Philadelphia Art Club and the City Club among his affiliations. Oilcloth manufacturer Thomas Potter was chairman of the Philadelphia School Committee for many years, an active member of the city's Common Council, and a member of the Academy of Fine Arts. Dozens of other Chestnut Hill residents boasted similar connections in the larger city, and thus maintained a dual identity, one

The Eldon Hotel, southwest corner of Bethlehem Pike and Stenton Ave. Since 1945 this structure has been part of the Fairview Nursing Home. *Local.*

with their homes in Chestnut Hill, and the other with their business and cultural activities in the city. For the time being, city and suburb could coexist in a happy equilibrium — at least for those who could afford a home on the Hill and the costs of commuting back and forth to the city.[48]

Meanwhile, Chestnut Hill was increasing its reputation as a fashionable summer resort. A few prosperous Philadelphians had been going to the Hill to escape the enervating heat and humidity of the city since the late eighteenth century, putting themselves up in the old stage hotels or boarding in farmhouses. The arrival of the railroad in 1854 then made Chestnut Hill much more convenient for vacationers. By 1880 there were several hotels that catered to summer guests. In North Chestnut Hill there was the Eldon, named (for now forgotten reasons) in honor of the British jurist Lord Eldon, and opened in 1884. It stood at the southwest corner of Bethlehem Pike and Stenton Avenue, where it commanded an impressive view of the valley below.[49] Since 1945 it has formed part of the Fairview Nursing Home. Across Stenton Avenue in Springfield Township there was also a water cure spa, built around a spring on the farm of Barclay

Lippincott (the exact location of the property is uncertain) and complete with a forty-room boarding house.[50]

Between the forks at Germantown Avenue and Bethlehem Pike stood the Maple Lawn Inn, a remodeled and enlarged older structure that opened in 1876. It was long nicknamed the Dust Pan, owing to its location on these busy thoroughfares. Demolished in 1927, it has since been the site of two gasoline stations, and at the time of this writing it is slated to be occupied by a cluster of new shops.[51]

Over on the West Side of Chestnut Hill, near the Wissahickon Creek, was the Park House, constructed about 1865. Destroyed by fire in 1877, its successor was the Wissahickon Inn, now home to Chestnut Hill Academy (see chapter 3). Just below the Park House in the Wissahickon gorge is the Valley Green Inn, built about 1850. Never a residential establishment, the inn, which continues to flourish, was famous for its waffles and catfish.[52] Further north along the creek was the now demolished Indian Rock Hotel, which sat on the Roxborough Township side, opposite a dramatic rock formation where local Lenni-Lenape (Delaware) Indians had reportedly held tribal councils before they were forced out by European settlers. The Indian Rock Hotel was a favorite stop for coaching parties — or for hikers on an expedition to Indian Rock itself.[53]

Besides being good for the hotel business, Chestnut Hill's reputedly healthy climate gave rise to several hospitals and charitable institutions. Short-lived but very impressive was the Mower General Hospital for convalescing soldiers, built beside the Chestnut Hill Railroad tracks during the Civil War. Opened in January 1863, the hospital and grounds occupied a tract of some twenty-seven acres between the rail line and Stenton Avenue. The hospital's entrance was near today's Wyndmoor station on SEPTA's Chestnut Hill-East line (the old Chestnut Hill and then Reading Railroad). The structure was built entirely of wood, with some thirty-four wards (containing 4,500 beds) radiating out from a central core. Over 20,000 patients passed through its doors before it ceased functioning in May of 1865. Demolished after the war, its site would later become part of the Randal Morgan estate and is now in the Chestnut Hill Village/Market Square development.[54]

Two decades later, the City Mission of the Episcopal Church,

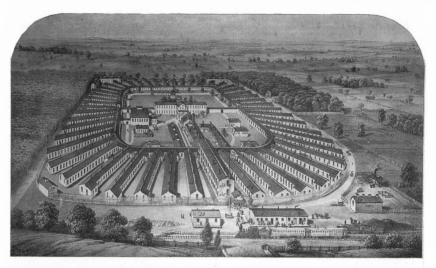

Lithograph of Mower General Hospital, 1863, which stood just east of the intersection of East Willow Grove Ave. and the Reading (Chestnut Hill-East) Railroad. CHHS.

attracted by the pure country air of Chestnut Hill, decided to locate
a tuberculosis hospital near the corner of Stenton and Evergreen avenues, just across the township/county line in Wyndmoor. The latest
treatment for this dread disease called for exposing patients to as
much fresh air as possible, placing their beds outside on porches during all but the coldest weather. Officially known as the Home for
Consumptives, the main structure was designed by Frank Furness.
Some local citizens protested the decision to locate the facility there,
but it remained a fixture of the community for decades and is now
part of the All Saints rehabilitation complex.[55]

A home for orphans was established in Chestnut Hill during its
early suburban period, the Bethesda Children's Christian Home, now
defunct. After occupying several sites, including the Park House Hotel, the home settled at the southeast corner of Willow Grove and
Stenton avenues in 1878 in a building (now demolished) that was
donated by Henry J. Williams, a wealthy Chestnut Hill lawyer. By
1883, there were 140 children living at the institution.[56]

With the increasing number of people in Chestnut Hill—whether
they were commuters, summer vacationers, consumptives, or or-

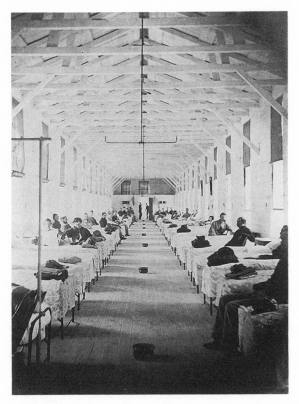

"A Ward," Mower General Hospital. Photo by John
Moran. LCP.

phans — there was an obvious need for additional utilities and institutions. Over a twenty-five-year period, leading residents established
a library, a waterworks, a private club, four new churches, and two
private schools.

Of utmost importance was a sufficient source of pure water. Although Chestnut Hill was now part of the consolidated city of Philadelphia, municipal authorities apparently could not or would not
supply the community with a waterworks. As local residents would
soon learn, city hall would often prove unresponsive to calls for public
services in their somewhat isolated corner of the city. Consequently,
several leading citizens established their own Chestnut Hill Water
Company, which was incorporated in 1856. Its president, Charles

Water tower and reservoir of the Chestnut Hill Water Company, now the site of the Water Tower Recreation Center and playing fields. Photo by Thomas Shoemaker, 1890. GHS.

Heebner, owned a forty-acre estate in Chestnut Hill that ran east of Germantown Avenue between Southhampton Avenue and Hartwell Lane.[57]

The water company built a small reservoir on Heebner's property near the intersection of Hartwell Lane and Ardleigh Street, where the Water Tower Recreation Center now stands. In 1859 the company erected a 125-foot-high water tower made of local stone. Nearly a century and a half later, the tower (though bereft of its wooden water tank at the top) stands as a local landmark. Just after the Civil War, the city of Philadelphia purchased the local waterworks and made it part of its own system of distribution.[58]

A supply of gas, largely for lighting purposes, had been obtained several years before when the Germantown Gas Company agreed in late 1853 to provide service to the Hill. Suburban residents might have reveled in Chestnut Hill's rural scenery, but they wanted to enjoy all the conveniences of city life at the same time, a typical sentiment of the suburbanite who wished to have the best of both worlds. Although there would be complaints about both the quantity and quality of gas piped to the Hill, it would be used to illuminate most prosperous homes in the community until the early twentieth century.[59]

It was also private initiative that led to Chestnut Hill's first library. The donor was Henry J. Williams, also the principal benefactor of the Bethesda Home. As a devout Presbyterian, he did not want any meetings or activities to take place on the premises that were not consistent with Christian principles, and he called his new institution the Christian Hall Library. He had the building constructed of local stone and appointed fourteen trustees to administer the library, with the Reverend Roger Owen, a Presbyterian clergyman, as its president. (As was true of many other early institutions in Chestnut Hill, the trustees operated under the common law rather than through a corporate charter.) Opening in early 1871, the Christian Hall Library functioned at first only as a reading room.[60] Several years later it became a subscription library and finally a free library. On the second floor of the building Williams provided space for a group called the Christian Hall Association, which held both religious services and social functions. Because purely secular activities were banned from the premises by its charter, Williams erected a frame structure behind the library where other organizations and clubs could hold their meetings. At his death in 1879, Williams left an endowment of $15,000 to support the institution he had founded. In 1896 the facility merged with the Philadelphia Free Library system, and in 1909 a new building, erected under a grant from the Carnegie Library Fund, replaced the original structure.[61]

Williams's insistence upon a Christian character for his library was much in keeping with the idea that the romantic suburb should be a thoroughly Christian community. The flurry of church building in Chestnut Hill between 1850 and 1860 attested to the popularity of

The Christian Hall Library, 1871–72. Photo c. 1900, after the library had been acquired by the Philadelphia Free Library. Harris Collection, CHHS.

this ideal. Three Protestant denominations and a Roman Catholic parish joined the preexisting Methodist and Baptist congregations. A community of Roman Catholic nuns, the Sisters of St. Joseph, also settled on the Hill during the decade.

The Presbyterians were the first to organize. Despite the older Baptist and Methodist congregations, the majority of residents in 1850 seem to have been either Presbyterians or Lutherans, thus leading several Presbyterians in the area to believe that they might start their own church.[62] The arrival of the Reverend Roger Owen that year, who had come to open a boys academy, encouraged the Presbyterians further. Owen was soon asked to preach regularly at the Union Chapel. The response was so encouraging that the faithful decided to establish the First Presbyterian Church of Chestnut Hill in May 1852. Owen became its pastor, a position that he would hold for the next thirty-three years. Among the names appearing in the charter were such important and prosperous local figures as Owen Sheridan, Joseph H. Hildeburn, and George V. Rex. For several

First Presbyterian (Rex Ave.) Church, designed by John Notman and built in 1852. Photo from Macfarlane, *Early History,* opposite p. 65, c. 1927.

years the Presbyterians met in the Union Chapel — or in the hall at the railroad station. They built their own church in the summer of 1852 at the northwest corner of Germantown and Rex avenues on a parcel of land donated by George Rex that now houses a Seventh Day Adventist congregation. Its designer was the famous John Notman, better known as the architect of Holy Trinity and St. Clement's churches downtown. Even at this early period, residents of the Hill were able to use their wealth to engage one of the region's top architects.[63]

If there were few Episcopalians in Chestnut Hill during the first half of the nineteenth century, the arrival of prosperous vacationers and suburban residents greatly augmented their numbers. Taking note of this fact, several members of the denomination began holding services whenever possible at the Union Chapel. In 1855, after two years of sporadic worship, they decided to form a parish. They held an organizational meeting at the railroad station in June of that year

and organized themselves as St. Paul's Episcopal Church. Among the
first vestrymen were prominent local men such as Cephas G. Childs,
Charles Taylor, and Joseph H. Hildeburn. Hildeburn, like several
others who had joined the Presbyterian fold only three years before,
had perhaps gone with the Presbyterians initially only because there
was not yet an Episcopal church on the Hill.

The Episcopal organizers decided to raise a chapel, which was
ready for use in September 1856. It still stands as part of a larger
structure on the south side of Chestnut Hill Avenue, opposite the
entrance to Norwood Avenue and just a block below Samuel Austin's
Summit Street development. They engaged as architects John E.
Carver and later the firm of Sidney and Merry. Although not as cel-
ebrated as Notman, all three architects were highly regarded prac-
titioners of the sort who would appeal to a wealthy and socially
conscious congregation such as St. Paul's.

After finding their first rector unsatisfactory, in part because of
his extreme youth, the St. Paul's vestry selected the Reverend J. Andrews Harris, who remained for the next half century. As the number
of well-to-do suburban residents increased on the Hill, the membership of St. Paul's grew apace. Although some of these newcomers
probably had not been Episcopalians when they arrived, they soon
converted to this prominent denomination in order to climb the social
ladder or to solidify their positions in the community. Since the colonial period, the Anglican church and its American successor, the
Episcopal church, had been the religion of the upper classes. In England, the Anglican church was the church of the king, the nobility,
and the landed gentry. For this and other reasons, St. Paul's would
remain Chestnut Hill's most fashionable church.[64]

The last Protestant group to establish themselves in Chestnut Hill
during the nineteenth century was the Lutherans. Started as a mission
of Christ Evangelical Church in Germantown, members on the Hill
organized themselves as Evangelical Lutheran Christ Church of
Chestnut Hill in late 1860. The congregation met at various locations
around the community until completing their own church in 1871, a
structure that remains at the northwestern corner of Southhampton
and Germantown avenues. Architect Charles M. Burns, Jr., was not

Our Mother of Consolation Roman Catholic Church, 1855. Drawing from Macfarlane, *Early History,* opposite p. 65.

as well-known as the designers of St. Paul's Episcopal and the First Presbyterian Church, a fact that may reflect the modest means of the congregation, as demonstrated by early membership lists. Most were of German ancestry. As German ethnic identity declined in Chestnut Hill over the decades, and especially in the twentieth century, the size of the Lutheran fold would dwindle. The Baptist and Methodist congregations would likewise suffer declining numbers as the farmers and laborers who made up the bulk of their congregations gradually disappeared from the area.[65]

Surprising to some is the fact that Chestnut Hill's Roman Catholic parish, known in recent decades as Our Mother of Consolation (OMC), was founded at the same time as the great Protestant expansion on the Hill during the 1850s. There had been few Catholics in the area, which had been populated almost exclusively by descendants of German, Scotch, Scotch-Irish, Welsh, and English Protestants. But accompanying the new suburban residents was a demand for domestic servants, many of whom were Irish Catholics who had come to Philadelphia in the wake of the potato famine.

Yet it was the prominent Chestnut Hiller Joseph Middleton, a convert from Quakerism to the Catholic faith, who founded the Hill's Catholic parish in 1855. It was he who purchased a lot for the church on the north side of Chestnut Hill Avenue, almost directly across the street from the future St. Paul's Episcopal, who provided the bulk of the funds for erecting a church, and who apparently designed the church himself. In selecting this site, Middleton placed the parish in the heart of North Chestnut Hill, destined to become a bastion of wealthy, Anglo-Saxon Protestantism where the vast majority of the Hill's first Roman Catholics (except for live-in servants) could not afford to settle. Anti-Catholic Know-Nothings in Philadelphia attempted several times to prevent the building of this Roman Catholic church in Chestnut Hill (see also chapters 4 and 5).[66]

Three years after the founding of Chestnut Hill's Catholic parish, a small group of nuns belonging to the Sisters of St. Joseph settled in Chestnut Hill. The order was founded in France during the early seventeenth century, and the sisters had originally come to Philadelphia in 1846. In 1858 they purchased Joseph Middleton's Monticello, a seven-acre tract with house that had once contained the old Deewees paper mill. There the sisters established their mother house, later the headquarters for a network of several thousand nuns who were assigned to missions throughout the Middle Atlantic States. By then specializing in education, the sisters founded Mount St. Joseph's Academy (for girls) in 1871 and Chestnut Hill College (for women) in 1924.[67] For decades the sisters kept largely to themselves, and were seldom seen around Chestnut Hill. Their students came from beyond the neighborhood for the most part, with the result that many Protestant residents of the Hill knew little or nothing about the academy or college for decades. The sisters' open, rolling grounds, augmented by further purchases of land, would do much to preserve the semirural flavor so important to the romantic suburb.[68]

If they were ignorant about the Catholic institutions in their midst, well-to-do Protestants in Chestnut Hill were quick to create or support a set of private schools for their own children. Over the

Springside School, which stood at the northeast corner of Norwood and Chestnut Hill avenues. Photo c. 1910. *Local.*

decades these schools would not only educate their boys and girls, but also serve as a means of inculcating a sense of upper- and upper-middle-class community. Children of well-to-do families would go to school with youngsters of a similar background and make lasting friends within that group. They might remain totally oblivious to other children on the Hill, who may have grown up only blocks away but who attended Catholic or public schools.

The first of the private schools was Chestnut Hill Academy, a boys boarding school founded in 1851 by the Reverend Roger Owen and his brother Joshua T. Owen. Although this institution closed about 1856, the name Chestnut Hill Academy was used by another school, founded in 1861, that remains the principal private school for boys in Chestnut Hill more than a century later.[69]

Several private schools for girls arose during the early suburban period, but the only one to last into the late twentieth century was the Springside School. Opened in 1879 in a house on Summit Street, this institution was originally known as Miss Bell and Mrs. Comegys' French and English Boarding School for Little Girls. Several years later it moved to the northeast corner of Norwood and Chestnut Hill avenues. Because a spring ran through the Norwood Avenue property, the school eventually came to be known as Springside. Its founders, Anna Loraine Bell (Mrs. Walter D.) Comegys and her unmarried sister, Jane Bell, were the Tennessee-bred daughters of Senator John Bell, who had run unsuccessfully for the presidency against Abraham Lincoln in 1860 as the Constitutional Unionist candidate. Following Walter Comegys' death in 1877, Anna joined with her maiden sister to open the school. Because of the family's connections in the South, many of their early boarders came from that part of the country. They also attracted day students from Chestnut Hill.[70]

In their early brochures the Bell sisters extolled the same conveniences and healthy atmosphere that had drawn prosperous residents to the Hill over the past two decades:

> Although within the city limits and consequently possessing all the advantages which Philadelphia affords, [the site] has been selected after mature consideration, as the best location for a school, on account of its extreme healthfulness and entire freedom from all malarial influences. Residence within three minutes walk of depot. Twenty-three trains daily, to and from the city.[71]

Like the Hill's other residents, the students could enjoy the best of two worlds — urban and suburban.

Socially prominent adults in Chestnut Hill founded the first of several exclusive clubs during the early suburban period, the Chestnut Hill Agricultural Society, incorporated in 1857 by an act of the state legislature. Its members purchased a five-acre tract on West Springfield Avenue that was not far from the future Wissahickon Inn. Its first president was the ubiquitous Owen Sheridan, with mill owner Charles Megargee as vice-president and merchant Daniel Brady as secretary. Membership was limited to 150. Far from being devoted to genuine agricultural subjects, the organization was something of an early day country club. A description of the new club in the *Germantown Telegraph* underlined the exclusionary nature of the Agricultural Society:

> A number of wealthy gentlemen have purchased a tract a little southward of Chestnut Hill and have enrolled themselves into a club or company. . . . The

select character of the company is guaranteed by balloting for every stock-holder — two negative votes being sufficient to exclude the applicant for membership.[72]

The article went on to say that each member might bring his family to the grounds and "mansion" on the site, where a "first-class steward" was on hand to serve meals or refreshments.[73] But most striking of all to the reader more than a century later, at a time when suburbanites are often apologetic or even defensive about their privileges, is the flagrant description in a local newspaper of the club's discriminatory practices.

Thus, by the mid-1880s North Chestnut Hill was a successful suburb in the far northwestern corner of Philadelphia. It was complete with dozens of romantic villas, private schools, a fashionable Episcopal church, an exclusive social club, and a convenient rail link to downtown, as well as supplies of gas and water. In Chestnut Hill prosperous Philadelphians could enjoy the wealth and culture of the city without having to live with its filth, disease, and poverty. Although they successfully identified with both city and suburb, their peaceful residences on the edge of the city allowed them and future counterparts to ignore many of the city's worst problems. At the same time, their drive for social and cultural homogeneity within Chestnut Hill would keep them from identifying with the interests of humbler residents and thereby contribute to community fragmentation on the Hill itself.

3

WISSAHICKON HEIGHTS / ST. MARTIN'S

The Planned Suburb

Although the villas of North Chestnut Hill remain attractive after nearly a century and a half, it is the housing on the West Side that locals and visitors alike associate with the residential look of Philadelphia's most fashionable suburb in the city. Of all the properties on the West Side, those commissioned between the 1880s and the 1930s by Henry Howard Houston (1820–1895) and his son-in-law George Woodward (1863–1952) are the most distinctive. Once completed, these properties became yet another piece in the residential ensemble that continues to characterize Chestnut Hill. The quaint streetscapes created by George Woodward, particularly in his Cotswold Village, provided a strong visual contrast to more urban areas of the city below and helped to emphasize the duality of suburban lives. At the same time, the beautiful dwellings and their prom-

MONTGOMERY COUNTY

1. Winston Court
2. Benezet Street
3. Pastorius Park
4. Cotswold Village
5. St. Martin's Church
6. Philadelphia Cricket Club
7. Chestnut Hill Academy
   (Wissahickon Inn)
8. Druim Moir
9. French Village

George W. Woodward Inc.

Woodward House Corp.

Open Space

SCALE IN FEET

The Woodward (and Houston) properties in 1990. ERG.

inent residents contributed to the social and cultural segmentation of Chestnut Hill.

Unlike the developers of North Chestnut Hill, who sold all but a few lots to individuals, Houston and Woodward built about 300 houses themselves, most of which they rented rather than sold. In this way they were able to maintain control over their properties and the neighborhood itself. In so doing, they provided all the elements that Chestnut Hillers and others have come to associate with the upper- and upper-middle-class suburban community: architect-designed houses, well-landscaped grounds, large open spaces, private schools, a well-appointed Episcopal church, recreational facilities, a homogeneous population, and convenient transportation. Far more than North Chestnut Hill, the Houston/Woodward development took on an English air that reflected the strong Anglophilia of many wealthy American suburbs in the late nineteenth and early twentieth centuries.

The original name for this development was Wissahickon Heights, chosen by Henry Howard Houston because of its site above the Wissahickon Creek. In the early twentieth century, George Woodward changed the designation to St. Martin's, in honor of the church of the same name.

Houston, the initiator of this development, was not a native son.[1] Born to a prominent family in Wrightsville, Pennsylvania, he had arrived in Philadelphia in 1847 to become an agent for David Leech and Company, a flourishing transportation business. In 1851 the nascent Pennsylvania Railroad hired Houston as its general (or head) freight agent. Houston succeeded well in organizing the Pennsylvania's freight department, and during the Civil War turned his talents to helping create a fast freight company using the Pennsylvania's main route and connecting lines. By 1865, with the war still in progress and the Union authorities dependent on the Pennsylvania Railroad to haul many of its troops and supplies, Houston had amassed a substantial sum of capital. He subsequently invested in mines, oil, shipping, various other railroad ventures, and in massive amounts of land, leaving an estate of just over $14 million at his death in 1895. During the last fourteen years of his life, Houston was also a director of the Pennsylvania Railroad.

Henry Howard Houston in 1884. Oil on canvas, by
David John Gué. FJD.

Although Houston came from a prominent family whose American ancestors went back to the early eighteenth century, his rapid
rise to wealth and entrepreneurial success did not make him an instant
member of Philadelphia's upper-upper class. For example, Houston
was not elected to the prestigious Philadelphia Club, and he was not
invited to subscribe to the equally exclusive Assemblies (an organization that has held annual balls since the colonial period), although
he was a member of several other distinguished clubs and organizations. Luckily, Houston had begun making his fortune just before the
end of the Civil War, a sort of unofficial deadline for the easy acceptance of one's heirs into Philadelphia's upper-upper class.[2] Accordingly, Houston's children and grandchildren became members of
Philadelphia's inner sanctum, including the Philadelphia Club and
the Assemblies.[3]

Whatever his precise social rank, Houston's real estate ventures
in Philadelphia began as early as 1853, when he bought a tract of land

in Germantown. In 1860, three years after his marriage to Sallie Sher-rerd Bonnell, Houston himself moved to Germantown. After living in a rented dwelling for several years, he bought a large Italianate villa (now demolished) at the northwest corner of Wayne Avenue and Tulpehocken Street, one of the most desirable locations in an already flourishing railroad suburb.

Tulpehocken Street had been developed a decade or so before, but there were still parcels of open land in the vicinity, some of which Houston purchased in the mid-1860s. In 1873 he also financed and built a neighborhood Episcopal church known as St. Peter's, Germantown.[4] Although Houston had grown up in his family's Scotch-Irish Presbyterian church, he converted to his wife's Episcopal faith a year after their marriage. Although by all accounts Houston was a sincere convert, his joining the socially prestigious Anglican confession paralleled the conversion of thousands of upwardly mobile individuals in Philadelphia and elsewhere in the nation.[5]

With St. Peter's completed in 1873, Houston may have already begun to look for other real estate investments beyond Germantown. According to family tradition, he had long been struck by the wild and rolling beauty of the Wissahickon gorge as it plunged through the western extremities of Chestnut Hill. He frequently climbed to the cupola of his Tulpehocken Street villa to admire the area, and he had allegedly vowed to acquire it for himself.[6] Whether or not this is apocryphal, Houston purchased more than 3,000 acres of land, totaling some four and a half square miles. Beginning at West Allen's Lane in Mount Airy, his land ran as far as Ridge and Butler pikes in Montgomery County, much of it contiguous property. The land bordered both sides of the Wissahickon Creek and occupied almost the entire West Side of Chestnut Hill, as well as most of Upper Roxborough on the opposite side of the creek.[7]

As a railroad man and as the resident of a railroad suburb like Germantown, Houston well understood that a commuter rail line was crucial to developing his land on the West Side of Chestnut Hill. He persuaded the Pennsylvania directors to build a subsidiary commuter line, to be known officially as the Philadelphia, Germantown, and Chestnut Hill Railroad. Houston himself donated $500,000 worth of land for the right-of-way and also may have put up a substantial amount of capital. Actual construction began in 1882, with the line opening to the present St. Martin's station on 1 June 1884.[8]

Meanwhile, Houston had been busy planning his Wissahickon Heights development. Unfortunately, any written documentation of his plans for Chestnut Hill has been lost, with the exception of a hand-drawn map, and no oral record has survived within the family. Perhaps Houston was simply not the sort of man who felt a need to explain himself to others.

One clue to Houston's motives for creating Wissahickon Heights may have been his joy at building and organizing things; he had been very successful in establishing the Pennsylvania's freight lines and then in setting up a railroad express company. It is also possible that he was inspired by the residential developments undertaken by various Pennsylvania Railroad board members on the Philadelphia Main Line, a string of semirural suburbs that still are located along the railroad's "main line" to Pittsburgh and the West. But it is just as likely that Germantown, over the quarter century that Houston lived there, provided something of an informal laboratory where he observed what real estate developers were doing and tried his own hand at real estate investment.

None of these assumptions rules out the possibility that Houston simply wanted to create a sylvan retreat for himself and for his family for generations to come. Houston had not grown up in the city, and he had moved to Germantown just a dozen years after his arrival in Philadelphia; a quarter century later he made his final move to Chestnut Hill. Somewhat like Venetian merchants of the sixteenth or seventeenth century, who retired from a hectic life in commerce to their estates in the nearby mainland, it may be that Houston saw Chestnut Hill as a retreat from the strident city that he and others like him had helped to create.[9]

Whatever his motives, the first of Houston's projects in Wissahickon Heights was the massive Wissahickon Inn, located just west of the present St. Martin's Lane, between West Springfield and Willow Grove avenues, on the site of the older Park House, which had burned in 1877.[10] Completed in the spring of 1884, its architects were

Wissahickon Inn. Commissioned by Henry Howard Houston, designed by the
Hewitt brothers, and opened in 1884. Photo c. 1895 by J. S. Johnson. LCP.

George W. Hewitt (1841–1916) and his brother William D. Hewitt
(1847–1924).

The Hewitts were one of the most distinguished and versatile
firms in the city. George Hewitt was a graduate of Burlington College
(New Jersey), had trained under Philadelphia architects Joseph C.
Hoxie and John Notman, and had been a partner of the legendary
Frank Furness before forming his own firm with his brother. William
Hewitt had also graduated from Burlington College and worked with
Furness. Houston would use the Hewitts to design virtually all his
projects in Wissahickon Heights.[11]

The Wissahickon Inn was a spacious, three-story U-shaped structure with wide wooden porches surrounding the entire ground floor.
Measuring 236 by 227 by 227 feet, the inn boasted 250 guest rooms,
many with their own fireplaces. The guests could also enjoy a ballroom, library, and commodious dining room. Like nearly everything
else that the Hewitts designed for Houston, the structure was in the
then popular Queen Anne style, which featured a variety of materials
and textures. The lower two stories of the inn were made of local

stone. The third story was constructed of wood made to simulate stucco and half-timbering. The roof line was punctuated by a profusion of turrets and tall chimneys.[12]

Houston doubtless had several reasons for building the inn. He wanted to take advantage of Chestnut Hill's popularity as a summer resort, and in the early years the Wissahickon Inn was a flourishing concern. For example, the *Germantown Telegraph* reported in July 1887 that "every room at the Wissahickon Inn has been occupied for two weeks back and the rush still exists. . . ."[13] Houston was able to rent the inn to its proprietor, J. E. Kingsley, for $3,000 a season.[14] He also must have seen the inn as a way of attracting prosperous Philadelphians to Wissahickon Heights. Later they might decide to buy land there or settle in one of Houston's houses.

Several other Houston projects were calculated to enhance Wissahickon Heights, or depended partly upon the inn's accommodations. One of these was Lake Surprise (now drained), which was located just below the inn along the present Cresheim Valley Drive. Houston created it by improving an old mill dam and pond along Cresheim Creek. On the lake guests could enjoy canoeing during the warmer months and ice-skating in the winter. He also landscaped an area just east of the inn called St. Martin's Green, an attractive arboretum where guests could stroll. The site is now the running track for Chestnut Hill Academy.[15]

Far more ambitious than either Lake Surprise or St. Martin's Green was the Philadelphia Horse Show, which Houston brought to Wissahickon Heights in the spring of 1892. Its first location was on St. Martin's Green, where Houston erected a grandstand for about 2,500 spectators. There were also arena boxes (with six seats each), 125 stables, and 140 stalls.[16] Several years later he moved the horse show to a larger site just across Willow Grove Avenue.[17]

Like the inn, one goal of the horse show was probably to introduce well-to-do folk, of the class who could afford to admire, keep, and show fine horses, to Wissahickon Heights. According to the *Germantown Guide*, a weekly newspaper of the period, Houston succeeded in doing just that. Describing the scene in May 1894, the *Guide* reported, "The great society event of the present week is the horse show at

JUDGING LADIES SADDLE HORSES
PHILADELPHIA HORSE SHOW

The Philadelphia Horse Show on Wissahickon Heights. CHHS.

Wissahickon Heights, where pretty women, noble men and blooded stock have combined to present the rarest of attractions." The article went on to say that the boxes and grandstands "were like a giant bouquet of American beauties, while the promenaders in their lovely spring gowns distracted the attention of many a one who was trying to settle in his or her mind which horse would carry away the blue ribbon." The horse show was a place to see and be seen for the Philadelphia upper class.

By 1896, according to the *Guide*, the horse show was attracting top exhibitors from Pennsylvania, New York, and Maryland, and from as far away as Chicago and Boston. Thereafter the event continued to grow in size and importance. In 1899 more than 800 horses were shown. Two years later, the total value of prizes was $11,715, with $1,750 in silver trophies and $9,965 in cash, altogether about twenty times as much as a factory worker could earn in an entire year. Beginning about 1898, the year of the Spanish-American War, various military groups put on equestrian displays. In 1898 there was a unit from the Pennsylvania Military College at Chester, which became a regular feature at the horse show in the years to come. The following year there was a performance by the Third United States Cavalry, which had reportedly shared the glory, with Theodore Roosevelt's Rough Riders, of fighting on San Juan Hill.

Among the Philadelphia exhibitors were such social lions as Alexander J. Cassatt, future president of the Pennsylvania Railroad and brother of the painter Mary Cassatt, and Anthony J. Drexel, the powerful investment banker. A later exhibitor was Edward T. Stotesbury, the immensely rich partner of J. P. Morgan and Anthony Drexel, and the future owner of a gigantic Trianon-style mansion just east of Chestnut Hill in Springfield Township.[18] With such socially important exhibitors and the display of fine clothes and expensive prizes, Wissahickon Heights was well on the way to establishing itself as a community for the social elite.

The horse show left Wissahickon Heights after 1908 because residents were concerned that the wooden stands were a serious fire hazard.[19] It moved to the Main Line and continues to exist as the Devon Horse Show. But by 1908 the show had served as a magnet to draw some of Philadelphia's most prominent citizens to Wissahickon Heights. Nor did the horse show's departure signal the end of sporting life in the neighborhood. In 1884, the same year that the Wissahickon Inn opened and the new rail line arrived, Houston's donation of land led to the opening of the Philadelphia Cricket Club on West Willow Grove Avenue, opposite the Wissahickon Inn. The original clubhouses, like nearly everything else in Wissahickon Heights, were designed in the Queen Anne style. These were destroyed in a disastrous fire in 1909 and were replaced shortly thereafter by the present colonial revival pavilions.[20]

The Philadelphia Cricket Club actually had been in existence since 1854, but it did not have a permanent home until Houston provided land for it on Wissahickon Heights. Cricket had been brought to Philadelphia by English hosiery workers, and it was soon adopted with great enthusiasm by wealthy Philadelphians who, like their colonial ancestors, continued to look to the British Isles for standards of culture and genteel behavior. Feeling insecure about America's status as a nation and still suffering from a lingering sense of colonial inferiority, many members of the middle and upper classes saw no

One of the early buildings (later destroyed by fire) of the Philadelphia Cricket
Club, designed by the Hewitt brothers, and opened in 1884. CHHS.

alternative but to keep imitating the fashions of their counterparts
and social betters in England. Furthermore, the United Kingdom remained the most powerful country in the world throughout the nineteenth century, and many Americans admired the British for it. Thus,
in a search for roots in a new and relatively rootless nation, the Anglo-
Saxon upper and upper-middle class naturally inclined toward British ways. Fears of the "new immigrants" from southern and eastern
Europe and an intensified race consciousness, fed by a twisted form
of social Darwinism, would exacerbate this Anglophilia in the late
nineteenth and early twentieth centuries.[21] Whatever its causes, Anglophilia would be expressed in many other ways in Chestnut Hill
over the years, and would become an integral part of the identity of
its wealthy families.

However important the Cricket Club, the horse show, and the
Wissahickon Inn were to the development of Wissahickon Heights,
Houston's centerpiece was St. Martin-in-the-Fields Episcopal Church,
completed in 1889. Houston took the name from St. Martin-in-the-

St. Martin-in-the-Fields Episcopal Church. Commissioned by Henry Howard Houston, designed by the Hewitt brothers, and completed in 1889. Photo c. 1890s. SMF.

Fields in London, a parish that had also once stood in the midst of open fields outside a great city. The name was thus another reflection of the Anglophilia among well-to-do Chestnut Hillers. So, too, was the church structure itself, designed by the Hewitt brothers in the Gothic Revival style. Executed in local stone, it was intended to look like a well-kept parish church in some quaint English village.

Besides providing land for St. Martin's, Houston assumed the entire burden of constructing and furnishing it, as well as providing a handsome parish hall and rectory. The total cost must have amounted to about $100,000. Houston also visited a number of Episcopal churches up and down the East Coast to select a rector, finally settling on the Reverend Jacob LeRoy, who shared his relatively high church views. As a final commitment to the parish, Houston agreed to pay LeRoy's salary of $2,500 per year. In the decades to come, Houston and his descendants often funded the parish's annual deficits, in addition to contributing a baptistery, an enlarged chancel, and several stained glass windows. Houston's only surviving son, Samuel Frederic Houston (1866–1952), served as rector's warden at St. Martin's for a record sixty-three years. Ironically, the senior Houston would never formally join St. Martin's, believing it to be his duty to remain as rector's warden at St. Peter's, Germantown, which he had built fifteen years before. Nevertheless, he frequently attended services at St. Martin's and was buried from there in 1895.[22]

Although Houston doubtless built St. Martin's as yet another feature of his suburban development, it is also clear that he was a devout man. Like the suburbanites who had built St. Paul's Episcopal Church in North Chestnut Hill a generation before, Houston intended St. Martin's to be the moral center of a neighborhood of Christian homes. Such was the intent of its rector, Jacob LeRoy, who wrote soon after the parish's founding that its mission was to help "create a good neighborhood and establish a wholesome Christian standard of intercourse against a narrow, worldly, and artificial substitute."[23] In case church services alone were not enough to effect this goal, Houston sponsored Sunday evening religious services at the Wissahickon Inn.[24] As to his own family, they invariably spent Sunday evenings around the piano singing hymns, a common practice among middle- and upper-class Protestants in Chestnut Hill and elsewhere during the Victorian age.[25]

It is also evident that LeRoy, Houston, and Houston's descendants wanted St. Martin's to be a force for good far beyond the neighborhood. In this sense one can associate St. Martin's charitable activities with the wider Social Gospel movement that was taking strong root among British and American Protestants, and especially among high Episcopalians such as Houston.[26] Houston thus used St. Martin's to funnel thousands of dollars into missions throughout the nation and the world. His daughter Gertrude Houston (Woodward) became devoted to American Indian charities, contributing heavily to them throughout her life. Closer to home, Houston established a lending library at St. Martin's, with many books of a spiritual nature. At the same time, Houston and St. Martin's reached out to black residents in the neighborhood, most of whom were servants at the Wissahickon Inn. Blacks were invited to use the library, as well as

Buttercup Cottage (demolished in 1958), Houston's summer retreat for working girls, which stood on the west side of Cresheim Valley Drive. GHS.

to attend services at the church. However, the services and library hours were segregated. The church's Social Gospel thus had its limits; it did not extend to overturning the racial customs of the day.[27]

St. Martin's also helped to sponsor a summer retreat in Chestnut Hill for white working girls from Philadelphia. This retreat was housed at Buttercup Cottage, a rambling old farmhouse (demolished in 1958) that stood along Cresheim Valley Drive, a property that Houston acquired about 1889. Houston's daughter Gertrude became president of the organization, and her sister-in-law Edith Corlies (Mrs. Samuel F.) Houston and cousin Sarah B. Houston, who lived with the family, joined the board of managers. Among the other managers, all of whom were female, were such socially prominent women as Mrs. J. Willis Martin, Mrs. Spencer Janney, and Miss Sophie Weygandt. Opened for the first time in June 1889, the cottage provided two weeks of relaxation in the country each summer for about 275 working girls, most of them shop clerks from the city. Although the cottage had no official connection with St. Martin's, the Reverend LeRoy served as its chaplain and two Episcopal nuns supervised the facility on a daily basis. Various members of the parish also helped to support Buttercup Cottage financially.[28]

Whatever the working girls may have thought of the facility, it was part of a local effort to practice the Social Gospel among the working classes of Philadelphia. Although a later generation might criticize it as an act of charity to the "deserving poor," those involved with Buttercup Cottage were sincere about a project that showed concern for less fortunate people in the city. The work at the cottage also may have helped them to identify emotionally with the city, despite their sheltered lives in a privileged suburban community. Finally, the effort put forth by Gertrude Houston and other well-to-do women at Buttercup Cottage anticipated the wide array of volunteer work that Chestnut Hill women would launch in the future.

As Houston was putting this and other institutions into place, he began to build some 80 to 100 houses on the streets radiating out from St. Martin's Church.[29] At first the streets running north and south went by numbers, a prosaic extension of the Philadelphia grid that city hall had projected all the way through Chestnut Hill. These ranged from 22nd Street on the far East Side of Chestnut Hill to 38th Street on the far West Side.[30] Houston disliked these uninspiring street designations, and even on the surviving map of Wissahickon Heights he had begun to suggest a more sylvan nomenclature.[31]

By the early twentieth century, all the numbered street designations had been changed in Chestnut Hill. In the Wissahickon Heights area, many of them were replaced by Indian names, a choice attributed by oral tradition to Houston's daughter Gertrude. For example, 27th Street became Shawnee Street, 29th Street became Navajo Street, and 30th Street became Seminole Avenue; other numbered streets became Towanda, Huron, and Cherokee streets. An exception was 31st Street, which was rechristened St. Martin's Lane. Such names were fitting for a late Victorian suburb like Wissahickon Heights which offered an idyllic alternative to the densely populated parts of Philadelphia—for those who could afford it. These name changes were a testament to the influence that men like Houston could wield at city hall. Although other sections of the city had to accept numbered streets whether they liked it or not, Chestnut Hillers were able to use their social and professional leverage to secure more appropriate names. Such leverage would be employed many times in the future by prominent citizens to get what they wanted from city authorities. But even Houston could not alter the grid pattern itself to create gently winding streets that in other American suburbs followed the natural contours of the land.[32]

Using the present street names, the residential portion of Wissahickon Heights was bounded on the west by St. Martin's Lane, and on the east, roughly, by Seminole Avenue and Pocono Street. Its northern and southern boundaries were Chestnut Hill Avenue and Mermaid Lane. The dwellings toward the Chestnut Hill Avenue end of the tract were generally larger and, in the early period particularly, separated by sizable parcels of land. There were smaller singles and semidetached houses at the opposite end of the development, along Springfield and Moreland avenues and Mermaid Lane. Houston also commissioned a number of double units along the 8300 block of Shawnee Street and in the first block of West Southhampton Avenue.

These houses in Wissahickon Heights, nearly all of them designed by the Hewitt brothers and still standing, were eclectic in style, with those of the 1880s in the Queen Anne mode.[33] They varied in size from the modest double units on the south side of the 300 block of West Springfield Avenue to a flamboyant Queen Anne residence at 8205 Seminole Avenue. The latter included a two-story porch in front, steep roofs, multiple half-timbered gable ends, and banks of casement windows, all characteristic of the Queen Anne style. It remains one of the most stunning Queen Anne houses anywhere in America.

Many of Houston's last commissions (in several cases completed by his estate managers) were executed in an early Colonial Revival mode. These include the double units on the north side of the 300 block of West Springfield Avenue. Several of these were rendered in a loose Dutch Colonial style, characterized by double-pitched gambrel roofs. These early Colonial Revival structures were not incompatible with the Queen Anne style, in that they also employed some neoclassical motifs. This compatibility was reinforced by the generous use of porches and balconies in the first generation of Colonial Re-

Stone twin house in the 300 block of West Springfield Ave., 1886. Commissioned by Henry Howard Houston and designed by the Hewitt brothers. Photo by author, 1984.

vival dwellings. Like St. Martin's Church, the Wissahickon Inn, and the original buildings of the Cricket Club, Houston's Colonial Revival houses were constructed in large part of local stone, adding a further degree of consistency.

Although Houston sold many of the larger single dwellings, he decided to rent the bulk of his houses, thereby retaining control over land use and occupants. Rents ranged from thirty dollars per month for the doubles to one hundred fifty dollars a month for the largest singles.[34] Such reasonable rates show that Houston was not interested in making a great deal of money from his rental properties, but rents were high enough to ensure that all the tenants would be of at least upper-middle-class standing. Of the residents in Wissahickon Heights in 1890–1891 whose occupations can be traced, six were substantial Philadelphia merchants, four were brokers, three were lawyers, one was a dentist, and one was steel magnate Nathan Taylor.[35] Given the tenants' occupations, it is evident that they shared the same dual identity with city and suburb as their counterparts over in North Chestnut Hill.

8205 Seminole Ave. Designed for Henry Howard Houston by the Hewitt brothers and built in 1885. Photo probably of the Sauveur children in the 1890s. CHHS.

This dual identity among the residents of Wissahickon Heights was demonstrated quite tellingly by the Samuel Porcher family. Born in Charleston, South Carolina, and descended from seventeenth-century French Huguenot settlers, Samuel Porcher (1857–1944) arrived in Wissahickon Heights in 1894. He and his wife rented a house at 322 Moreland Avenue from Houston for forty dollars a month and lived there with their three children for about fifteen years, until Porcher built his own house several blocks away. Porcher made a good living as the assistant and then chief purchasing agent for the Pennsylvania Railroad. He served on the boards of several subsidiary lines of the Pennsylvania, and during World War I he became the assistant director of purchasing for the United States Railroad Administration. Porcher commuted daily on the train to his office downtown, and sometimes made trips out of town on railroad business.[36]

Although Porcher went downtown to work each morning, his wife, Maria, and their children, Eleanor, Mary, and St. Julian, remained in the sheltered world of Wissahickon Heights. Nearly a cen-

The Samuel Porcher family poses for a photograph in the backyard, c. 1905. Left to right: younger daughter Mary (later Mrs. James Bond), baby St. Julien, mother Maria, father Samuel, and older daughter Eleanor. MWPB.

tury later, Mary Wickham Porcher Bond (b. 1898) remembered their peaceful house and yard on Moreland Avenue:

> "Home" meant an iron gate in a fence with a mass of lilacs on the right and on the left a tangle of wistaria in which I used to snuggle and watch the bees gathering pollen from the dangling lavender blossoms. Home meant the number 322 on the top step to our Moreland Avenue front porch. It meant rushing home from Miss Landstreet's kindergarten across the street and finding Mother seated in one of the French windows in her bedroom, sewing. . . . *Home* . . . was an opening door to life based on an unshakable sense of security.[37]

Mary's secure childhood was one of beauty and prosperity, made possible by her father's well-paying job in the city and the family's attractive home, far removed from the unpleasant realities of urban life. It was also a world in which middle- and upper-class children could be assured that their Victorian mothers would be at home, per-

Druim Moir, the Henry Howard Houston residence, designed by the Hewitt brothers and completed in 1886. CHHS.

haps sitting in a window seat sewing, when they walked in from the neighborhood school.

It was these same two worlds of city and suburb that the Houston family enjoyed on a much more lavish scale in Wissahickon Heights. Henry Howard Houston continued to commute to his office downtown until the very end of his life. In fact, he made the trip down and back on the day he died in 1895, returning to the mansion that he built on a bluff overlooking the Wissahickon Creek. Moving to Wissahickon Heights from Germantown in 1886, Houston called his impressive dwelling Druim Moir, a Gaelic name meaning great ridge.[38]

Druim Moir was designed by the Hewitt brothers and contained some thirty rooms. In many ways it resembled a medieval castle. There was a five-story tower (now demolished), with embattlements, on the south side of the mansion. Beside the front entrance, there

stood an oriel with a steep conical roof. Inside, the walls and ceilings
were paneled in wood. According to a contemporary description, the
front hall and stairs were "in oak; the parlor in butternut; the recep-
tion room in mahogany; the library and dining room in quartered oak;
the office in cherry; the servants quarters in white pine; and the principal bedrooms in oak, cherry, and sycamore."[39]

Surrounding the residence were fifty-two acres of lawn and wood-
land, including a small deer park. There were also vegetable gardens,
as well as a small farm with chickens, pigs, cows, and horses. Three
greenhouses supplied both Druim Moir and St. Martin's Church with
flowers throughout the year. Houston also bred Irish wolfhounds on
the property. In addition, there were several small houses dotting the
grounds, including an older farmhouse, an entrance lodge, and two
dwellings for employees. Together these buildings made the estate
look something like a small village.[40] As late as the 1930s, as one em-
ployee remembered, the place "was like a little town":

> We had our own rubbish collection; we had cows; we had greenhouses; we
> had formal gardens. . . . We had truck gardens [and] . . . people to maintain
> the lawns. . . . [T]here were four men in the greenhouse[s] all year
> round. . . .[41]

Although it was located within Philadelphia, Druim Moir was as far
removed in spirit from the city as one could imagine, insulated by its
fields and trees from the dirt, noise, and crime of Philadelphia streets.
Yet Houston and his heirs could travel to town for business or pleasure in less than half an hour on the train.

Houston also acted to provide a direct access by road from Druim
Moir to West Mount Airy and from there to downtown Philadelphia.
In July 1890 he decided to build a bridge to carry McCallum Street
across the deep valley carved out by Cresheim Creek. He then gave
the new bridge (only recently replaced) to the city of Philadelphia as
part of a project to provide a continuous carriageway from downtown
to Chestnut Hill that followed the Schuykill River and Wissahickon
Creek.[42] Houston's ambitious plans to extend the Chestnut Hill
branch of the Pennsylvania Railroad into his Roxborough lands
failed, however, when high costs and then the panic of 1893 forced
him to abandon the project.[43]

As to Druim Moir itself, there was an obvious element of conspicuous consumption. It is also probable that Houston was making a conscious attempt to imitate the British country gentleman. Several blocks to the east of the mansion was Houston's own village of tenant houses, along with his own parish church. Yet the continuing romanticism of the age would have allowed Houston and others like him to view their large houses and grounds as expressions of their own sense of beauty — natural as well as human.

Wissahickon Heights was notable for its amenities. It had a convenient rail link to downtown, and from there to trains and ships that could carry its residents most anywhere in the world. There were also the neighborhood church (St. Martin's) and recreation centers (the Wissahickon Inn and the Philadelphia Cricket Club). Just as important was Houston's realization that the continuing success of his suburban development depended upon maintaining the semirural atmosphere that had made it so attractive in the first place. This he provided through St. Martin's Green, Lake Surprise, the spacious Cricket Club grounds, and his own estate on the western edge of Wissahickon Heights. The large plots that he set aside for his children would play a role in future efforts to maintain an open, rural atmosphere in Chestnut Hill, as would the family's donations of land to adjoining Fairmount Park. By trying to assure that his development would remain a beautiful semirural retreat, Houston also sought to protect his family's wealth from environmental degradation through overbuilding on the land.

In the years immediately following Houston's death in June 1895, it appeared that the development of Wissahickon Heights would extend no further. Houston left just over $14 million in trust for his children, the principal to be divided among his grandchildren once the last of his own offspring had died. The last of these was his daughter Gertrude (Mrs. George) Woodward, who died in 1961. By the time her father's estate was finally settled in 1964, it was worth between $160 and $200 million.[44] His son, Samuel F. Houston, the eventual inheritor of Druim Moir and principal trustee of the estate, turned out to be a very conservative businessman who was not interested in further development on Wissahickon Heights. This left

Dr. George Woodward in the state senate at Harrisburg c. 1930, wearing his favorite knickers and knee stockings. TUL.

Henry Howard Houston's two daughters, Sallie and Gertrude, to
carry on the tradition, if they so desired. Sallie had married Charles
Wolcott Henry and lived immediately south of Druim Moir on a fifty-
acre estate, complete with a French chateau-style mansion (now destroyed) that was designed by the famous beaux-arts architects,
McKim, Mead, and White. Known as Stonehurst, the house had been
a wedding gift from Henry Howard Houston in 1887.[45]

As it turned out, it was Houston's daughter Gertrude and her
husband, George Woodward, who continued the family's real estate
interests in Chestnut Hill. The two married in 1894. Like her sister,
Sallie, Gertrude received a large parcel of land from her father that
stood just above the Wissahickon Creek, directly adjacent to the Hen-
rys at Stonehurst. Houston also gave her $75,000 with which to build
a house on the property. Instead of building immediately, the Wood-

Krisheim, the home of George and Gertrude Woodward, designed by Peabody and Stearns and completed in 1912. *Local.*

wards spent fifteen years landscaping the grounds. They called their home Krisheim, a Tudor-Jacobean mansion (still standing) begun in 1910 that was designed by the Boston firm of Peabody and Stearns.

It was Gertrude who provided the money for their real estate ventures. She also took some part in the planning, but, as a good Victorian wife, she was content to have her husband carry out their projects.[46] Any consideration of their additions to Wissahickon Heights should thus begin with an introduction to George Woodward himself, a man who would prove highly influential in the community, city, and state for over half a century.[47]

Like his father-in-law, Houston, Woodward was not a native Philadelphian. Born in Wilkes-Barre, Pennsylvania, to parents of Connecticut Yankee stock, Woodward could claim a long line of distinguished ancestors, including three colonial governors. After graduating from Yale University in 1887 and then doing a year's study at Yale's Sheffield School, he entered the University of Pennsylvania Medical School, receiving his M.D. degree in 1891. While there, he studied under Dr. William Osler, who went on to be one of the great medical educators and public health reformers of the age. Although

Woodward admired physicians and had intended to make a career in medicine, he found himself unsuited to the field and quit medical practice after several years. Yet Woodward would identify himself with the scientific side of medicine and sign himself "George Woodward, M.D." for the rest of his life. Like Houston, Woodward was a religious man who was devoted to the Social Gospel. He became an active member of and generous contributor to St. Martin's Church, serving as accounting warden and a vestryman for many years.[48]

With his New England background, strict Protestant upbringing, upper-class standing, scientific curiosity, and devotion to the Social Gospel, Woodward possessed nearly all the characteristics that Americans have come to associate with leaders of the nation's Progressive movement of the early twentieth century. Although he came to Philadelphia as a Democrat, he soon became a Republican, the party of most other Progressive reformers in the country.[49] Woodward went on to become a Progressive reformer on the local and state level. The list of his accomplishments would include his role in ridding Philadelphia of typhoid fever; his leadership in the campaign to obtain a new municipal charter for Philadelphia in 1919; his creation of the Bureau of Municipal Research, which studied urban problems and suggested workable solutions; his fight for laws against child labor; his sponsorship of Philadelphia's municipal wage tax; and seven consecutive terms as a Pennsylvania state senator (1919–1947).

But Woodward's most consuming interest was decent housing for all citizens. He was a director and then president of Philadelphia's Octavia Hill Association, which renovated or built low-rent housing for the working classes. He also commissioned a model tenement in South Philadelphia and put up the money for Inasmuch Mission, a haven for the homeless in the 1000 block of Locust Street. He joined others in successfully lobbying for the licensing and inspection of tenement houses in Philadelphia.[50]

Thus, in addition to his father-in-law's example of planned development, Woodward's own real estate ventures in Chestnut Hill must be seen partly within the context of his Progressive ideas. Above all, he believed that intelligent professionals like himself could improve urban conditions by studying their causes and proposing practical solutions. This belief had led him to found the Bureau of Municipal Research and to spend much time and money trying to upgrade the city's housing stock through the Octavia Hill Association, as well as through demanding stricter and more effective building regulations from the city council. He would also apply to Chestnut Hill the Octavia Hill Association's habit of expecting only a modest return on its real estate investments. There, as well as in poorer neighborhoods, he hoped that his example of building attractive and affordable housing would inspire other private investors who, through their own actions, might solve the housing problem. During the New Deal and then after World War II, he would even offer ambivalent support for public housing. Yet like most Progressives, he continued to hope that private funds and free market forces could provide decent housing for nearly everyone, a goal that was not realized in Woodward's day — or in the years since.[51]

Woodward was also influenced by the aesthetic theories of English artists and art critics such as John Ruskin and William Morris. Ruskin had provided initial funding for the Octavia Hill Association in London, after which the Philadelphia organization had been modeled, and Woodward may have learned of Ruskin's ideas through the local group. As to Morris, he and Gertrude owned a well-thumbed volume of arts and crafts essays that were introduced by Morris. The Woodwards also belonged to the Arts and Crafts Society of Philadelphia.[52] In any case, they shared Ruskin's and Morris's preference for natural building materials and skilled craftsmen. Woodward engaged the most talented masons, carpenters, and cabinetmakers in the area for his houses in Chestnut Hill: he and Gertrude brought the Willet Stained Glass Studio from Pittsburgh to Chestnut Hill. For fine ironwork, they patronized the highly regarded firm of Samuel Yellin. Their masons were local craftsmen, virtually all of whom had immigrated to Chestnut Hill from northern Italy (see chapters 4 and 5).[53]

Yet another influence on Woodward was the English Garden City movement, which had its origins in Ebenezer Howard's ideas for planned communities.[54] Howard wanted to move workers out of large cities such as London and relocate them in small garden cities that were surrounded by greenbelts of farm land. The houses in these communities were to be built in clusters around courtyards or other green spaces. Many of these concepts were put into effect at Letchworth, England, a project begun in 1903 and designed by Barry Parker and Raymond Unwin.[55] The experiment at Letchworth, as well as the Garden City movement in general, attracted much attention in the United States.[56] Woodward heard about these ideas at the annual meetings of the National Housing Conference, which he attended between 1911 and 1929.[57]

Finally, it appears that Woodward was attracted for a time by the City Beautiful movement, a nationwide phenomenon in the very late nineteenth and early twentieth centuries. Reacting to the physical ugliness of American cities, the movement called for tree-lined parkways bordered with monumental public buildings in a neoclassical style[58] In his *Memoirs*, Woodward praised the Benjamin Franklin Parkway, Philadelphia's most noted contribution to the City Beautiful movement.[59] In Chestnut Hill, Woodward would apply some of its principals to initial but unrealized plans for Pastorius Park.

Woodward undertook his first ambitious real estate venture in Chestnut Hill with the idea of building low-cost housing for the local working class. As he related in his *Memoirs*, it was Sister Ruth, for years the supervisor of Buttercup Cottage, who suggested the project. She pointed out a group of dilapidated houses just east of Germantown Avenue and persuaded him to build new units (located on the present Benezet Street), which would be "rented to working people, . . . at low [rates]."[60] Yet, as Woodward maintained, the "white collars came along and rented every house in sight."[61] He could have easily reserved them for the local working class, but he chose not to. After the fact, he even seemed pleased that middle-class families had taken them up so quickly: "They were exactly the people," he wrote, "who pay their bills, and seldom complain."[62] In this sense he joined other advocates of the Social Gospel in admiring the middle-class resident, the "upright, property-owning, unobtrusive citizen," as Robert Wiebe has described him.[63] This decision was regrettable for a man like Woodward, who had expended so much time and money to provide housing for the working class in Philadelphia, and who earnestly hoped that his housing ventures might inspire others to build low-cost housing, with only modest return to the investor.

In light of Woodward's support for good housing elsewhere in Philadelphia, it is likely that he subscribed to the contemporary "organic" view of the metropolis, a way of viewing large cities that was common among Progressives of the day.[64] Accordingly, he saw Philadelphia as a large body with many organs: its commercial and governmental center was downtown, whereas industrial areas were in North Philadelphia and along the Delaware and Schuykill rivers. Scattered throughout the metropolitan area were numerous residential neighborhoods that varied according to the incomes, tastes, and backgrounds of their inhabitants. It is also probable that Woodward agreed with writers who hoped that trolleys and trains could allow most residents of the city, including all but the poorest, to live in essentially suburban neighborhoods, however modest they might be.[65] As a result, most urban dwellers could escape from the worst ravages of disease, overcrowding, and crime. Consistent with such thinking, Woodward undoubtedly saw nothing wrong with Chestnut Hill's being a suburban community for upper-middle- and upper-class Philadelphians, however false the reality of an organic city proved at the time, as well as in later decades.

By the time Woodward had begun to build on Benezet Street, styles in American architecture had shifted from the Queen Anne motifs that predominated when his father-in-law Houston was active in the mid-1880s. Since then, the American Colonial Revival had gained prominence and achieved what many critics consider its greatest level of creativity. At the same time, architects on the East Coast in particular were turning to English and French vernacular styles for inspiration. All three of these modes seemed fitting for suburbs such as Chestnut Hill, where many residents had fled from what they considered the more distasteful realities of urban life. Among these were the thousands of poor immigrants from southern and eastern Europe who began coming to the United States in large numbers after 1890. The Colonial Revival was a visual statement through which wealthier suburbanites could assert their native American roots. En-

One of George Woodward's quadruple houses, designed in 1910 by Duhring, Okie, and Ziegler and built on Benezet St., Chestnut Hill, and Nippon St., West Mount Airy. Photo by author, 1984.

glish vernacular styles likewise attested to their owners' British backgrounds, in addition to satisfying their Anglophile tastes. Rural French motifs, on the other hand, had been associated for several decades with sophisticated country living. Woodward commissioned houses in all three styles.[66]

To serve as architects for the Benezet Street project, executed between 1909 and 1912, Woodward chose the firm of Duhring, Okie, and Ziegler. Their designs were in a controlled eclectic style that made use of both English and American colonial traditions. For the north side of the street they created seven three-story twins, all in a vaguely Colonial Revival style, with certain English Jacobean features, such as stucco and half-timbering on several second-story gables. On the south side of the street they designed two quadruple houses that also combined Jacobean and Colonial motifs.

Chief architect H. Louis Duhring (1873–1953) was born in Philadelphia and held a degree in architecture from the University of Pennsylvania. He worked briefly in the offices of Mantle Fielding, who specialized in Colonial Revival designs, and then for a short time with Frank Furness. A traveling scholarship in 1897 allowed him to visit Italy, where he did extensive sketching.[67]

It is not clear whether it was Duhring or Woodward himself who came up with the idea for the quadruple houses, but Woodward was personally excited about what he considered to be a novel design. He contributed an article about the "quads" to the July 1913 issue of *The Architectural Record* that accompanied a second piece on the Benezet Street development.[68] In Woodward's opinion, the quad was "a logical development of the semi-detached or twin house" that had long been accepted by middle- and even upper-class Philadelphians as a respectable and economical solution to high urban land prices.[69] The quads simply extended these economies by including four units instead of two under one roof and eliminating the expense of two more external walls. As a result, Woodward could rent each unit for about forty dollars a month. The quad also solved a number of aesthetic problems so far as Woodward was concerned. By constructing two sets of twins side by side and back to back, he eliminated back alleys, back lots, and backyards — all of which were particular banes to Woodward. The quads appeared identical on the sides and ends and could be surrounded with pleasant gardens and trees.[70]

Woodward was so pleased with the quads that he built three more sets, of four units each, in nearby Mount Airy, on the 200 blocks of West Nipon Street and West Mount Airy Avenue. In January 1916 he also proposed four more quads on West Gravers Lane in Chestnut Hill as a gift to St. Martin's Church, which could then rent them out as part of a permanent endowment. For unexplained reasons, these never were built.[71]

Meanwhile, Woodward had begun his extensive development on the lower West Side of Chestnut Hill on land adjacent to Houston's Wissahickon Heights, all of which he and his wife Gertrude had to purchase from the Houston estate or from private owners. A decade earlier he had waged a successful campaign to change the neighborhood's name from Wissahickon Heights. In his own words, the name had "always seemed a cheap [one] for [such] a pretty country."[72] He began his campaign in 1906 by persuading the Pennsylvania Railroad to rename the Wissahickon Heights Station the St. Martin's Station, a success that doubtless owed to the family's long connection with the railroad.[73]

The earliest of Woodward's houses in St. Martin's were erected about 1904 on the 100 block of West Springfield Avenue. They were four sets of twins in a bulky, undistinguished early Colonial Revival style.[74] Much more impressive was the ambitious Pastorius Park development, begun about 1915 and located between Graver's Lane and Cresheim Valley Drive. Woodward named the park after Francis Daniel Pastorius, the founder of Germantown. Although Woodward admired Pastorius as a historical figure, the use of the name was yet another way of associating suburban Chestnut Hill with its rural colonial past.[75]

Woodward told *The Architectural Record* that his inspiration for the Pastorius Park undertaking had come to him several years before, during a visit to London's Hyde Park.[76] He had also been delighted by English architecture during several trips to the British Isles.[77] Returning to Chestnut Hill, he decided to buy an abandoned field and several rundown houses and donate the property to the city as a park. Because the city had already projected two major roads through the site, Woodward had no choice but to accommodate them in his plans for the park and the residential development around it. Such wide boulevards, lined on either side with trees, were also consistent with the City Beautiful movement. According to the city plan, Lincoln Drive would continue up from Mount Airy, run through the park, and link up with Bethlehem Pike at the forks with Germantown Avenue. A major east-west highway would intersect Lincoln Drive in the park and create a direct connection between Chestnut Hill and the Philadelphia Main Line. Early plans for Pastorius Park, none of which were executed, also show the influence of the City Beautiful movement, including monumental gates and a neoclassical fountain in the center.

As it turned out, the roads were never built, although a segment of Lincoln Drive was constructed between Cresheim Valley Drive and the entrance to Pastorius Park. The highway plan was not officially abandoned, however, until the 1960s — in part because of successful pressure from the Woodward family itself (see chapter 7). The park proper would not be landscaped until the mid-1930s, under a grant from the WPA.[78]

Woodward's architects for the housing project around Pastorius Park were Louis Duhring, Robert Rodes McGoodwin (1886–1967), and Edmund Gilchrist (1885–1953). Gilchrist was born in nearby Germantown and studied at the Drexel Institute and the University of Pennsylvania. He then did apprenticeships with Wilson Eyre, one of the most highly regarded residential architects of the day; and Horace Trumbauer, who was known for the huge, neoclassical country houses that he designed for nouveau riche clients. Later Gilchrist became much interested in the English Garden City movement and in town planning generally.

McGoodwin was born in Bowling Green, Kentucky, but came to Philadelphia at a young age. He received a degree in architecture from the University of Pennsylvania and, like Gilchrist, he worked for a time with Horace Trumbauer. A traveling scholarship allowed him to visit Belgium, France, England, and Italy. He also studied for a year at schools in Paris and Rome.[79] According to a persistent oral tradition, Woodward sent McGoodwin, Gilchrist, and Duhring to England and France to study country architecture before beginning the Pastorius Park project.

The three architects and their patron worked well together. According to Woodward, the four of them met in his office once a week: They were "a happy, harmonious group; working for the common good. . . . Each architect had to submit his designs to the other two and to myself for criticism."[80]

The Pastorius Park development was actually composed of several residential groupings. Just south and west of the park, along Hartwell Lane, Navajo Street, Lincoln Drive, and Crefeld Street, was what Woodward called his Cotswold Village, constructed largely in 1915 and 1916. Houses along these streets were built of rough-cut local stone and were topped with steep roofs that recalled the cottages that Woodward had admired during his trips through England's Cotswold hills. He also used this Cotswold style later at Roanoke Court, Winston Court, and in several houses on the south side of East Springfield Avenue that adjoined the Benezet Street development.

Another significant grouping in the Pastorius Park ensemble was

Three houses in George Woodward's Cotswold Village, designed by Edmund B. Gilchrist and built in 1921 on the 8000 block of Crefeld St. Photo c. 1920. AAUP.

located on the northeast corner of Willow Grove Avenue and Lincoln Drive. This was Gilchrist's Linden Court (1915–1916), one of the few Woodward commissions ever done in red brick — or brick of any color. Designed in a simple Colonial Revival style, its six units bordered a central courtyard, with two semi-attached dwellings at either end and two in the middle. Further south along Lincoln Drive lay the so-called half-moon group (1916–1917), composed of six stone twin houses arranged in a crescent shape around an open court and designed by Louis Duhring. Directly across the street from the half-moon group was a replica of Sulgrave manor, the country home of George Washington's English ancestors. The Colonial Dames had built it for the Sesquicentennial Exhibition held in Philadelphia in 1926. Afterwards, Woodward bought it, had it dismantled, and trucked it from its site in far South Philadelphia to Chestnut Hill, where it was reassembled. For many years Woodward rented it to Robert McLean, publisher of the *Philadelphia Evening Bulletin*.

George Woodward's Linden Court, northeast corner of Willow Grove Ave. and Lincoln Drive, designed by Edmund B. Gilchrist and built in 1915–16. Photo c. 1920. AAUP.

Still other houses in the greater Pastorius Park development betrayed a definite French flavor. The Woodwards became enamored of the old stone farmhouses that they had seen in Normandy. This affection was reflected in what some have called the Anglo-Norman style of the court and three houses (1915) that McGoodwin designed on the southwest corner of Willow Grove Avenue and Lincoln Drive.[81]

But it was just across the McCallum Street bridge in West Mount Airy that Woodward gave full vent to his taste for French architecture. There, in the mid-1920s, he and McGoodwin created the French Village, located immediately north of Allen's Lane between Emlen and McCallum streets. On both corners of Emlen Street and Allen's Lane there were two stone gatehouses, with stone arches extending across heavy slate sidewalks. Around the corner to the west on Allen's Lane there was even a stone wall with the phrase so familiar to anyone who has lived or traveled in France, *Défense d'Afficher* (Post No Bills). McGoodwin designed eight modest-sized houses for Woodward along Gate Lane. Larger lots were sold with stipulations in the deeds that their owners must build in a French style. Sixty years later, the French Village remains a place of great charm.[82]

Much of this attractiveness owed to the special style of landscaping in the French Village and elsewhere in Wissahickon Heights/St. Martin's. According to Carol Franklin, who has made a detailed study of the so-called Wissahickon style, its basic goal is to bring the three main elements of the Wissahickon gorge — rocks, water, and trees — into the community itself. This was accomplished in Wissahickon Heights/St. Martin's through the use of locally quarried stone as a building material and by surrounding each house with a gradient of foliage that begins far out in the plot with native trees and then descends to shrubs and smaller plants, also native to the area, in spaces closer to the dwelling. Equally important is the creation of stone-lined drainage ditches along streets (instead of the regular cement curbings) that become stream-like extensions of the Wissahickon Creek as rain water flows down them on its way to the gorge.[83] Exactly who or what was responsible for this appealing style remains uncertain.

In all, Woodward commissioned about 180 houses in Chestnut Hill and neighboring Mount Airy, virtually all of which remain standing with very few alterations at the time of this writing. Like his father-in-law, Houston, he decided to rent the bulk of them to suitable tenants of his own choosing. In an article that he wrote in 1920 for *The Survey* magazine, a publication aimed at municipal reformers and social scientists, Woodward was remarkably candid about his rental practices. His ownership of all the houses, he explained, "assures the tenant against undesirable neighbors." He added that he had even rented some of the houses "at cost" to young married people "who were decidedly in the class of social assets. . . ." "I have always inquired into antecedents," he continued, "I have never taken a Jewish family or allowed one to be taken as a subtenant."[84] Given Woodward's later horror over the Nazi slaughter of millions of Jews, it is difficult to understand his refusal to rent to Jewish tenants.[85] Either he changed his attitudes over time, or his rental policies were more determined by a desire for neighborhood homogeneity than by a thoroughgoing hostility toward Jews, an inconsistent attitude that has been explored in recent scholarship on anti-Semitism.[86]

Although the *City Directory* does not indicate the precise social or religious backgrounds of Woodward's tenants, it does reveal most of their occupations. In 1930, Woodward's Linden Court, in the 100 block of West Willow Grove Avenue, included a lawyer, a broker, an architect, and a corporate executive; two of these appeared in the *Social Register*. That same year, Woodward's Cotswold houses in the 8000 block of Navajo Street contained two lawyers, a university professor, a clergyman, two insurance company executives, and a corporate manager. Six of the ten tenants on the street, some of whom did not report an occupation to the *City Directory*, were also in the *Social Register*.

Although the *Social Register* has been adopted by historians as an acceptable but less-than-perfect guide to upper-class standing, many members of Philadelphia's upper-upper class have held that it is far too inclusive, insisting that only about one-tenth of the families listed in the register truly belongs to the upper-upper class.[87] Whatever their precise social designation, Woodward evidently believed that social homogeneity among his tenants was necessary for a strong sense of community in St. Martin's. As he put it in his *Survey* article, "I have always striven for that essential, if somewhat intangible factor, good will [among neighbors]."[88]

Besides the rental policies, there were several other features of Wissahickon Heights/St. Martin's that engendered social homogeneity. Among them was St. Martin's Episcopal Church, which, with the increase in population from Woodward's houses, became more of a neighborhood church than ever before. Directly west of the church, the Philadelphia Cricket Club functioned as an exclusive country club for local residents. (Oral tradition holds that Woodward's tenants were almost assured membership in the club.) The horse show had left the area by the time Woodward began his most important projects, and even the Wissahickon Inn had failed as a summer resort, as prosperous Philadelphians went further afield for their vacations. But through the initiative of Woodward's brother-in-law, Charles W. Henry, the inn became home to the growing Chestnut Hill Academy in 1898. At first the academy and inn shared the structure, with the inn using the facility during the summer season and the school during the rest of the year. After two years of joint occupancy, however, the inn closed altogether in 1900 and the academy became the sole tenant. Over the decades, the Woodwards as well as other members of the Houston family would sit on the academy's board and subsidize it in various ways. Wissahickon Heights/St. Martin's thus added a private boys school to its already impressive array of amenities.[89]

In 1904 Gertrude Woodward and her sister, Sallie Houston Henry, took the initiative for erecting a new building for the Wissahickon Heights School, an institution for girls that had been founded some years before.[90] The handsome Dutch Colonial structure, executed in the local stone, stands at the northwest corner of Seminole and Willow Grove avenues. Although its official name was the Wissahickon Heights School, everyone fell to calling it Miss Landstreet's School, after its well-liked headmistress. When Miss Landstreet's closed in 1918, the building was acquired by Springside School for its junior department, while the senior (upper) school remained for the next forty years in North Chestnut Hill at Norwood and Chestnut Hill avenues. In 1957 the upper school would also move to the West Side, combining with the junior school to occupy a new facility on the Druim Moir grounds, yet another example of the Houston/Woodward families' support for private education on the Hill.

Thus by the time George Woodward finished the bulk of his building projects in the late 1920s, Wissahickon Heights/St. Martin's (then known solely as St. Martin's) had overshadowed the first railroad suburb over in North Chestnut Hill. St. Martin's was better planned, architecturally more distinctive, and better served by recreational, religious, and educational institutions. As time would show, it was better situated to resist heavy automobile traffic and overdevelopment in future decades. This last factor owed to the Wissahickon gorge on its westernmost borders, which was now safely part of the city's vast Fairmount Park system. The continuing success of this development also stemmed from the fact that Woodward and Houston descendants continued to own much of the land and were thereby able to resist encroachment by real estate developers or expansionist institutions.

The question of uniqueness is more difficult to assess for the Houston/Woodward developments. Certainly none of the other wealthy suburbs in or around Philadelphia, then or later, was quite like St. Martin's. There was no such planned suburb anywhere on the famous Main Line (a collection of suburbs west of Philadelphia), where the land was generally sold to individuals, who then built their own homes. Because the land on the Main Line was initially cheaper than that in Chestnut Hill, individual properties tended to be much larger than on the Hill—often as large as several acres. Thus when rising property values and taxes emerged in the post–World War II period, many owners on the Main Line were lured by financial gain or forced by rising expenses into subdividing their parcels into smaller and smaller lots for tract homes that look little different from those in upper-middle- and middle-class suburbs all over the United States. Lot sizes in St. Martin's, in contrast, were always modest. Many were under a quarter of an acre, and very few exceeded an acre. Thus even the properties that the Houstons or Woodwards sold were not likely to be subdivided in response to rising taxes and land values.

One might also compare St. Martin's to planned suburbs elsewhere in the United States, such as Llewellyn Park and Short Hills, New Jersey; Riverside and Kenilworth, Illinois; and Garden City, New York. All were intended as prestigious residential developments that featured attractive, architect-designed houses and carefully landscaped grounds. Several of them included clubs or recreational facilities not unlike those in Chestnut Hill. But none of them remained under the ownership of a single family for as long a period as much of St. Martin's, and none has succeeded in attracting and then retaining so many renters from the upper-middle or upper class.[91]

The reasons for the success of the Houston/Woodward development for more than a century would appear to stem from several factors. One is the decision of several family members, now fourth- and fifth-generation descendants of Henry Howard Houston, to live in the community and to take a personal interest in maintaining the properties at a high level. Until recently, another compelling factor has been modest rents, which were very attractive to young couples, and even to older ones, who might have come from prominent families but who were not wealthy themselves. The fact that Dr. Woodward did not raise rents for the duration that a tenant remained in a given property was an additional inducement. Indeed, Woodward often specified that the lease would run "indefinitely," without an increase in rent. The only exception was if the city raised property taxes, in which case the full amount was passed on to the tenant. Woodward's reasoning was that this would force renters to become tax-conscious voters.[92] Finally, there was the prestige that many attached to living in one of Woodward's houses, not to mention the near guarantee of acceptance into the Philadelphia Cricket Club, which served as a neighborhood country club. Understandably, many tenants stayed for decades, some for fifty years or more. As Woodward himself put it, "Death, removal from the city and promotion to a larger house are about the only causes for change."[93]

With the virtual completion of Woodward's projects by 1930, wide portions of Chestnut Hill took on both the visual and social characteristics that would distinguish it as an upper-middle- and upper-class Philadelphia suburb for many years to come. Its very attractiveness set it apart from the rest of Philadelphia, as well as other portions of Chestnut Hill, and perhaps made it easier for residents to ignore the poverty and despair in other areas of the city. George Woodward, for one, was fully aware of these problems and hoped that programs such as the Octavia Hill Association would be imitated widely enough to provide decent housing for all. But the idea was not taken up on a large scale, leaving Wissahickon Heights/St. Martin's and North Chestnut Hill as islands of beauty and privilege on the edge of the city. The concept of an organic city seemed good in theory, but in practice it meant a metropolis that was divided along social and economic lines. At the same time, the economies of real estate development and the wage levels of many workers did not allow them to live in even modest suburban neighborhoods, separated from the factories, sounds, and other annoyances of the city.

Willing to accept such divisions as unavoidable, Woodward and Houston spent a half century making meticulous plans for their suburb on the West Side of Chestnut Hill. Their persistence and that of their descendants in maintaining Wissahickon Heights/St. Martin's would be paralleled by the planning and activities of the Hill's two Improvement Associations and the much later Community Association. But before exploring these groups, it is necessary to come to terms with the social divisions in Chestnut Hill as they emerged during the first three decades of the twentieth century.

4

SOCIAL CONTOURS

The Divided Community

Although it was located within a large city with many diverse peoples, an important part of the suburban ideal in Chestnut Hill, as elsewhere, was social homogeneity. This emphasis upon living with social equals was partly in reaction to the social, ethnic, and racial diversity that characterized large cities such as Philadelphia. Fearing that ethnic newcomers were introducing unsavory and even dangerous habits into urban life, and unfairly blaming urban problems upon such alien groups, many well-to-do families of British descent continued to seek havens in expensive suburban developments such as those in Chestnut Hill. They may have sought homogeneous enclaves also because of their own social insecurity,

Tables containing data relevant to the discussion in this chapter are found in the appendix.

especially if they had become wealthy or successful in recent years. The move to an upper-middle- or upper-class suburb could in itself help to still self-doubts and solidify the family's new status through close associations with other successful families.[1]

In reality, of course, Chestnut Hill was home to many residents who did not live in the prestigious developments in Wissahickon Heights/St. Martin's and North Chestnut Hill. Thus, in addition to separating themselves from less privileged individuals outside the community, wealthier suburbanites sought to insulate themselves from servants and working-class families on the Hill itself. Here again, the motive may have been their own feelings of social insecurity, along with a desire to associate with only the "right people" in Chestnut Hill.

Yet these habits of social separation were also pursued by local servants and artisans, many of them recent immigrants, who self-consciously banded together in certain areas of Chestnut Hill and insisted that their children marry within strict ethnic and religious backgrounds. In this way Chestnut Hill continued to be an aggregation of communities that overlapped only at certain points.

In addition to the dual identity that commuters felt in Chestnut Hill, there were thus conflicts of identity on the Hill itself. One result was a fragmentation of local identity that would endure into the late twentieth century and combine with other factors to weaken a wider sense of community in Chestnut Hill. This chapter will seek to define different social groups numerically by making use of the *City Directory*, the *Social Register*, *Who's Who in America*, and other guides to socioeconomic standing. It and the following chapter will also attempt to bring these differences to life through oral histories and contemporary newspaper accounts.

During the first three decades of the twentieth century, social divisions in Chestnut Hill had established themselves firmly. At the upper end of the scale, Chestnut Hill was home to a large concentration of socially and professionally prominent Philadelphians. According to E. Digby Baltzell, in his *Philadelphia Gentlemen*, Chestnut Hill was "more . . . exclusively upper-class" than any other community in the whole metropolitan area.[2]

A careful study of the *Philadelphia City Directory* for 1930 and editions of the *Social Register* for the late 1920s and early 1930s shows that Chestnut Hill was in fact home to more upper-class residents than any other single community in the region. Although the *City Directory* for 1929 would have been better as a guide to Chestnut Hill's population on the eve of the Great Depression, only the 1930 edition included a street index for the entire city, thus making it possible to identify the addresses and occupations of many heads of households in Chestnut Hill. Because the depression did not become truly severe until late 1930 and early 1931, the 1930 *City Directory* should be little different from the year before.

Because the *Social Register* had long been regarded as a reliable but not wholly perfect gauge of class prestige, it is an acceptable indication of how many socially prominent adults lived in Chestnut Hill around 1930.[3] Approximately 550 entries of the 9,000 or so from the greater Philadelphia area were in fact from Chestnut Hill — or just over 6 percent of the total. Considering that the Hill's estimated 8,500 people represented less than one-half of one percent of the region's total population, these figures are revealing. More startling, perhaps, was the fact that there were more Chestnut Hillers listed in the *Social Register* than residents of Haverford and Bryn Mawr combined, even though these were among the most prestigious addresses on the Main Line. (There were about 220 entries from Haverford and 130 from Bryn Mawr, for a total of 350.) Of course, both communities were smaller than Chestnut Hill, given the fact that Lower Merion Township, in which both were located, had a total population of just under 5,900 in 1930.

Among the *Social Register* listings for Chestnut Hill, there were also at least twenty-six heads of households who descended from Philadelphia First Family Founders, as defined by Baltzell in his *Philadelphia Gentlemen*. These included the names of Biddle, Borie, Bullitt, Cadwalader, Clark, Dallas, Disston, Houston, Lea, Lippincott, McLean, Morris, Pepper, Strawbridge, Wistar, and Wood.[4]

Chestnut Hill also contained more than its fair share of the nation's meritorious elite, as measured by *Who's Who in America* for 1930. At least forty of the approximately nine hundred entries from Philadelphia, or 4.4 percent of them, lived on the Hill. The occupations of the 40 were: banker (9); architect (7); lawyer (4); engineer (4); physician (3); capitalist (2); artist (2); publisher (2); economist (1); chemist (1); educator (1); author (1); insurance executive (1); manufacturer (1); and symphony orchestra conductor (1). In this category, too, Chestnut Hill was ahead of either Bryn Mawr, with thirty-three entries in *Who's Who*; and Haverford, with thirty-four. If the faculty living at Bryn Mawr and Haverford Colleges were removed, there were twenty-seven and twenty-eight, respectively.

Whether or not they were counted in the guides and directories, Chestnut Hill was home to some of the most successful and influential individuals in the region. Officers of many of the leading banks, for instance, lived in Chestnut Hill in the late 1920s and early 1930s. These included Joseph Wayne, Jr., president of the Philadelphia National Bank; Levi L. Rue, chairman of the board, Philadelphia National Bank; William J. McGlinn, president of the Continental Title and Trust; Livingston E. Jones, president of the First National Bank of Philadelphia; Albert Atlee Jackson, president of the Girard Trust; Marshall S. Morgan, chairman of the board, Fidelity-Philadelphia Trust; Samuel F. Houston, president of the Real Estate Trust; Thomas Sovereign Gates, vice-president of Drexel and Company and soon to become president of the University of Pennsylvania; Richard L. Austin, chairman of the Federal Reserve Bank of Philadelphia; and Herbert E. Amidon, assistant manager of the Philadelphia Clearing House Association.[5]

Several insurance executives also lived in Chestnut Hill at the time: John L. Cornog, president of the Philanthropic Mutual Life Insurance Company; Gustavus Remak, president of the Insurance Company of Pennsylvania; Harry S. Bradley, president of the Indemnity Company of America; and William H. Kingsley, vice-president of the Pennsylvania Mutual Life Insurance Company.[6]

Among Chestnut Hill's corporate executives, there were Frederic H. Strawbridge, senior director of the Strawbridge and Clothier department store; T. Morris Perot, president of Perot Sons Malting Company; Harvey Miller, president of Southern Steamship Company; John E. Zimmerman, chairman of the board, Phildelphia

Boxly, near the northwest corner of Seminole Ave. and St. Martin's Lane. This
Georgian Revival house, designed by Mantle Fielding and built in 1903–04, was
the home of Frederick W. Taylor, founder of industrial management. Portions of
the house survive in 1991. CHHS.

Electric Company; Charles Bromley, president of Quaker Hosiery
Company; Mahlon C. Kline, president of Smith, Kline and French
pharmaceuticals; Samuel Porcher, chief purchasing agent for the
Pennsylvania Railroad; Thomas H. Addie, president of the American
Manganese Bronze Company; William D. Disston, vice-president of
Henry Disston and Sons saw works; and William McLean, Jr.,
secretary-treasurer of the *Philadelphia Bulletin*. Until his death in 1915,
the founder of industrial management, Frederick W. Taylor, lived in
Chestnut Hill.[7]

Also among Chestnut Hill's most successful residents were its architects. These included the three men who had worked with George
Woodward: H. Louis Duhring, Edmund Gilchrist, and Robert Rodes
McGoodwin. Two other architects who made important contributions in Chestnut Hill and elsewhere were Walter Mellor and the
nationally known George Howe, both of whom collaborated for a
number of years with Arthur I. Meigs in the firm of Mellor, Meigs
and Howe. Howe was also co-designer of the spectacular Philadelphia Savings Fund Society (PSFS) building at 12th and Market

Street, which was commissioned just before the Great Depression and was one of the first international/modernist-style structures in the United States. In addition to these architects, the muralist Violet Oakley and the painter Jessie Willcox Smith made their homes on St. George's Road, just across Cresheim Creek in West Mount Airy. Yet another talented resident was Leopold Stokowski, famed director of the Philadelphia Orchestra, who lived on the lower end of St. Martin's Lane in a Woodward house.[8]

These talented men and women were generally well known throughout the Philadelphia area and thus easily identified themselves with the metropolitan region as a whole. A search of the *Social Register* also shows that many of them belonged to clubs and civic organizations in the city, which reinforced their sense of a dual identity with Philadelphia and Chestnut Hill.

The question of exactly how these and other Chestnut Hill residents should be categorized with regard to social class is not always easy to answer. Considered in European terms, there was no true upper class in Chestnut Hill — or anywhere else in America — because there was no titled or hereditary nobility. In this sense, the so-called American upper class was really an *haute bourgeoisie,* or upper-middle class, made up of families who could claim roots going well back into the nation's history (preferably to the colonial period), along with some ancestor who had gained wealth or high occupational status. If the wealth were too new or the family founder still a little "rough around the edges," it might take several decades for the family to be accepted into polite society. But if the family founder had established himself by 1865, few questions were asked about his descendants.

In Chestnut Hill there could be little doubt that the twenty-six heirs of pre–Civil War Family Founders formed the inner core of its upper class. Beyond that, it is difficult to say precisely where a prominent individual belonged in the upper class. However, by comparing the names of Chestnut Hillers who were listed in the *Social Register* with the 1,051 male heads of household in Chestnut Hill whose addresses and occupations appeared in the 1930 *City Directory,* it is possible to create a category of upper-class occupations for Chestnut Hill.[9]

The inclusion of several non-upper-class occupations, such as

"elected office holder," "scientist/researcher," and "college professor," in the *Social Register*, was a local aberration explained by the fact
that particular persons ranked high socially because of their family
backgrounds rather than because of their occupations. However, the
forty-eight lawyers in Chestnut Hill were significant enough numerically to allow conclusions about the social status of their occupation.
Twenty-eight, or 58.33 percent of them, were listed in the *Social Register*. Bankers came next (20 of 35 — 57.14 percent listed), followed
by brokers (12 of 22 — 54.55 percent), physicians (10 of 19 — 52.63
percent), insurance executives (5 of 11 — 45.45 percent), and corporate executives and substantial business owners (52 of 116–44.83
percent). It is also interesting that six of the nine architects (66.67
percent) in Chestnut Hill were in the *Social Register*. This was probably because only affluent parents could then afford to send their sons
off to study architecture, and because a successful architect had to
be acceptable to the wealthy and socially prominent clients who commissioned architect-designed structures.

Other occupations that were found among individuals listed in
the *Social Register* were: real estate broker, manager, statistician, government bureaucrat, manufacturer's agent, artist, sales manager,
salesman, insurance agent, engineer, and clergyman. Of the 462 persons in these occupations from Chestnut Hill, 185 (40 percent) were
in the *Social Register*.[10] Comparing these 185 to the 1,051 heads of
households listed in the *City Directory*, one might conclude that about
18 percent of Chestnut Hillers belonged to the upper class.

It would seem reasonable to categorize the 287 Chestnut Hillers
in high-prestige occupations who did not appear in the *Social Register*
as members of the upper-middle class. They amounted to just over
27 percent of the 1,051 households. Adding this to the 18 percent for
the upper class, one finds that about 45 percent of those residents
listed in the *City Directory* were from the upper or upper-middle
classes.

The question of who belonged to the middle-middle or lower-
middle classes presents some difficulties, too. Local tradition holds
that there never has been much of a true middle class in Chestnut
Hill, and in several interviews the author heard individuals from vary-

ing backgrounds assert that there really have been only two classes on the Hill: "the upper classes and those who served them." Although this is a gross exaggeration, the numbers of householders in what might be considered middle-middle- and lower-middle-class occupations were comparatively small in 1930.

Beginning with officers of eleemosynary institutions and ending with local shopkeepers, Chestnut Hill's middle-middle class comprised some 131 heads of households — or about 12 percent of the total.[11] This categorization is admittedly somewhat arbitrary and unsatisfactory, particularly at the upper and lower ends. Among the forty-five shopkeepers, for example, there was undoubtedly a variation in income and status, depending upon the size and nature of their businesses. Pharmacist Frank Streeper, for instance, was obviously better educated and much more prosperous than Harry Mackrives, who ran a small shoe repair shop. Indeed, because the Streepers were among the original settlers of Chestnut Hill and had been modestly successful members of the community for over two centuries, one might well consider Frank Streeper to be a member of the community's upper-middle class — or to be in a category all his own.[12]

Also somewhat arbitrary is the categorizing of some occupations as lower-middle class; these begin with bookkeeper and end with apartment superintendent. There were seventy-five in this group, just over 7 percent of all the heads of households in the *City Directory*. Particularly difficult to categorize in this group were the forty-eight individuals listed as clerks, because the definition of clerk was then in transition. Some were obviously clerks in stores or shops; others were clerks in an older sense, in that they were more like male secretaries or office clerical workers.

Chestnut Hill's working class in 1930 (excluding domestic servants) included skilled workmen, some of whom may have made more money than certain individuals in lower-middle-class occupations. But given the prevailing belief that men who did not "work with their hands" belonged to the middle class, it would make sense to place skilled workers on the upper rungs of the working class. These occupations included printer, electrician, tile setter, mason,

Frank Streeper's Drug Store (now Battin and Lunger)
at the southwest corner of Germantown and Evergreen
avenues. This Tudor-style structure is attributed to architect George T. Pearson and was built for Streeper in
1891–92. *Local.*

plumber, roofer, and tinsmith. At the other end of the working class
were the unskilled workers, many of whom may have done manual
labor in the construction trades. There were 234 individuals in the
local working class, or a little over 22 percent of the male heads of
households who listed occupations in the *City Directory*.

Finally, there were 139 householders in the upper ranks of the
domestic servants who made enough money to live in their own
homes and, presumably, to marry and have children. These were but-
lers, valets, stewards, housemen, cooks, chauffeurs, and gardeners.
The large number of gardeners (70) and cooks (57) was a testament

to local wealth and the attention given to property in Chestnut Hill. The 139 individuals in this category made up approximately 13 percent of the total.

It was thus evident that the lower-middle and middle-middle classes were the smallest social groups in Chestnut Hill, with 7 percent and 12 percent, respectively. Next in order of size were domestic servants, with 13 percent; the upper class, with 18 percent; the working class, with 22 percent; and the upper-middle class, with 27 percent. (Because of rounding to the nearest whole percentage, these figures total only 99 percent.) Thus the local saying that there were only the upper classes and those who served them was partly grounded in reality. This is especially true if one sees local shopkeepers and skilled workers as servants of sorts, who were able to make a living only if they catered to the wishes and tastes of their social betters. Several older shopkeepers have indeed said that they were servants in this sense during the pre–World War II period. According to William Gillies, whose family owned a well-known fish market on Germantown Avenue for many years, some local shopkeepers were virtually "on call" twenty-four hours a day. It was thus not unusual for Gillies to receive a telephone call in the early hours of the morning asking him to deliver several dozen oysters to a party at one of the wealthier households.[13] In the late nineteenth and early twentieth centuries, it had been typical for a well-to-do matron to be driven in her carriage from shop to shop, and to have the owners run out to the carriage to take her orders, which would be delivered later in the day.[14] To this degree shop owners and their employees really were servants of a sort.

Chestnut Hill's many live-in servants did not, of course, appear in the *City Directory* sample, because they did not inhabit households of their own. Unable to afford their own dwellings, they had little choice but to live in their employers' homes. Until the actual manuscripts from the 1930 census are made public early in the next century, there will be no way of counting these men and women with any accuracy.[15]

The degree to which the class structure in Chestnut Hill differed from normal patterns is most striking. In most communities, then and

Gillies Oyster, Game and Fish Market, which once stood at the southeast corner of Germantown and Evergreen avenues, now the site of the First Pennsylvania Bank. CHHS.

now, a diagram of the social classes would look like a pyramid, with the fewest number of people at the top, representing the upper classes, and many more people at the bottom of the pyramid, representing the lower-middle and working classes. Such would have been the pattern for Philadelphia as a whole in 1930. But in Chestnut Hill the typical pattern was completely distorted, with the upper-middle and upper classes together accounting for 45 percent of the *City Directory* sample, and the working class making up only 22 percent — or 36 percent if one included the heads of household who were domestic servants. Of course, adding the uncounted live-in servants would have made it far larger than that. Even so, the result would still be a tremendous distortion of the usual configuration, especially since the middle-middle and lower-middle classes in Chestnut Hill were comparatively small, at only 19 percent of the sample. A diagram of social stratification on the Hill would look more like an hourglass than a pyramid, with the great majority of its residents in the upper and lower categories, and relatively few in the middle.

Another way to appreciate this distortion is to compare the class percentages in Chestnut Hill with percentages from the nation at large. According to the social historian Edward Pessen, a normal distribution of classes would be: upper (3 percent); upper-middle (9–10 percent); middle (32 percent); upper-lower (34 percent); and lower-lower (21 percent). But in Chestnut Hill the upper-class distribution of 18 percent was six times the national norm, and the upper-middle class distribution of 27 percent was about three times the norm. Pessen combines the middle-middle and lower-middle into one middle class. Nevertheless, the 19 percent making up those categories in Chestnut Hill is little more than half the size of a more typical community. For the two lower classes Pessen assigns the figure of 55 percent. If one includes in this category heads of household in Chestnut Hill who were workers and those who were domestic servants, then the figure for the lower (or working) class, as stated earlier, would be 36 percent.[16]

Because the *City Directory* for 1930 gave both occupations and addresses, it is also possible to discover how the various classes were distributed geographically with some degree of accuracy. Local opinion has loosely divided Chestnut Hill into the West and East sides, with the dividing line at Germantown Avenue. The fact that Germantown Avenue also separates the streets and house numbers into east and west has doubtless reinforced this convention. However, an examination of house size and architectural style, along with figures culled from the *City Directory*, shows that the residential divisions were (and are) more complex.

A carefully drawn map would show four main residential zones. The area north of Rex Avenue, along with a thin strip that lay along the easternmost segment of the community, is North Chestnut Hill. This portion of the Hill was the first area to be developed after the Chestnut Hill Railroad (later the Reading and now the Chestnut Hill-East line) arrived in 1854. Although its southeast extension lay east of Germantown Avenue and thus seemed to defy the points of a compass, it had much more in common with North Chestnut Hill than with the neighborhood just a bit further west. In any case, North Chestnut Hill remained an area of attractive single-family homes

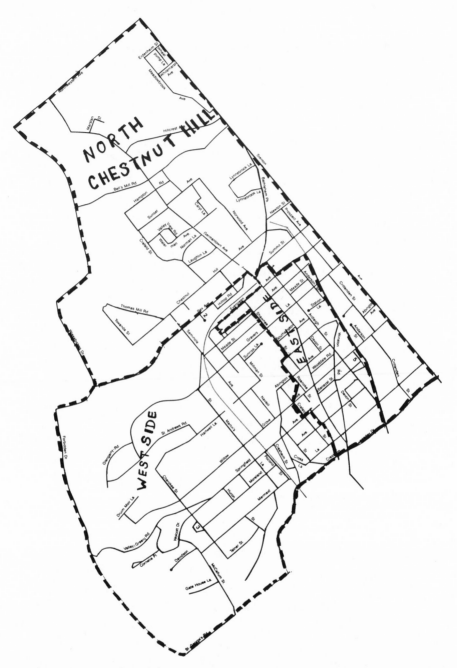

Approximate residential divisions of Chestnut Hill. The commercial district is located along Germantown Ave. and the upper portions of Bethlehem Pike. Note that the small enclave of Woodward houses on the East Side is not shown here. Map adapted by Mary Contosta.

Aerial view of Chestnut Hill, looking southwest to northeast and taken in 1926.
The Philadelphia Cricket Club can be seen near the center of the photograph.
This picture also gives a good view of the many open spaces on the West Side.
LCP.

where many members of the upper and upper-middle classes continued to live in 1930. It should be reiterated, however, that the bulk of
the population in North Chestnut Hill lived south of Bell's Mill Road:
North of that line, most of the land was occupied by large estates or
institutions such as the Morris Arboretum or Chestnut Hill College.

Wealthy and socially prominent residents of the Hill also lived on
the West Side, much of which had been developed by Henry Howard
Houston and George Woodward. The West Side began a block or
two west of Germantown Avenue and reached all the way to Fairmount Park along the Wissahickon Creek, and was bordered on the
north by Chestnut Hill Avenue and on the south by Cresheim Valley
Drive. As in North Chestnut Hill, the streets closer to the railroad
and nearer to the center of Chestnut Hill were more densely popu-

lated than those further away. West of St. Martin's Lane, the land had been given over to large estates such as Druim Moir, Stonehurst, and Krisheim, and to institutions such as the Philadelphia Cricket Club and Chestnut Hill Academy (the former Wissahickon Inn).

The East Side, where most of the workers and better-paid domestic servants lived, began on the streets slightly west of Germantown Avenue and continued east in a jagged pattern to the tracks of what was then the Reading Railroad. However, an island of Woodward houses protruded into the East Side along Benezet Street, East Springfield Avenue, and Winston Road. Thus for purposes of this study, they have been included as part of the West Side. Thus, the East Side resembled two islands. The lower island began at Chresheim Valley Drive and ended at the Woodward developments on the corner of Springfield Avenue and Winston Road. The second island started just north of there along East Willow Grove Avenue and extended up to East Evergreen Avenue and then jogged west to Ardleigh Street, where it continued north again to the edge of Summit Street.

The fourth residential zone was actually part of the commercial district along Germantown Avenue, which extended as far north as Rex Avenue and then down Bethlehem Pike to the railroad station at the foot of Chestnut Hill Avenue. As the *City Directory* indicates, many shopkeepers lived above their establishments at that time. On the lower end of Germantown Avenue (south of Southhampton Avenue) there were also a number of residential properties that were home, for the most part, to the same kinds of people who lived on the East Side.

Table 5 (in the appendix) shows that the great majority of residents who worked in the more prestigious occupations lived in North Chestnut Hill or on the West Side. Of the lawyers, 34.69 percent resided in North Chestnut Hill and 59.18 percent on the West Side; only 6.12 percent reported addresses on the East Side. The great majority of physicians (73.68 percent) lived in North Chestnut Hill, with only 15.79 percent on the West Side and 10.53 percent on the East Side. These figures can probably be explained by the fact that the Chestnut Hill Hospital was located in North Chestnut Hill and was

The east side of Germantown Ave. between Evergreen and Highland avenues, c. 1900. The second and third floors of such buildings often were homes for local shopkeepers. CHHS.

within easy walking distance for the doctors who lived there. The 10 percent of physicians on the East Side doubtless carried on practices in houses there, a common arrangement in those days all over the city of Philadelphia.

At the other end of the occupational scale, 100 percent of the masons, mechanics, truck drivers, and laborers lived on the East Side. Chauffeurs and gardeners showed a slightly more mixed pattern because some of them lived in small houses on or near the large estates in North Chestnut Hill or the West Side. Even so, the great majority of them (87.72 percent and 88.57 percent, respectively) had East Side addresses.

Although the *City Directory* did not designate ethnic backgrounds, an examination of surnames gives some measure of the ethnic contours of Chestnut Hill in 1930. It might be argued that these family names gave no indication of the ethnic provenance of married women, but there was so much pressure at the time to marry within one's

The intersection of Highland and Seminole avenues, showing a
deeply shaded streetscape that remains typical of North Chestnut Hill
and the West Side. Photo c. 1970s. *Local.*

ethnic group that this factor was not as significant as it might have
been two generations later. Other names posed a problem because
they could have been derived from several linguistic traditions. As a
result, the author did not try to differentiate among English, Welsh,
Scotch, or Scotch-Irish surnames, choosing instead to place them all
in the less-than-ideal category of "British." Likewise German, Austrian, Scandinavian, and certain Swiss names were lumped together
in the less-than-perfect category of "Germanic." More serious than
any of these problems was the understandable failure of the *City Directory* to include live-in servants. Despite these flaws and the inac-
curacies that they have produced in the count, this examination of
surnames gives at least a crude indication of ethnic backgrounds.

The 8100 block of Ardleigh St. These neat row houses, with their small front yards, are indicative of Chestnut Hill's East Side. Photo by author, 1991.

Of the 1,051 heads of household, 667, or 64.41 percent, appeared to bear British surnames. Next came Irish (128 — 12.18 percent); Germanic (124 — 11.80 percent); Italian (94 — 8.94 percent); French (20 — 1.90 percent); and "other" (8 — 0.76 percent). As might be expected, there were strong correlations between ethnic background and occupation in Chestnut Hill. Nearly 92 percent of the lawyers appeared to have British surnames. Another 8 percent bore Germanic names, whereas none carried identifiably Irish, Italian, or French names. Ethnic distribution among bankers was very similar: Almost 83 percent were British; 8.57 percent were Germanic; and 8.57 percent were French. One of the physicians was French (5.26 percent); one was Irish (5.26 percent); and two were Germanic (10.53 percent). The remaining fifteen were British (78.94 percent). These figures are not surprising, because men of Protestant, British backgrounds dominated the professions all over the United States at the time, though not always so overwhelmingly as in Chestnut Hill.

At the other extreme, 100 percent of the tile setters and quarriers were Italian, as were over 70 percent of the masons. The greatest variation came within the occupations of contractor/builder and local shopkeeper. Half the shopkeepers had British surnames, 20.45 percent were Italian, 15.91 percent were Germanic, and 13.64 percent were Irish. These figures would lead one to conclude that it was possible for less prosperous residents to open a local business and thereby rise into the ranks of the lower-middle class.[17]

A comparison of surnames with addresses also shows that some ethnic groups were heavily concentrated in certain neighborhoods. On Summit Street, in the heart of upper-class North Chestnut Hill, all the residents were either British or Germanic (81.25 and 18.75 percent, respectively). Even greater areas of British dominance were St. Martin's Lane on the West Side (87.50 percent British surnames), and George Woodward's Benezet Street development (88.89 percent British surnames). The largest concentration of Irish names (57.89 percent) appeared in the unit block of West Highland Avenue, which was part of the East Side extension across Germantown Avenue. There were also a considerable number of Italians (42.86 percent) in the 200 block of West Highland. But the greatest concentration of Italians was in the lower East Side, and especially on the 7700 block of Devon Street, where 83 percent were Italian. There was also an Italian enclave just west of Germantown Avenue in the 8100 block of Shawnee Street (66.67 percent) and in the 8000 block of Roanoke Street (31.57 percent), both defined in this study as East Side neighborhoods.

Looking at Chestnut Hill as a whole, it becomes clear that North Chestnut Hill and the West Side were overwhelmingly British, whereas the East Side was home to nearly all the Irish and Italians. Residents with Germanic surnames, some of whom could trace their American ancestry back to the eighteenth century, were also concentrated in the North and West, as were the handful of French who, like the Germans, most likely had old roots in the region and were fully assimilated.

The *City Directory* gave no figures for religious affiliation, but the large number of British surnames would point to a substantial Protestant population in Chestnut Hill. According to Roman Catholic leaders in the community, 30 to 35 percent of Chestnut Hillers have been Catholic in the twentieth century, a figure that corresponds roughly with the numbers of Irish and Italians in the community, particularly if one could consider live-in servants who were of Irish background.[18] This would leave 65 to 70 percent for the Protestants, a figure that is close to the 64 percent of residents with British surnames. The remaining Protestants could have come from the 12 percent with Germanic last names, a portion of whom may also have been Catholic.

A breakdown of the Protestant denominations, which made up 65 to 70 percent of the Hill's religious population, is more difficult for the period in question. One might estimate that the small Baptist, Methodist, and Lutheran congregations did not account for more than 10 percent of the church population in Chestnut Hill.[19] Even the small group of Chestnut Hill Quakers, who founded a meeting in 1924, might be included in that 10 percent figure, although the Quakers came from more socially prominent backgrounds than the Baptists, Methodists, or Lutherans. The considerable number of upper- and upper-middle-class residents would, of course, point to a substantial membership for the two Episcopal churches, perhaps as high as 35 to 40 percent of the church membership on the Hill. This would leave 15 to 20 percent for the Presbyterians, many of whom were also prosperous residents of the Hill.

Considered together, the demographic figures from the *City Directory* and *Social Registers* indicate that Chestnut Hill was one of the wealthiest and most socially elite suburbs in the nation, as well as Philadelphia's most exclusive suburb in — or outside — the city. The prosperous suburbanites who lived on the Hill, among them the leaders of Philadelphia's most important commercial and cultural establishments, maintained strong connections with the entire metropolitan area — and in some cases with a national or even international network of interests. At the same time, Chestnut Hill remained home to many families of humbler background, who had little social connection with the upper-middle- and upper-class suburbanites. Even less prosperous residents, divided as they were by ethnic and religious differences, frequently failed to find a common ground among themselves.

5

DIFFERENT WORLDS

Chestnut Hill Lives

During the first three decades of the twentieth century, distinct social patterns had emerged in Chestnut Hill. Although demographic figures for 1930 provide a static and quantitative picture of these social contours, the personal accounts of men and women from these years add a vital dimension to understanding life on the Hill. They also help to illuminate the various loyalties of local residents, both between Chestnut Hill and the rest of Philadelphia, and within Chestnut Hill itself.

Divided as they were by occupation, religion, ethnic background, and social class, the inhabitants of Chestnut Hill lived in separate worlds during the first decades of the twentieth century. They attended different churches, went to different schools, courted and married within different groups, and spent their leisure time in dif-

138

St. Paul's Episcopal Church, showing the 1928 structure
by architects Zantzinger, Borie, and Medary. *Local.*

ferent ways. There were thus four or five distinct communities in
Chestnut Hill at the time — communities that would continue to exist
to varying degrees into the 1990s.

Where Chestnut Hillers spent Sunday mornings and how they
felt about other religious groups give one indication of how they
viewed their own and the other worlds of Chestnut Hill. The two
Episcopal churches, St. Paul's in North Chestnut Hill and St. Martin's on the West Side, attracted more upper- and upper-middle-class
residents than any other denomination. Of the two, St. Paul's was
and remains the more uniformly upper class.[1] This was particularly
evident in the 1920s. In 1924, St. Paul's chose the Reverend Mal-
colm E. Peabody to be its rector. He was the son of the Reverend
Endicott Peabody, famed headmaster of Groton School and the very

epitome of the Episcopal establishment in America. Four years later, St. Paul's laid the cornerstone for a splendid new Gothic Revival church, designed by Chestnut Hill architect Clarence C. Zantzinger. St. Martin's, by contrast, almost failed during the 1920s after rector's warden Samuel F. Houston insisted on selecting a former army chaplain as rector in 1919. Unfortunately, the man had been born and reared in rural Alabama and was not well liked by his upper-crust parishioners. Eventually, the vestry, with support from the bishop, forced him to resign, yet another example of how influential Chestnut Hillers were able to have their way with higher authorities, in this case ecclesiastical ones.[2]

The Presbyterian church also attracted a number of prominent Chestnut Hillers. It, too, was an established denomination, having originated in the Presbyterian Church of Scotland. However, the local Presbyterians had suffered a split in 1889, when a group from the First Presbyterian Church had bolted to form Trinity Presbyterian Church, with new facilities, now demolished, on the northwest corner of Germantown Avenue and Gravers Lane (known in 1990 as the Jones Oldsmobile site). After a series of protracted negotiations, the two congregations reunited in 1929 as the Presbyterian Church of Chestnut Hill, and following World War II they erected a large, attractive stone building just north of the Chestnut Hill Hospital on Germantown Avenue. Although there is no documentary explanation for this split, older members of the congregation attribute it largely to social cleavages. According to this explanation, less prominent members of the faith, some of them servants of Scotch-Irish background, charged that the more well-to-do brethren were running the church too much to suit themselves. Angry at the constant slights, humbler members of the congregation left the fold and started Trinity.[3] If this account is more or less true, it is one of at least two local examples of how social divisions were substantial enough to create serious problems in individual churches.

The other example of social disruptions at church occurred among the Hill's Roman Catholics when Italians began to arrive in the late nineteenth and early twentieth centuries, only to find that Our Mother of Consolation (OMC) was dominated by an Irish clergy and

Our Mother of Consolation Roman Catholic Church, c. 1900. *Local.*

Irish parishioners. Not speaking any English at first, the local Italians did not even have a priest to whom they could confess. As a result, some Italians did not bother to go to church at all, and many refused to send their children to the "Irish nuns" at the parish school.[4] Had there been more Italians in Chestnut Hill, they probably would have tried to start their own "national parish," as Italians and other ethnic groups did all over Philadelphia at the time.

Relations among the Protestant denominations in Chestnut Hill were generally cordial. Indeed, some individuals remember that they thought nothing of attending the youth group at another church, especially if it seemed more interesting than their own.[5] But there was considerable ill feeling between Protestants and Catholics, and by both of them against Jews.

Local Catholics continued to remember attempts by the Know-Nothings to keep them from building a church in Chestnut Hill, long after the events were forgotten by Protestants. They also harbored considerable misgivings about the theology and spiritual standing of Protestants. Reflecting on his experience in the 1920s and 1930s, one Catholic remarked:

Back in those days, the Protestant was a "Protester." We all thought you
were no good if you went to St. Paul's [Episcopal]. . . . We weren't even allowed to go to any services in a Protestant Church. I mean the nuns, and the
priests, and my family, too, [wouldn't allow it]. . . . If one of your playmates
died and was being buried from St. Paul's or the Presbyterian Church, you
dared not step your foot on those premises. . . . I never could understand it,
but I had to follow the rules. . . .[6]

Joseph McLaughlin recalled that his membership in a Boy Scout
troop that met at St. Martin-in-the-Fields caused him trouble with
the principal at OMC's parish school:

I guess we were in the scouts a couple of years and one day the Mother Superior sent for me . . . , and she wanted to know what Boy Scouting was
about. . . . When it came to the climax she [asked], "Have they tried to convert you?"[7]

Another Catholic, who did not want to be identified, also related
her childhood feelings about Protestants:

I remember going past Jenks [public] School on the way home [from OMC]
and praying for all those poor children in there because they really didn't
know [the truth]. . . . When I look back on that I can laugh and hope that I
didn't show that kind of prejudice to anyone.[8]

From the Protestant side, Henry Disston II recounted how his
parents objected when they discovered that two servants were in the
habit of taking him to the Catholic Church with them:

The Irish maid and the Irish nurse . . . spent a lot of time with me, and at tea
time they would take me down into [their] dining quarters off the kitchen and
we would have tea and Irish bread with caraway seeds. And when they'd
want to go to Our Mother of Consolation . . . they would sneak me off with
them. . . . My mother and father found out and read the riot act to them. In
those days Roman Catholics and Episcopalians were a little more divided than
today. . . .[9]

Many Protestants were prejudiced against Catholics because they
associated the church with the working and servant classes in Chestnut Hill. They also criticized Catholics for "obeying orders from the
pope" and "not thinking for themselves" in religious matters. Some

of the more prejudiced Protestants also vented themselves verbally against the Sisters of Saint Joseph, whose mother house was at the foot of the Chestnut Hill College campus. Referring to the creek that runs through the grounds, they dubbed the nuns "witches of the Wissahickon."

Out of ignorance more than prejudice, many local Protestants did not even realize that the nuns operated a four-year liberal arts college on the site. If they thought about Chestnut Hill College at all, they supposed that it was some sort of indoctrination program for new nuns. Even in 1990, residents of Chestnut Hill would be introduced to faculty members from the college and, upon meeting them again, would ask, "How is everything over at Chestnut Hill Academy," thereby revealing that they were still only vaguely aware of the college's existence. Historian John Lukacs, who has taught at the college since 1947, contends that certain Chestnut Hillers have maintained an almost "willful ignorance of the college."[10]

Sister Mary Julia Daley, who has lived at the college for nearly sixty years, reflected at length on this isolation of the sisters and the college, and attributed some of it to the nuns' way of life:

> I came here when I was 26 years old. So I've had my entire life here. . . . I think, on the whole, [that] we weren't and still aren't . . . acceptable. And I can understand it. You see, there is a great deal of blue blood in Chestnut Hill. They are elegant people and historically associated with the founding of the city, and we just did not move in that class of society. And when we were nuns in those days, it was less possible for us than it is now . . . to go out. . . . We had rules . . . that kept us out of public life. . . . Because of not knowing what we could do and not do, there was this feeling, "We don't understand the nuns and we don't know what they can do." And so that was an obstacle.[11]

Chestnut Hillers have been more reluctant to talk about prejudice against Jews, perhaps because of the shame that many have felt about anti-Semitism in the aftermath of World War II and the Nazi Holocaust. One individual, who for many years has been associated with Chestnut Hill Academy in various capacities, deplored the way in which local realtors tried to discourage Jewish families from settling on the Hill:

Aerial view of Chestnut Hill College in 1928. LCP.

> The real estate agents really made an effort not to sell to Jews in those days.
> [The prospective Jewish buyer], after looking over a house, would say, "Do
> you think that I and my family would be happy here?" And that was an op-
> portunity for him to find out and for the agent to say, "No, I don't think you
> would be."[12]

He also related that during his student days the local hotel keepers
would not let rooms to Jews, and that this caused considerable trouble at Chestnut Hill Academy when parents with German (and seem-
ingly Jewish) last names were turned down for reservations at local
hotels. It apparently never occurred to school officials that one way
to deal with this situation was to protest against the anti-Semitic practices of hotels in Chestnut Hill.[13]

Distinct school populations also marked the Chestnut Hill experience during the early decades of the twentieth century and
continue to exist at the time of this writing. Upper- and upper-middle-
class parents usually sent their children to one of the local private

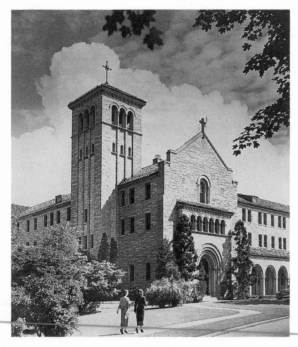

Fournier Hall, Chestnut Hill College, constructed 1927–28. Photo c. early 1950s. CHC.

schools, such as Springside for girls or Chestnut Hill Academy for boys. Another popular school among this set was Miss Catherina Zara's, now defunct, which took both boys and girls in the early grades, and girls alone in the upper elementary years. Then there were some parents who preferred private schools elsewhere in Philadelphia, such as Episcopal Academy, which was then downtown, or Germantown Academy and William Penn Charter School in Germantown—all of which were exclusively male. There were also the coeducational Quaker schools, such as Germantown Friends.

Very few children from Chestnut Hill went to private schools on the Main Line, however, a custom that was and is reciprocated by youngsters on the Main Line, who seldom cross the Schuykill River and Wissahickon Creek to attend schools in Chestnut Hill. Some have attributed this pattern to a paucity of bridges across the Schuykill and Wissahickon, but others have pointed to a polite but very real social rivalry between Chestnut Hill and the Main Line.

There were also those parents who sent their sons off to New England boarding schools at age twelve or thirteen. Philadelphians had never taken to this tradition as enthusiastically as their Yankee counterparts, preferring to keep their children at home in day schools. But some of the wealthier families in Philadelphia (and Chestnut Hill) did adopt the boarding school tradition. Without question, the most favored of these for boys were St. Paul's School in Concord, New Hampshire, and the St. George's School in Newport, Rhode Island, both run as closely as possible along the lines of an English "public" (in reality, private) school.[14]

After secondary school, well-to-do Chestnut Hillers sent their sons to a select list of colleges, confined for the most part to the University of Pennsylvania, Haverford, Swarthmore, Harvard, Yale, and Princeton. Princeton had the greatest prestige among Philadelphians at the time. For aspiring lawyers, many believed that the perfect combination was an undergraduate degree from Princeton and a law degree from Penn. Until after World War II, Chestnut Hill women generally did not go to college. Because their main missions in life were thought to be rearing children and superintending a large household, college seemed pointless.[15]

Catholic children in Chestnut Hill attended their own set of schools. Most went to the parish school at OMC, but those who lived below Springfield Avenue were members of Holy Cross parish in Mount Airy, a somewhat arbitrary decision made by the archdiocese that had the effect of splitting the Hill's Catholic population. However, some of the more prosperous Catholics sent their children to private academies run by religious orders. The Sisters of St. Joseph have operated two such elementary schools in Chestnut Hill: Norwood for boys and Fontbonne for girls. They also have run a secondary school for girls known as Mount Saint Joseph's Academy. Catholic boys could commute to LaSalle High School, run by the Christian Brothers, to St. Joseph's Preparatory School, operated by the Jesuits, or to Roman Catholic High.[16]

Those who attended the Jenks Public Elementary School in

John Story Jenks Public Elementary School, built 1922–23. Photo c. 1970s. *Local.*

Chestnut Hill, and its predecessor, the Gilbert School, seem to have been largely Italians and not-so-wealthy Protestants. After graduating from Jenks, these children went on to Germantown High School. Although Jenks was an attractive and well-equipped facility built in the early 1920s, upper- and upper-middle-class Chestnut Hillers generally would not consider it for their children. This was partly because of a weak public school tradition in Philadelphia, probably because the first public schools, with the exception of Central High, had been part of a drive to educate the poor. Sending one's children to the proper private schools would also help to ensure that they mixed with youngsters of their own background. In any case, there were never enough students from Chestnut Hill to fill Jenks School, forcing authorities to bring children in from neighborhoods beyond the Hill.

As a consequence of these different school traditions, children belonged to five educational groups in Chestnut Hill: private day schools, private boarding schools, private Catholic schools, Catholic

parish schools, and the local public schools. It was thus entirely possible for youngsters growing up within several blocks of one another
to never meet in school—or anywhere else on the Hill. This fact,
combined with strict courtship rules, meant that there was little
chance that they would marry someone of a different background.

The most elaborate courtship customs were practiced by the upper classes in Chestnut Hill. Here parents presided over an elaborate
process that began its familiar course as soon as a daughter was born.
In some families, a special trip was made to Caldwell's jewelry store
in downtown Philadelphia (which maintained registries for wed-
dings, coming-out parties, and the like), within several weeks of the
baby's birth in order to reserve a date for the child's coming-out
party—a full eighteen years in advance. If this were not done right
away, they worried, all the more attractive dates on the social cal-
endar would be spoken for.

The next step was securing an invitation to Miss Louise Lockwood's dancing class at the Philadelphia Cricket Club. Boys and girls
from the best families could expect to go as a matter of course, but
other parents might have to worry a bit. For them it was essential to
enroll their children in one of the Hill's private academies; the schools
sent a list of youngsters to a committee of mothers, who chose from
among them for the dancing class.[17]

After Miss Lockwood retired in the 1940s, she was succeeded by
Miss Mary Waln Graham and later by Margaret Harris Dale, the
latter a granddaughter of the former, long-time rector of St. Paul's
Episcopal Church, J. Andrews Harris. Mrs. Dale remained head of
the dancing class until the mid-1970s.[18]

Children in grades three through six danced on Wednesday after-
noons; the older children went on Friday evenings. Most of them
were already familiar with the Cricket Club's row of neocolonial pavilions, but they must have felt awkward at first in the Georgian Revival ballroom, with its large Palladian doorways that opened onto
the terraces and tennis courts beyond. Here they were supposed to
master the art of formal dancing, along with the finer points of ballroom etiquette.[19]

Mary Wickham Porcher Bond, who went to Miss Lockwood's
during the early years of the century, remembered the class vividly:

We all went to dancing class, which the boys hated and the girls loved. We'd walk over in every-day shoes, and we always had a pretty little silk bag to carry our slippers in, and when we got to the Cricket Club we'd put on our patent leather slippers . . . and we had a wonderful time.[20]

After completing Miss Lockwood's sequence, the youngsters graduated to the yet older "Friday Evening" and then to the "Saturday Evening" classes downtown at the Bellevue Hotel (and later the Warwick Hotel), conducted first by a Mrs. Wurts and later by Mrs. E. Naudain Duer. There they mixed with social contemporaries from the Main Line and other communities. After three years at the "in town" subscription classes, a young lady was ready for her debut.

The debut, or coming-out party, had originated in England and France, when young ladies were presented for the first time at court. The practice had been adopted and simplified by colonial Philadelphians and had continued ever since. Its purpose was twofold: to introduce young women to socially prominent Philadelphians of the older generation, and to find a mate among the most recent crop of suitors. If all went well, she fell in love, got married, and began the process all over again of rearing children and introducing them into polite society.

The girls typically came out at age eighteen. A round of parties and balls began in the fall, with a flurry of events clustering around the Thanksgiving and Christmas holidays. The pace slowed during the winter months and then picked up again in the late spring. Parents or friends might sponsor a variety of events, all with their own set hours and activities. There were tea dances in the late afternoon, followed by dinners, dinner dances, and balls in the late evening. At the height of the season, the more popular debutantes went from one party to another and arrived home not so early the next morning. After several hours of sleep, they were up and preparing for the next round of dining and dancing.

A bachelor's role in the coming-out process was not so well defined. The young ladies were presented and the men were there to meet and court them. Parents always tried to round up more boys than girls, so that each debutante had numerous partners in the course of an evening. If there were an equivalent to the debut for young gentlemen, it would be an invitation to join the First City

Troop, a Philadelphia cavalry unit that dates back to the eighteenth century.[21]

A coming-out party could be a major ordeal for the girl's family, and most engaged a social secretary to help. She arranged the details and provided the all-important list of acceptable young men. Chestnut Hill parents called on the indispensable services of Mrs. J. Edward MacMullan or Mrs. Wirt L. Thompson. As Emily Rivinus Bregy remembered it:

> Mrs. MacMullan and Mrs. Thompson were the social hostesses [i.e., social secretaries] of Philadelphia, and whatever Mrs. MacMullan said went and whatever Mrs. Thompson said went. They would give you a list of all the eligible bachelors because you didn't know all those people.
>
> Mrs. Thompson was a lady herself—and a very close friend of my mother and father—who fell on hard times and got into this business of being a social hostess. . . . You called them and said, "The date is the 14th of June, and would you see that you line up Jimmy Duffy [the caterer], and line up Albers [parking service], and will you line up Robertson's for the flowers?" They arranged for all that. And if a boy got drunk at a party—and they used to get drunk at a lot of parties—they were crossed off the list or else you were told, "He's no good. . . ." And if they did anything else, or if their parents weren't quite up to it, they just weren't on those lists. So they were in charge. They had a lot of power.[22]

Some of the debutante balls were elaborate. Mary Bond described one such affair during the 1916 season:

> [It was on] the roof garden of the Bellevue. . . . The scene was a hunt, and all the waiters had to dress in hunt clothes. And they had live horses! They had stalls up there with straw in them and we could lean over a fence . . . and pat [them]. I always wondered how they got the horses up there in the Bellevue elevators. . . .
>
> At the Assembly [Ball] there was always plenty to eat. There were eggs and champagne. When the champagne showed up the fights began and the boys would rush from table to table trying to snatch a bottle away. . . .[23]

Italian parents in Chestnut Hill were just as strict in their own way about courtship as were the socially prominent families. They expected their children to marry others of Italian descent and went to great lengths to bring about the desired results. The experience of

Joseph Galante, owner of a local food
market, who came to Chestnut Hill from
his native Sicily as a child. Photo by
author, 1985.

Joseph Galante, who came as a boy from Sicily in 1914, was fairly typical:

> The family was quite strict. The family — my father — had friends that had
> children and this was the way of meeting young girls and young fellows. . . .
> We were supposed to go out with the daughters of my father's friends from
> South Philadelphia or West Philadelphia. . . . And then, of course, they tried
> the matchmakers. But it didn't work. . . . I married an American girl of Ger-
> man background. [My parents] didn't like it. . . . But after . . . our first child
> was born, that mellowed everything.[24]

Galante's rebellion was unusual, because for decades the Hill's Italians generally married within their own set. Some even went back to ancestral villages to find wives, and the practice continued to some degree into the post–World War II period. Sante Romano, a popular tailor in Chestnut Hill, was one who followed this tradition. He and a friend went back to Italy in the summer of 1955, and both returned married:

> We rented a car and we traveled all over Italy and then we decided that we
> wanted to get married. And we fortunately, I guess, had met two nice girls.

> In the same town—you know how it is—everybody knows each other's family. And this young woman was available and I asked for the hand. I knew her when she was young. I knew the family. . . . And then we just went together for four months and we got married.[25]

Youngsters of middle-class and non-Italian working-class backgrounds seemed to have the most freedom in courting, at least in the 1920s and 1930s. Joseph McLaughlin remembered that he and others met girls on the number 23 trolley while on their way to Roman Catholic High downtown:

> You got to be social with them. They knew who you were and you knew where they were from. The problem was that there wasn't enough money around [during the depression]. A lot of us would ask them for a date and they'd say, "I'll see you inside."[26]

Others spoke of fraternity and sorority dances at Germantown High or of big-band entertainments at Sunnybrook, outside Pottstown.[27]

The ways in which people spent their leisure time also reflected the distinctions among the different communities of Chestnut Hill. Wealthier and more socially prominent residents, of course, had the most time to spare for such activities, and many of their free hours were devoted to sports. These sports, like their homes, schools, and personal manners, continued to be influenced by British models.

In addition to an affection for British ways, upper-class Chestnut Hillers and their counterparts in other American suburbs had also taken to sports in the nineteenth century as a part of the romantic/transcendental ideal. For it was not enough merely to escape from the crime and disease of the city; one also needed to counteract the physical degeneration that resulted from too much sedentary office work. Some religious spokesmen in England and America even associated physical weakness with sin and promoted what has come to be known as "muscular Christianity." These men recommended team sports in particular, at school and later in adult life, so that players could built their bodies at the same time that they learned the values of team spirit and fair play.[28]

One such example was cricket, which was played in Chestnut Hill until the 1920s, after which faster-paced team sports replaced it. An-

Aerial view of the Philadelphia Cricket Club in 1922. Lawn tennis courts are visible in center of photograph. St. Martin-in-the-Fields Church appears near the upper left corner. LCP.

other British import on the Hill, and in other elite suburbs, was golf. Golf was originally a Scottish game and was so closely identified with Scotland that American golfers commonly donned woolen caps and tweed suits with knickers, or the cotton equivalents in warm weather, when they went onto the links. Playing golf gave an individual some social distinction, because it was played on courses that were expensive to build and maintain, and that until recently belonged almost exclusively to private country clubs. The Philadelphia Cricket Club built its first golf course in 1895, and in 1905 the club held the first in a series of national golf tournaments, including the United States Open in 1907 and 1910. In 1922, the cricket club inaugurated a much larger course outside Flourtown. The older greens remained in Chestnut Hill, but by 1990 were reduced to a single nine-hole course.

Many prominent Chestnut Hillers also joined the Sunnybrook Golf Club, located initially in Springfield Township near Oreland and later in Whitemarsh Township near Militia Hill.[29]

Prosperous Chestnut Hillers likewise adopted the British affection for tennis, another expensive sport that required special equipment and well-tended courts. Local residents started a Chestnut Hill Tennis Club in the mid-1880s, with courts somewhere along Bethlehem Pike. Among its early members were Alexander W. Biddle, Eli K. Price, Jr., and Mrs. J. Willis Martin. In 1895 the club began holding an annual "open tournament." The Cricket Club also built tennis courts and a clubhouse in 1909, replacing much smaller facilities that had been built across the street near the Wissahickon Inn in the late nineteenth century. For decades the Cricket Club hosted important competitions, such as the Women's National Tennis Tournament, the Women's Atlantic Seaboard Tournament, and the Girls National Tournament.[30]

The creation of such tennis, cricket, and golf clubs was itself an integral part of the suburban ideal. The club grounds — particularly the golf courses — were planted to look like romantic parks where members could enjoy being in the out-of-doors — hence the name "country club." In the future the various clubs' open spaces would play an important role in maintaining the semirural atmosphere of Chestnut Hill.

Even more than golf or tennis, the mania for fox hunting among a few of the wealthiest residents demonstrated an attachment to British sporting life among upper-class Chestnut Hillers. Requiring wealth, leisure, and abundant land, it was the supreme gentleman's sport on both sides of the Atlantic. As early as 1891, upper-class residents from Chestnut Hill helped to organize the Pennbrook Hunt, which met on John R. Fell's estate near Fort Washington. In order to ensure authenticity, the group imported a dozen hounds from England.[31] By the early twentieth century, Chestnut Hillers were participating in the Whitemarsh Valley Hunt, held on the estate of George D. Widener, located just north of Chestnut Hill and now known as Erdenheim Farms. A hunt held there in October 1925 was described by the *Chestnut Hill and Mount Airy Herald*:

A wealthy Philadelphia woman in Paris, 1907. Author's collection.

> Throngs of men and women prominently identified in social, club, financial, and professional circles, were augmented by many of the hunting set, from New York, Long Island, Washington and Baltimore. . . . Several officials . . . met on horseback, in their pink riding coats.[32]

Yet another sign of wealth and leisure among Chestnut Hillers was their penchant for travel abroad. Every summer the newspapers were full of the comings and goings of local residents to England or the Continent. Typical of these was an obsequious notice in the *Germantown Telegraph* in July 1930. It projected a stay at an English country house, followed by leisurely automobile trips through Scotland and southern Europe:

> Mrs. J. Wilmer Biddle, of "Binderton House," Chestnut Hill, who sailed for Europe last Saturday on the Belgenland with her daughters . . . will, upon her arrival in England, go to Henley-on-Thames to be the guest of her son-in-law and daughter, Mr. and Mrs. Howard Gwynne Kepple-Palmer. Later Mrs. Biddle and her daughter will visit Scotland and then will motor through southern Europe before returning about October 1.[33]

In its own polite way, the article attributed every characteristic of upper-class life to the Biddles: enough wealth and leisure to undertake a prolonged visit to England and the Continent; marriage of a

Francis and James Bond (standing) building a sand castle at the New Jersey shore, 1905. James Bond would
later wed Mary W. Porcher of Chestnut Hill. Ian Flem-
ing would take the name for his fictional "Agent 007"
from this James Bond. Author's collection.

daughter into the English upper class; and attendance at the aristo-
cratic Henley Royal Regatta.

If other prosperous Chestnut Hillers did not join the summer ex-
odus to Europe, it was likely that they would spend July and August
in Maine. Although local residents went to several spots on the Maine
coast, Northeast Harbor on Mount Desert Island was the most
proper place to go — so much so that it was dubbed "Philadelphia on
the rocks." There they could escape the semitropical heat of many
Philadelphia summers.[34]

For a large and well-equipped household, the annual move to
Maine was a major undertaking. Dr. George Woodward's son Stanley remembered the whole experience with some amusement: "We
were all packed off — family, cook, maids, horses, carriages, coach-
men, . . . a sweet grandmother, and [the nurse] Miss Blong."[35] When
Stanley's uncle, Samuel F. Houston, went off to Maine with his family, he took along a couple of Druim Moir cows so that the children's
digestion would not be upset by strange milk.[36]

Members of Chestnut Hill's working class, as might be expected,
spent their summers very differently, back in Chestnut Hill. In the
nineteenth and early twentieth centuries, boys swam behind the aban-

White City amusement park, which stood near the corner of Bethlehem Pike and Paper Mill Road in Erdenheim. Harris Collection, CHHS.

doned mill dams along the Wissahickon. They and their families also went picnicking in the Wissahickon woods on Sundays or, if they were lucky, visited any of several soda fountains along Germantown Avenue. During the 1910s, 1920s, and 1930s, there was the annual July excursion by rail to Atlantic City, organized by the Chestnut Hill Businessmen's Association.[37]

Another treat for those left behind in Chestnut Hill was a short trip to White City, an amusement park in nearby Erdenheim at the northwest corner of Bethlehem Pike and Paper Mill Road. Also known as Chestnut Hill Park, this pleasure center was one of many trolley-car parks that were built at the ends of trolley lines all over the country as a way of attracting riders on evenings and weekends. Centered by a small lake and covering about sixteen acres, White City belonged to H. B. Auchey, who later owned the famous Philadelphia Toboggan Company, which made high-quality carousels and other amusement rides.

Many well-to-do inhabitants of Chestnut Hill objected to the park, claiming that it brought a rowdy group of visitors through the Hill. Thus, in early 1912 a syndicate of wealthy local residents, made up of George C. Thomas, Jr., Charles N. Welsh, Wilson Potter, and

Jay Cook III, bought the property for approximately $500,000 and demolished the park. They maintained that the park "lowered the tone of the entire suburb; that it depreciated the value of the land and that its existence kept desirable persons away from Chestnut Hill."[38] This was another example of a group of Chestnut Hillers using their wealth and influence to control development in or around their community. The men planned to use the park site to build "high class houses." For unexplained reasons, these were never built, and in 1923 they sold the land to Springfield Township as the location for a new public high school. All that remains of the park is the miniature lake along Montgomery Avenue.[39]

During the winter months, less prosperous Chestnut Hillers could attend the movies, at least after July 1914, when the Belvedere Theater opened its doors. Ten years later the Chestnut Hill Theater, another movie house, was established at 8320 Germantown Avenue.[40] There were also frequent dances on the second floor of Joslin's Hall at 8434 Germantown Avenue, a building that now houses the offices of the Chestnut Hill Community Association and the *Chestnut Hill Local*.[41]

Members of Chestnut Hill's middle and working classes could join a variety of clubs. In 1889, for example, the Knights of Pythias built a new lodge hall at Highland and Germantown avenues. The following year, the Ancient Order of Hibernians, an Irish fraternal order, opened a branch in Chestnut Hill.[42] Local Italians formed their own clubs. In 1924, Italians from northern Italy, most of them quarriers and stone masons who were born in or around the village of Pofabbro, some forty miles north of Venice, founded the Venetian Club in an old house at 8030 Germantown Avenue. In 1930 they erected a three-story addition to the front of the structure (still standing), equipped with a bowling alley, lodge and game rooms, and a large ballroom with stage on the upper floor. Considering themselves to be distinctly different from the southern Italians on the Hill, many of whom made their livings as gardeners, they excluded the latter from membership. The southern Italians responded by forming their own Bocce Club, whose present headquarters are on East Hartwell Lane.[43]

In addition to this split within the Italian community, there was continuing friction between the Irish and Italians on the Hill. Besides Italian resentment over Irish domination of the local Catholic church, there were name callings and fistfights between Irish and Italian boys. Both groups, however, could agree on disliking individuals whom they considered to be snobs or social climbers in North Chestnut Hill and the West Side. These were not people who already belonged to the Hill's upper class; rather, they were those who desperately wanted to break into it or who pretended to belong. East Siders took to calling them "half-cuts," meaning people who were "phony" or "a cut below" the real upper class. Over time, however, this definition became less precise and was used in a mildly derogatory way to describe anyone who did not live on the East Side — anyone who was not "none of us."

Nobody whom the author interviewed in North Chestnut Hill or the West Side had ever heard of the term half-cut. This is not surprising, because Chestnut Hillers usually have known very little about the real lives and thoughts of workers and domestic servants in their midst — although they sometimes liked to think that they did. In contrast, East Siders knew (and still know) a great deal about upper- and upper-middle-class residents, but usually will not discuss it outside their own trusted circle, a habit of domestic servants in particular, who proved the most difficult to interview.

Such distinct ways of viewing themselves and others reveal that there were several communities within Chestnut Hill during the first decades of the twentieth century. Although each of these groups depended to some degree on the others, and although there was little outward hostility, this suburban neighborhood in the northwest corner of Philadelphia did not function as an integrated community. Powerful effects of these different worlds would influence events for decades to come.

6

COMMUNITY IMPROVEMENT

The Progressive Suburb

As residents of a suburb in the city, the inhabitants of Chestnut Hill had discovered soon after the city/county consolidation of 1854 that they could not depend upon Philadelphia's government to provide all the services and public works that they might want or need. Three decades later little had changed. Partly in response, local leaders created two different improvement associations, one in the 1880s and the other soon after the turn of the century. By raising its own funds for improvements, the earlier of these organizations provided a number of public works for the Hill. The second association was formed in cooperation with residents of Mount Airy and Germantown, thereby reaffirming the common history and common circumstances of these suburban communities within the city of Philadelphia. By lobbying the city to achieve their goals, and by becoming active in city reform movements, the three communities (Chestnut Hill, Mount Airy, and Germantown) also exhibited their belief in an organic city, with separate but mutually dependent parts. Other local organizations, some of which remain active at the time of this writing, also joined in improvement activities.

Although similar improvement groups existed in other urban neighborhoods and in suburbs outside the municipal limits, those in Chestnut Hill, Mount Airy, and Germantown became partial instruments of local autonomy and laid the groundwork for quasi government in Chestnut Hill several generations later. Such organizations emphasized the dual identification that commuters felt between their jobs in the city and their homes and community activities back on the Hill. They also demonstrated the persistence with which the inhabitants of Chestnut Hill worked to maintain a privileged way of life for themselves and their descendants.[1]

In virtually all such undertakings, it was the upper-middle- and upper-class residents of the Hill, or their counterparts in Germantown and Mount Airy, who took the lead. These were men — and sometimes women — who prided themselves on their abilities to discover problems and provide rational solutions. As bankers, lawyers, manufacturers, and corporate executives, they had presided over an industrial and urban revolution that literally changed the face of America.[2] This experience of success, combined with a habit of working on a problem until they had solved it, doubtless contributed to their persistence in creating and sustaining a high quality of life in Chestnut Hill. Also, because they were successful in their careers, the leaders of local civic groups were unlikely to be impressed or intimidated by politicians downtown. Their high social standing conditioned them to expect a degree of deference from others and gave them a large measure of self-confidence. All these factors led Chestnut Hillers to demand, maintain, and realize a pleasant and privileged way of life in their suburb in the city.

Such efforts, whether at work in the city or at home in Chestnut Hill, depended very little upon government initiative. According to Sam Bass Warner, E. Digby Baltzell, and others, this insistence upon private rather than public actions has been particularly noticeable in

Philadelphia, where a strong opposition to governmental compulsion may stem from early Quaker traditions of voluntarism, combined with a distaste for powerful government at any level.[3] It is also true that business managers and executives at the time had an almost religious devotion to the principles of laissez-faire economics, except for the contradictory issue of protective tariffs, which they generally favored. Somewhat paralyzed by their own political and economic philosophies, many well-to-do Philadelphians moved to suburbs outside the city, where they could take voluntary action to control their surroundings and provide themselves with the most advanced services.

Such a restricted approach to urban problems was consistent with the thinking of moderate reformers during the Progressive Era of the early twentieth century (c. 1900–1917).[4] These Progressives were largely Republican in politics, Protestant in religion, and upper-middle to upper class in social background.[5] They crusaded against political corruption and inefficiency, supported limited public health measures, advocated parks and municipal beautification projects, and supported private reform efforts such as settlement houses and the Social Gospel movement. But by emphasizing private or largely local measures, moderate Progressives often failed to understand that most problems in the urban/industrial age were regional, national, and even international in scope.[6] On the local level, as in Chestnut Hill, their Progressivism was often, though not always, a self-serving attempt to preserve their comfortable way of life. But if these Progressives shared an opposition to strong government with the Quaker/Pietist settlers of the old German Township, they most certainly did not agree with their ancestors' egalitarian principles and disdain for elite leadership in the community. The men and women who would run Chestnut Hill's civic and improvement groups believed that professionally skilled and socially prominent residents should dominate the organizational life of the community.

From the late nineteenth century until World War II, Chestnut Hill's improvement efforts were in fact characterized by a spirit and form that many would associate with the Progressive Era, even though that period of national history has been associated with the first two decades of the twentieth century. This survival of Progressivism in Chestnut Hill thus lends support to the argument that Progressivism is as much a state of mind as it is a movement that took place within a brief period of American history.[7]

The continuing appeal of Progressivism also stemmed from the fact that Chestnut Hill remained inside the city of Philadelphia, a municipality that was notorious for its corrupt political machine. Unlike prosperous Philadelphians who moved to suburbs on the Main Line, where they were free from the city and could create their own government and local services, Chestnut Hillers had to improvise ways of working around or through the city hall machine. In the process, Chestnut Hill residents were forced, more than suburbanites outside the city, to examine their relationship to the larger metropolis.

For these reasons, civic-minded residents of the Hill organized themselves during the late nineteenth and early twentieth centuries. These organizations helped them to pave and maintain streets, secure a new public school, launch conservation and beautification projects along the Wissahickon Creek, and battle attempts by the machine in city hall to divide their ward and weaken their strength as independent Republicans. During both world wars and the Great Depression, Chestnut Hill's improvement groups also became involved in war work and in private relief efforts.

The earliest of Chestnut Hill's improvement groups actually anticipated the Progressive Era by two decades. Founded in 1882, it was called the Village Improvement Association.[8] The organization was also known in the press as the Improvement Company, the Village Improvement Company, and the Chestnut Hill Improvement Association. Whatever its precise designation, this local group was not unique; there were hundreds of improvement associations being founded all over the United States at the time. In fact, local residents may have been influenced by an abundance of books and articles on the subject.[9]

As these writings made clear, there was a growing disgust in the latter half of the nineteenth century with the ugliness of rural villages. Such sentiments were particularly evident among successful businessmen, who placed a premium on tidiness and order. As they fled

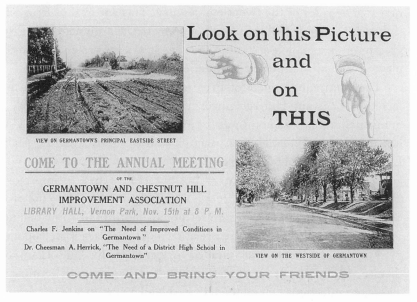

One reason that Chestnut Hillers joined improvement associations was to obtain
better streets. This poster, from around 1910, advertises an annual meeting of the
Germantown and Chestnut Hill Improvement Association. GHS.

from urban ills and into the gateway villages that surrounded cities
such as Philadelphia, they were determined to rid their new homes
of rural slovenliness. Although they wished to live in "the country,"
they also wanted to transform it into the sort of picturesque village
that existed more in their imaginations than in reality. The early improvement associations were thus important vehicles for creating the
suburban ideal.[10]

What distinguished Chestnut Hill's improvement association was
its persistence and resourcefulness. According to the *Germantown
Guide,* which reported on its founding, the goals of the organization
were:

> The trimming of trees on the highways, planting trees at proper places, the
> removal of those improperly placed . . . , compelling laws and the health,
> safety or convenience of the inhabitants to be enforced, procuring the side-
> walks to be kept in a safe, proper and neat condition, and, as far as it lies in
> their power, endeavoring to introduce and maintain a general attention to the

comfort and neatness of the streets and other thoroughfares in and about Chestnut Hill.[11]

The article went on to point out that the association wanted to have the city pave Germantown Avenue from Gorgas Lane in Mount Airy to the present Northwestern Avenue at the municipal limits. A recent investigation of the lower portions of the avenue had revealed serious "damage to teams and injury to horses occasioned by the billows of mud and beds of mire through which they are compelled to pass. . . ."[12]

The principal force behind this ambitious improvement association was Colonel Samuel Goodman (1834–1914), one of its early presidents. Goodman was a Civil War veteran who had grown up on a farm near Limekiln Pike and Washington Lane, in the present West Oak Lane section of Philadelphia. After the war he was associated with a New York City textile firm. Other early leaders of the organization were Samuel Y. Heebner (1857–1917), president of the Market Street National Bank and son of pioneer suburbanite Charles Heebner; and the Reverend J. Andrews Harris (1834–1922), the influential long-time rector of St. Paul's Church.[13]

Minutes, correspondence, and other records of the Chestnut Hill Improvement Association have apparently not survived, forcing the investigator to rely on newspaper accounts. These reveal that Goodman and his fellow improvers dedicated themselves primarily to paving and maintaining roads in Chestnut Hill. By 1893 they had resurfaced or constructed over fifteen miles of roadway and had collected some $200,000 in private funds ($2 to $3 million in 1990) in order to finance them.[14] In 1886 and 1887, for example, they applied several layers of crushed stone to Gravers Lane and Highland Avenue, employing a method of street paving known as the macadam process, named for its Scotch inventor, John MacAdam. The following year, the association "macadamized" both Stenton and Evergreen avenues. In 1892 they shared with the Philadelphia city government the expense of resurfacing Germantown Avenue from Gorgas Lane to Northwestern Avenue — a distance of almost three miles. They had been pressing for this improvement since their establishment ten years before, but it was the decision to install the first electrified trolley cars on the roadway that probably did more than anything else to force the city into action.[15]

Once the roads were resurfaced, the association did its best to maintain them. Each spring it filled hundreds of potholes that had broken numerous axles and buggy wheels during winter thaws.[16] In the early 1890s the group organized itself to combat clouds of dust thrown up by horse-drawn vehicles during dry summer months along the Hill's dirt and gravel roads. They bought ten wagons equipped with water tanks, which they employed to sprinkle the roads whenever possible. They even constructed their own reservoir in Mount Airy to ensure enough water for sprinkling.[17]

The association also set aside funds for building sidewalks, then generally constructed of wood and known as boardwalks. In 1898 they built a boardwalk from Stenton Avenue on the far East Side of the Hill to Houston's Wissahickon Inn on the West Side, which coincidentally provided a walkway along Willow Grove Avenue to St. Martin's Church.[18] Because both the church and the inn had been created by Houston, it is likely that the Houston family helped to finance this undertaking and was a regular and substantial contributor to the association.

The Chestnut Hill Improvement Association proved so effective that a writer for the weekly *Germantown Guide* regretted in June 1889, "that the city government itself cannot be transferred to such management," an obvious reference to the increasing belief by reformers that government should be run like an efficient business.[19] Two years later the same newspaper asserted that the association "would be justified in applying for an act of separation from the city. . . ."[20] This would not be the last time that Chestnut Hillers, frustrated with a lack of municipal services, contemplated secession from Philadelphia.

Instead of breaking away from the metropolis, which even then would have been difficult if not impossible, the local improvers decided to pressure the city to assume more financial responsibility for Chestnut Hill. Association president Samuel Goodwin himself won a seat in the city's Common Council in 1892, a position that he held until ill health forced him to resign in 1899. His place was then secured for the Hill by Dr. George Woodward.[21]

For Common Council
GEORGE WOODWARD, M. D.,

Of Chestnut Hill,

Subject to the Rules

OF THE

REPUBLICAN PARTY

Advertisement in the *Germantown Telegraph*, 19 August
1899, for George Woodward's campaign for Philadelphia
Common Council. GHS.

It is impossible to determine just how successful the improvers
were in their lobbying efforts with city hall, but it appears that the
municipal government did begin to allocate more funds for Chestnut
Hill streets and roads in the 1890s. This greater cooperation from the
city, combined with Goodman's ill health, may also explain the apparent decline in the Chestnut Hill Village Improvement Association
by the end of the century. Although there was no public announcement of its official demise, no further stories about its activities appeared in the local newspapers, leading one to conclude that it had
become inactive or was disbanded altogether. Although Chestnut
Hillers have shown a remarkable persistence in using such organizations to preserve their way of life, such efforts have been punctuated by periods of decline, followed by bursts of civic renewal.

One of these renewals was prompted in the early twentieth century by the escalating corruption of Philadelphia's city government.
Despite improvements in city services to Chestnut Hill, Philadel-

phia's city government remained one of the most corrupt and inefficient in the nation. As journalist Lincoln Steffens put it in his *Shame of the Cities,* Philadelphia had one of the most "corrupt but contented" governments in America.[22] Although Steffens may have exaggerated, Philadelphia's municipal government was in the grips of a corrupt Republican machine that cared far more about distributing patronage and staying in power than it did about addressing urban problems.

Indeed, many of the same conditions that had caused prosperous citizens to leave the city a half century before for places like Chestnut Hill continued to exist. Although Philadelphia had now fallen to third place in population (behind Chicago), the city's expanding economy continued to attract thousands of newcomers each year. Between 1901 and 1915, its population rose from 1,293,000 to 1,684,000, approximately one-quarter of them foreign born. About one-third of them were so-called new immigrants from southern and eastern Europe. For these most recent arrivals, home might be a back-alley shack with primitive sanitary conditions.[23] Under the circumstances, with teeming slums and a city government enmeshed in patronage, no section of the city could expect that municipal funds and services would be distributed on a rational, nonpartisan basis. Instead, neighborhoods that commanded the greatest political influence usually enjoyed a larger share of appropriations.[24]

It was partly for this reason that several dozen men from the old 22nd Ward, made up largely of Chestnut Hill, Mount Airy, and Germantown, met in December 1906 to found the Germantown and Chestnut Hill (G&CH) Improvement Association.[25] In its initial letter to solicit members, the officers wrote that the purpose of the association was "to concentrate and intelligently direct all efforts for improvements of whatever sort needed to receive complaints and remedy them. . . ." It went on to propose that the recent and rapid growth of the ward made improvements more urgent than ever before:

> Germantown and Chestnut Hill, now comprising the Twenty-second Ward of our city, have a population upward of 70,000, and covers an area of [10.7] square miles. It is nearly twice as populous as Lancaster, Pa. Harrisburg, Pa.,

and Charleston, S.C. have about the same population as this one ward. If it were not part of a city, it would, by virtue of its size and population, be ranked as a city itself. Its outlying position gives it a peculiar character, and the steady opening up of new sections and the development of its suburban life, bring with them a constantly increasing multiplicity of needs.[26]

It is clear that the organizers of the G&CH Improvement Association saw their ward as a suburban neighborhood that was somewhat different from the rest of the incorporated city. For by now rural Mount Airy, just south of Chestnut Hill, was also undergoing rapid development as an attractive suburb in the city. Except for the unofficial and somewhat arbitrary division separating it from the Hill, it was difficult to discern much visual difference between the two. This was particularly true of Mount Airy's West Side, which shared the banks of the Wissahickon gorge with Chestnut Hill, along with the lush Wissahickon style of landscaping and gardening. Although Chestnut Hill had more socially prominent residents, Mount Airy (like Germantown below it) was an attractive and prestigious place to live at the turn of the century. Besides recognizing their common demographic characteristics, the organizers of the new G&CH Improvement Association were inspired by their connections with the old German Township, whose boundaries had been nearly coterminous with the 22nd Ward since the city/county consolidation of 1854. "We are proud of our ward," they wrote. "It has an honorable past. Part of the richest history, not only of the city, but of the whole country finds its home in Germantown."[27]

Finally, the organizers committed themselves to a nonpartisan stance in politics, promising that it would have "nothing to do with any political party." One motive was to attract all interested residents, regardless of their political affiliations. But their nonpartisan position also reflected the 22nd Ward's growing tradition of political independence and opposition to the city's corrupt machine. As an extension of this nonpartisanship, membership was open to anyone, whether an official resident of the ward or not, who was interested in the welfare of the region — Germantown, Mount Airy, and Chestnut Hill. Dues were set at a modest one dollar per year. General membership meetings were held semiannually, in May and November. There was also an executive board of nine (and later fifteen) directors.[28]

By the spring of 1907, the new association listed 370 members, roughly 20 percent of whom were from Chestnut Hill. Because the Hill, with approximately 6,000 people, then represented less than one-tenth of the total ward population, its participation was twice what might have been expected by numbers alone, a testament to the progressive-mindedness of many Chestnut Hillers and their determination to preserve their community as a comfortable and attractive suburb in the city. Among the Hill's charter members of the G&CH Improvement Association were several prominent men, some of whose descendants were still active or well-known in the community at the time of this writing. These included Henry H. Bonnell (a nephew-in-law of Henry Howard Houston); Walter A. Dwyer (whose family has owned a coal and then a fuel-oil company for over a century); Edgar Dudley Faries (a lawyer, as well as a trustee and manager of the Henry Howard Houston estate); the Reverend J. Andrews Harris (who had been active in the old Chestnut Hill Improvement Association and was thus a personal link between the two groups); Samuel F. Houston (son of Henry Howard Houston); Walter E. Rex (a lawyer and descendant of one of the Hill's earliest land-owning families); and, of course, Dr. George Woodward.[29] As clergymen, lawyers, businessmen, and physicians, these were the sort of men who created and sustained the Progressive movement throughout the United States.

Unlike the earlier Chestnut Hill Village Improvement Association, the successor group did not seek to raise its own funds for large projects. Instead, it concentrated on gathering information about physical conditions in the ward, serving as a clearing house for complaints, and putting all the pressure it could on Philadelphia authorities to make improvements, deliver services, and remedy a variety of problems and nuisances. This decision to act as a lobbying group before city government showed that most thoughts of leaving the city had been discarded and that members of the association probably accepted the prevailing idea of an organic city, with its separate yet mutually dependent parts.

An outing of the all-male Germantown and Chestnut Hill Improvement Association. The group's president, William H. Emhardt, Jr., is seated in the center of the front row, wearing a white suit. GHS.

The guiding personality behind the G&CH Improvement Association was William H. Emhardt, Jr. (1876–1951), a native Germantowner and head of the Germantown Mutual Fire Insurance Company, who left an estate of over $250,000 (then a respectable sum) at the time of his death. Emhardt was the association's first secretary, and in 1914 he was elected president, a position that he held without interruption for the next three decades.[30] Such dedication was an important factor in the group's long success, in contrast to many other improvement associations that originated in other Philadelphia neighborhoods during this period and that failed or became inactive within several years. Unlike these, the Germantown and Chestnut Hill organization would remain effective into the early 1930s and would manage to survive into the post–World War II period.

Yet another reason for the association's success was the decision to open a permanent headquarters with a paid executive director. This office initially was on the second floor of the Vernon Building at Germantown and Chelton avenues, and later at 5555 Germantown Avenue, both locations in Germantown rather than Chestnut Hill. The first executive director, whose official title was actually special representative, was Jacob C. Bockius (1848–1940), who was hired in 1909 and remained in that position until resigning in 1932. Bockius was a native Germantowner who, with his father, had operated a flourishing clothing store, the Bockius Bazaar.[31] Bockius's main job was to receive complaints from ward residents, forward them to the proper authorities downtown for solution, and monitor responses from city hall. From all accounts, he was very resourceful: in 1922, when about 400 complaints were registered with his office, the summary list of acceptable adjustments filled fifty typed pages.[32]

Serving as Bockius's eyes and ears was another important institution known as the Auxiliary Committee of the G&CH Improvement Association. It was made up of one or more appointed representatives from each of the voting districts in the 22nd Ward, the number varying from forty-nine in the early period to eighty by the 1930s. Among the district representatives from Chestnut Hill were John B. Lear, a property manager and the father of John B. Lear, Jr., and Polly (Mrs. Samuel J.) Randall, both of whom lived in Chestnut Hill in 1990. Another was Howard S. Kneedler, grandson of early Chestnut Hill suburbanite Jesse Kneedler and himself a prosperous textile company executive. These and the other representatives collected comments and concerns at the grass-roots level and forwarded them to Special Representative Bockius.[33] Ironically, the Auxiliary Committee somewhat resembled the hated Republican machine at city hall, which was well organized at the neighborhood level with ward bosses and precinct captains. It was impossible to tell whether there was any conscious imitation of the system by the Improvement Association.

In any case, the Auxiliary Committee met once a month to set priorities for their requests to city hall and to plan overall strategy. Men from the auxiliary group (there were no female members) also joined individuals from the general membership to serve on a number of functional committees. During the first years of the organization these committees were: highways, lighting, and street cleaning; street and steam railways; health, charities, sewage, and water (with Dr. Woodward as chairman); police and fire; public education and libraries; parks, playgrounds, public bathhouses, and amusements; and publicity (whose chairman was Henry H. Bonnell). Additional committees came later, such as one for public adornment and another for shade trees.[34]

Given the 70,000 to 90,000 people (depending on the precise time) who lived in the 22nd Ward, it is understandable that only a portion of the improvements secured by the association benefited Chestnut Hill directly. Even so, a list of accomplishments on behalf of Hill residents would fill several pages. Among the more impressive were the removal of ugly and dangerous grade crossings on both the Pennsylvania and Reading lines (completed in the early 1930s); the opening of emergency hospitals during the 1918 influenza epidemic; the building of a district high school in Germantown (which remains the public high school for Chestnut Hill); the building of a new public elementary school in Chestnut Hill (the present Jenks facility); the construction of the Water Tower Recreation Center (with generous financial assistance from Dr. and Mrs. Woodward); the purchase of up-to-date fire-fighting equipment for the Chestnut Hill station; the repaving of many local streets, along with the installation of curbings and storm sewers; better trash removal; the augmentation of city water supplies on the Hill; and the institution of an annual property inspection and spring cleanup.[35]

With such accomplishments, the G&CH Improvement Association was more effective than any other local civic group in the early twentieth century. Although not as impressive, the Chestnut Hill Businessmen's Association supported many of the same causes. Its precise origins are unclear, but this group seems to have been founded very early in the century as part of a nationwide movement of businessmen's associations. After becoming inactive for several years, it was reorganized in Chestnut Hill during the spring of 1913. Its early presidents were two local building contractors, James McCrea (1878–1973) and Pringle Borthwick (1861–1948). Borthwick also served for several years as a city councilman from Chestnut Hill. Howard S. Kneedler, who was active in the Improvement Association, was another of the early leaders of the businessmen's group. In addition to enrolling local merchants in Chestnut Hill, the Businessmen's Association included doctors, lawyers, dentists, realtors, contractors, and anyone else who might do business on the Hill.[36] Although the organization included some socially prominent members, one has the impression that its membership was largely middle-middle to upper-middle class in background. This was in contrast to the G&CH Improvement Association, which appeared to draw members more from the upper-middle and upper classes.

During a half dozen years or so after its reorganization, the businessmen campaigned for many of the same projects as the G&CH Improvement Association, including the elimination of grade crossings on the two commuter railroads serving Chestnut Hill and the erection of a new public elementary school on the Hill.[37] They similarly petitioned the city to resurface local streets and to provide additional water supplies as the population grew.[38] In early 1915 the businessmen endorsed an ultimately unsuccessful plan put forward by Dr. Woodward to have a new firehouse and post office erected at Germantown Avenue and Mermaid Lane opposite the gateway to Cresheim Valley Drive (yet another example of Woodward's debt to the City Beautiful movement).[39] A year earlier the Businessmen's Association had also rallied local residents to save the old stone water tower at Ardleigh Street and Southhampton Avenue, then in a state of decay and threatened with demolition.[40]

During this period the Businessmen's Association began sponsoring a day-long rail excursion to Atlantic City each July, an event that was aimed at giving less prosperous residents an affordable day at the shore. Beginning in the summer of 1913 and continuing until World War II, the group reserved cars on the Pennsylvania Railroad for the trip. In 1925, when the two-way fare was $2.30 for adults and $1.25 for children, nearly 1,000 inhabitants took advantage of this outing. Virtually all businesses on the Hill shut down for the day.[41] It was also in 1913 that the businessmen began sponsoring a Fourth of July celebration in Chestnut Hill, at first on the Chestnut Hill Academy grounds and later at the Water Tower Recreation Center. The celebration featured speeches, a military band concert, athletic contests, and the singing of patriotic songs.[42] As with the shore excursion, this event seemed to attract less prominent residents of the Hill, as upper-class inhabitants enjoyed their own celebration at the Cricket Club. Even the observation of the nation's birth was not enough to bridge social cleavages for a few hours on Independence Day.

The Businessmen's Association also mobilized itself during World War I. As early as May 1917, one month after the American declaration of war against Germany, some thirty-five members of the association met in the barn of president Pringle Borthwick to cut seed potatoes for planting in victory gardens. They cooperated with several local organizations in establishing victory gardens throughout the Hill, with many of the plots donated by Dr. Woodward on land that he owned. The businessmen also organized a series of "send-off" parties for departing local soldiers.[43]

After World War I the association seemed to falter. This may have had something to do with the spirit of complacency that overtook the entire country in the 1920s, but it is more likely that the Businessmen's Association suffered from a lack of energetic leadership and effective organization. Unlike the G&CH Improvement Association, it did not have a paid director or a mechanism such as the Auxiliary Committee to gather ideas and plot strategy. Although it would continue to exist into the post–World War II period, the Businessmen's Association would follow an uneven course of activity and eventually become a moribund group that confined itself largely to organizing the annual Fourth of July celebration and excursions to Atlantic City.

Chestnut Hill wives and daughters also became active in civic affairs during the early decades of the twentieth century. This was part of a national trend that saw upper-middle- and upper-class women campaigning for a host of Progressive reforms, including women's suffrage. This was nowhere more evident than in their creation of the Chestnut Hill Community Center just after World War I.

The Community Center, which continues to function seven decades later, had its immediate origins in war work. At the instigation of Mrs. George Woodward and Mrs. Walter E. Clark, wife of a wealthy investment banker, a group of socially prominent women

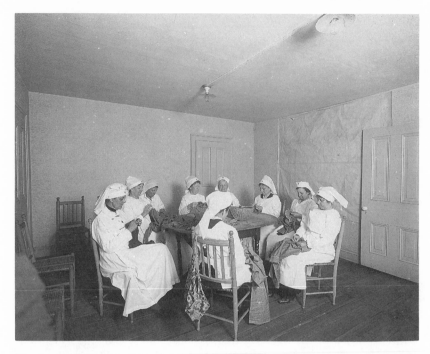

Chestnut Hill women sewing for the National League for Women's Service during World War I. CHCC.

founded a Chestnut Hill branch of the National League for Women's Service during a meeting at the Cricket Club in July 1917. For head-quarters they rented a large three-story stone house at 8419 Germantown Avenue, parts of which may date to the early nineteenth century. There the women sewed bandages, knitted socks for the troops, made clothing, raised money for war refugees, canned and sold vegetables and preserves, made soup for settlement houses, al-lotted war gardens, baked cakes for military hospitals, staffed canteens, gave luncheons for departing troops, and supplied automobiles for nurses. During the influenza epidemic, they also "visited, nursed, fed, and if necessary, buried the unfortunate [victims]."[44]

It was as if the League for Women's Service had touched off an explosion of pent-up energy in these local matrons, many of whom leapt at the chance to use their talents outside the home for the first time. In this sense, Chestnut Hill women appeared to lag behind

National League women baking during World War I. CHCC.

women in other parts of the country, who had become very involved in social service activities a decade or two before. It is impossible to say why this was the case, though it may have stemmed from lingering romantic notions about women's place in the home as guardians of morality, combined with a concerted effort to maintain proper domestic models in Philadelphia's most prominent suburb.

Whatever the reasons, Chestnut Hill's unit of the League for Women's Service demonstrated an energy and persistence that had already marked local civic organizations dominated by men. Not content with war work alone, the women began to assist settlement houses in Philadelphia and to care for the poor in general.[45] After the war ended, they kept working at these projects, and by 1919 they were involved in about twenty separate programs. These included a Visiting Nurse Society, classes in cooking and dietetics, and a housing committee that was dedicated to improving housing conditions throughout the city. Under the circumstances, it seemed logical to form themselves into a permanent organization. As Mrs. Woodward explained it, "The time has now come when this house should be

Headquarters of the Chestnut Hill Community Center, 8419 Germantown Ave.
This Italianate structure was built about 1854, although parts of it may date from
the early nineteenth century. CHHS.

taken over by the Community, to be the center of all those better-
ments of living and opportunities for . . . service that Chestnut Hill
stands for."[46] In Gertrude Houston Woodward's mind, at least,
Chestnut Hill represented progress in modern living and civic altru-
ism. For her there was no obvious conflict between the dual identity
with suburb and city.

Agreeing with Mrs. Woodward's advice, the women formed
themselves into the Chestnut Hill Community Center, with a charter
from the state of Pennsylvania, and bought the building at 8419 Germantown Avenue for $13,000. Most of the purchase price came from
Mrs. Woodward. Among those signing the charter, in addition to
Mrs. Woodward, were Ellis Ames Ballard, a socially prominent Philadelphia lawyer who lived in Chestnut Hill, and Albert Atlee Jackson, president of the Girard Trust.[47] Although they were dedicated
and energetic, the women apparently thought that they needed the
moral support of leading men in the community.

Besides continuing with their various urban projects into the 1920s, the women of the Community Center organized classes in current events, psychology, and French, along with programs to heighten the interest of newly enfranchised women in politics and voting. Through the Visiting Nurse Society, the center established a clinic for preschool children. The center also provided funds for dental care and milk for poorer children on the Hill.

As members of wealthy families, who had both time and money to expend, the women from the Community Center saw their role in the organic city as enlightened dispensers of private charity. With their belief in study and organization, they also showed themselves to be faithful to the Progressive spirit well into the 1920s and 1930s. Yet it is obvious that the women's activities could be viewed as nurturing efforts and thus as extensions of motherhood, endeavors that were acceptable among their age and class. In contrast, none of the members of the Improvement Association or the Businessmen's Association appear to have been women. This was typical of women's relative lack of involvement with Progressivism in Chestnut Hill.[48]

In addition to their social work through the Community Center, many well-to-do women in Chestnut Hill volunteered their time and energy to a variety of charitable groups organized by the churches in Chestnut Hill. Such was the case with the women at St. Martin-in-the-Fields. Organizing themselves into the Women's Auxiliary, the women collected money and clothing in the 1890s for settlement houses, Indian missions, and a variety of other charitable causes. In 1916 Gertrude Woodward, who was active in the Women's Auxiliary at St. Martin's, began holding an annual "Fete and Garden Party" at Krisheim in order to raise money for church work in Germantown. During World War I and World War II the auxiliary rolled bandages and cooperated with other womens groups in the church to give and attend courses on home gardening and the preservation of foods. During the Great Depression the women sewed clothing for the poor and collected money for relief work in Germantown.[49]

In addition to these charitable activities, there were organized efforts during the first few decades of the twentieth century in Chestnut Hill that focused on health and education. These were the Chestnut Hill Hospital and the new Jenks Elementary School. Inspiration for

Norrington (now demolished), which became the Chestnut Hill Hospital in 1907. Photo from the 1970s. CHHS.

the Chestnut Hill Hospital came from four local physicians: Drs. Radcliffe Cheston, J. Murray Ellzey, Russell H. Johnson, and John F. McCloskey. In 1904 they leased a double house at 27 West Gravers Lane. Facilities were so primitive that the physicians had to carry nonambulatory patients to the second floor. This hospital became inadequate almost immediately, and in 1907 some $31,000 was raised in a community drive to buy the large Norris house, known as Norrington and located on the east side of Germantown Avenue, just above Chestnut Hill Avenue. In 1921 a new stone structure was built on the site and the old Norris house was converted into a maternity ward. Six years later the hospital opened a nursing program with a new nurses dormitory.

From the first, the hospital received financial support and managerial advice from Chestnut Hill's wealthy families, who were interested in providing themselves and their community with good medical care. The hospital also represented the sort of practical philanthropy that progressive-minded Chestnut Hillers admired. Among the early supporters of the hospital were Dr. and Mrs. Woodward,

Samuel F. Houston, Mrs. Charles W. Henry, Ellis Ames Ballard, C. Stuart Patterson, Judge J. Willis Martin, and the Reverend J. Andrews Harris. Over the decades its board of trustees would read like a local social register. As time passed the hospital also added to Chestnut Hill's attractiveness as a suburb in the city. In the late twentieth century, however, the hospital's need for additional space would clash with historic preservationists' and neighbors' desire to save the residential character of Norwood Avenue, which passed directly behind the hospital grounds (see chapter 9).[50]

In this era of improvement, civic-minded Chestnut Hillers, such as Pennsylvania's own Gifford Pinchot and many other thoughtful Americans during the Progressive Era, became interested in conservation. Receiving the bulk of local attention was, understandably, the Wissahickon Creek and its wooded gorge. Efforts to protect this all-important western boundary to Chestnut Hill would also lay the foundation for conservation efforts later in the century. Such preservation efforts, like the improvement organizations, were additional examples of how prosperous and capable members of the community cooperated to maintain an important ingredient of their suburban lives. In this case they strove to preserve the natural or seminatural surroundings that remained essential to the suburban ideal.

Since 1868, and largely through the efforts of Fairmount Park Commissioner Eli Kirk Price (whose family owned a summer house on Bethlehem Pike and some of whose descendants continue to live in Chestnut Hill), the city had acquired the entire Wissahickon Creek within the municipal limits. The Park Commission subsequently demolished all the mills and most of the other structures along the creek, leaving only the dams and ruined foundations as a clue to future generations that the valley had once been a thriving center of industry. With the goal of returning the land to its pristine state, the commission doubtless gave little thought to the possibility that industrial historians and the general public alike might some day profit from seeing a restored mill or two along the creek banks.[51]

It was in this same spirit of harkening back to a romantic past that Chestnut Hillers became interested in restoring and improving the Wissahickon during the first years of the twentieth century. In

The marble Indian chief placed on Indian Rock high above the Wissahickon Creek by Charles Wolcott and Sallie Houston Henry in 1902. GHS.

fact, a sort of inauguration for such efforts took place in June 1902 when Mr. and Mrs. Charles W. Henry presented a large marble statue of the area's half-legendary Indian chief, Tedyescung. It stands atop Indian Rock, where Joseph Middleton had placed a wooden Indian back in 1854. Poised in a half-crouch, the marble chief, in full headdress, still surveys the valley that had once been home to his tribe.[52]

This heightened interest in the Wissahickon included architectural restoration, or what was understood as restoration at the time. The first building to be renovated was the Valley Green Inn, undertaken by yet another group of prominent women who belonged to the Society of Colonial Dames. In 1901 they obtained permission from the Fairmount Park Commission to repair the old inn and to open it as a "first-class refreshment cafe." Heading their committee was Miss Lydia T. Morris, who, with her brother John T. Morris, had already begun to create their arboretum in Chestnut Hill. Joining her in the group were the equally prominent Mrs. Alexander Van Rensselaer, Mrs. Samuel Chew, Mrs. Mitchell Harrison, Mrs. Francis H. Bohlen, Mrs. Alfred C. Harrison, Miss Margaret L. Corlies and Mrs. John B. Morgan (both sisters of Mrs. Samuel F. Houston), Mrs. Alexander Biddle, and Mrs. Randal Morgan (who lived with her husband on the large estate known as Wyndmoor at Mermaid Lane and Stenton Avenue in Chestnut Hill).[53]

Given the interests of the Colonial Dames, a patriotic lineage society that had been founded in 1890 in order to honor the pre-Revolutionary ancestors of fellow members, it is not surprising that they were attracted by a series of myths about the Valley Green Inn. Although the structure then standing dated from about 1850, an apparently false local legend held that a pre-Revolutionary inn had stood on the site and that George Washington and the Marquis de Lafayette had dined there during their retreat from Barren Hill to Valley Forge.[54]

The Dames proposed to remodel the inn "along original lines," but photographs of the 1850 structure show that they had no intention of doing an exact restoration of the midcentury building.[55] Instead, the women and their architects decided to use their imaginations and to create what they thought a colonial inn should be. Like much so-called colonial restoration of the day, the resultant Valley Green Inn was largely fantasy. Among its more charming but unauthentic features were leaded glass windows on the upper story, stylized picket gates, and built-in porch benches with large scrolled shoulder rests. Inside the inn there was a newly built "colonial-style" fireplace. Whatever liberties were taken with the architectural past, the Dames created a picturesque facility that now stands as a good example of the early Colonial Revival style. The "restored" Valley Green Inn, now a full-fledged restaurant, continues to be a favorite with visitors to the Wissahickon. For nine decades it has provided a focal point for other preservation projects along the Wissahickon.

Another conjectural restoration was done on Glen Fern, the old

Valley Green Inn (Hotel) c. 1875, before its renovation by the Colonial Dames.
LCP.

Thomas Livezey house at the foot of West Allen's Lane and the Wissahickon Creek, which had once stood beside the pre-Revolutionary
Livezey grist mill. It was purchased, along with seventy-five acres,
by the Fairmount Park Commission in 1908. A year later the house
was rented by the newly formed Valley Green Canoe Club. They used
the pond behind the Livezey mill dam for canoeing and the house for
social events. By 1912 they had added a second-story "colonial" balcony, a supposed restoration of the one that had been there originally.[56]

While such renovations were being carried out at Glen Fern and
the Valley Green Inn, the Fairmount Park Commission continued to
acquire land in Chestnut Hill along both the Wissahickon Creek and
its tributary, Cresheim Creek. Through systematic purchases and
gifts, for example, Dr. and Mrs. Woodward (and Mrs. Woodward's

Women in colonial dress in front of the Valley Green Inn some years after its remodeling in the Colonial Revival style. CHHS.

sister, Mrs. Charles W. Henry) enabled the commission to extend
the park along Cresheim Creek almost as far as Chestnut Hill's eastern boundary on Stenton Avenue. In 1909 Mrs. Henry and the
Woodwards also donated a monumental stone gate in the City Beautiful style for the entrance to Cresheim Valley Drive at Germantown
Avenue, complete with a watering trough for horses and an overhanging trellis for wisteria vines. Even so, it looks somewhat out of
place at the entrance to a wooded extension of Fairmount Park.
Twenty years later, in 1929, Dr. and Mrs. Woodward spent $500,000
to purchase a 100-acre estate on the northwest corner of Allen's Lane
and McCallum Street known as Medlock Wold. They then donated
it to Fairmount Park and it is now the site of the Allen's Lane Art
Center. In the meantime (1920) the Park Commission purchased the
first of its properties along the Wissahickon in adjoining Montgomery
County as an initial step toward protecting the creek outside city limits. In 1928 it also bought several houses on the south side of North-

western Avenue at the end of the park and then demolished them, a last step in taking the park to the very edge of the city.[57]

As these boundaries were being rounded out, the first debate over automobiles in the Wissahickon portion of the park emerged. The G&CH Improvement Association took the lead in late 1910 when it successfully protested against a proposal before the Fairmount Park Commission to allow motor vehicles on the upper Wissahickon Drive (the present Forbidden Drive that passes in front of the Valley Green Inn). Sharing opposition to automobile traffic along the creek were the Pennsylvania Forestry Association, the Pennsylvania Botanical Society, the Civic Club, and the Automobile Club of Philadelphia. Five years later the idea of opening the drive to cars was renewed. This time the Park Commission was deluged with a pile of protest letters some two feet high. Meanwhile, petitions opposing automobiles on the drive were placed in every drug store in the 22nd Ward.[58] A letter to the Park Commission from William H. Emhardt, Jr., on behalf of the G&CH Improvement Association stated its objections to automobiles in the upper park:

> [It] will necessitate the widening of the drive, taking out trees and cutting and filling. This will create scars in the present wooded scenery for many years to come. . . . Foot travel on Sundays and holidays in this part of the Wissahickon is large, and [there] would be a considerable source of danger from automobiles.
>
> We therefore cannot express our feelings too strongly for the retention of the upper Wissahickon in its present condition. It is a wonderful natural piece of scenery, with the quiet that is so fitting for a proper appreciation, and we desire that it remain so.[59]

The opponents again won a stay of execution, only to have the park commissioners reconsider automobile traffic again in the early 1920s. This time local residents formed two permanent organizations to combat the recurrent threat. The first of these was the Philadelphia Riders and Drivers, founded in 1920 and reorganized in 1952 as the Riders of the Wissahickon, Inc. In order to draw attention to their cause, the group held an equestrian demonstration in late October of 1920. About 200 riders and drivers turned out, assembling at the Valley Green Inn and parading down to Lincoln Drive and back. In May

Riders along "Forbidden Drive" pause before the Valley Green Inn, 1920s. *Local.*

of the following year they held the first annual Wissahickon Day Parade, an event which has been held each spring ever since, except for a hiatus during and just after World War II. Over 600 riders and 12,000 spectators turned out for the first spring event in order to show their support for keeping motor cars off the drive. In future years celebrities appeared in the parade, including silent screen star Tom Mix and his horse, Tony, who came for the 1924 event. Early presidents of the Riders and Drivers were Judge J. Willis Martin and Frederic H. Strawbridge, both of whom were frequently seen driving their four-in-hand coaches through the valley. In 1934 the equestrian organization was joined by a second preservation society called the Friends of the Wissahickon, a group that continues to exist nearly sixty years later.[60]

This local victory over automobiles along the upper Wissahickon would prove very important to Chestnut Hill, for it helped to protect the semirural atmosphere that was so essential to the suburban ideal. Another contemporary movement that contributed to the suburban atmosphere of the community was the establishment of the Chestnut Hill Horticultural Society in 1898. Among its early presidents was

John and Lydia Morris, the brother and sister who
created Chestnut Hill's Morris Arboretum. *Local.*

John T. Morris, cocreator of the Morris Arboretum at the northeast
corner of Germantown and Hillcrest avenues. The group awarded
prizes each year for outstanding gardens, flowers, and plants, and
also heard lectures on subjects of mutual interest. In January 1909,
for example, they listened to a paper on "How to Beautify the Garden
Cottage."[61] Later garden clubs would continue programs of this
nature.

Supporting such activities were the Andorra Nurseries, so named
for an earlier estate on the site and established in 1897 on a 120-acre
tract of land at the intersection of Forbidden Drive and Northwestern
Avenue that was originally rented from the Houston estate. Eventually the nurseries acquired about 1,000 acres of land, much of it in

An example of the Wissahickon style of landscape gardening. Included are the three main elements of that style: water, local stone, and native vegetation. *Local.*

adjoining Montgomery County. The company specialized in the sorts of native trees and shrubs that Chestnut Hillers continued to plant as part of the Wissahickon style of landscape gardening.[62]

Some local improvers became actively involved in city politics, if only to pressure officials to provide better services for the community. Others joined the fight for political reform in the early twentieth century. In this respect, too, many Chestnut Hillers shared the broader goals of the Progressive Era.

So far as partisan politics were concerned, the majority of local residents were confirmed Republicans. This was partly because the Democratic party was virtually nonexistent in Philadelphia, where a Republican machine enjoyed a monopoly that would not be broken until the post–World War II period. As an example, voter registration in 1919 for the 22nd Ward, to which Chestnut Hill belonged, was 7,892 for the Republicans and a mere 571 for the Democrats.[63] Thus even domestic servants and other workers on the Hill, who might have voted Democratic in cities such as New York or Boston, could be counted on to support the GOP. For prosperous Chestnut Hillers, the Republican party (at least on the national level) represented progress, respectability, and support for business interests. Accordingly, the Republicans dominated election after election in Chestnut Hill.

Yet many well-to-do Chestnut Hillers were disgusted by the waste and dishonesty of Philadelphia's Republican bosses and joined with their counterparts throughout the 22nd Ward in battling the machine and in supporting reform candidates for municipal and state elections. As early as January 1898, for example, the *Germantown Guide* published a long, unsigned letter condemning the city hall machine:

> The people of the Twenty-second Ward have made up their minds that they will stand by their rights and will allow "no boss rule in this town." Doorbells are being rung constantly by the heelers as they go the rounds, with their same old threadbare rags and promises in search of pledges. Why cannot men be men always, and vote for the welfare of the city and State without throwing away a vote simply because some heeler, who is paid for his trouble in dollars and cents argues that the boss delegate of his division is a perfect gentleman and only interested in the purification of his division politics, notwithstanding the fact that this styled gentleman carries a bottle of whiskey in his pocket to get followers by buying up rumsoaks when he thinks he is going to be defeated. . . .[64]

Just one year later, in 1899, reform-minded Republicans of the 22nd Ward unanimously nominated and elected Dr. George Woodward to the Philadelphia Common Council, to fill the unexpired term of Samuel Goodman.[65] In 1897, as a member of the Philadelphia Board of Public Health, Woodward had taken on the machine over the subject of filtering the municipal water supply. For years city hall had denied that devastating typhoid epidemics were caused by dumping raw sewage into the Schuykill River and then pumping untreated river water into city mains. Woodward had responded by testing the water in the Schuykill all the way to Reading and publishing in a pamphlet his incriminating results, which proved beyond doubt that polluted river water was the primary cause of recurrent typhoid fever in Philadelphia. The mayor and both councils had no choice but to begin filtering the water.[66]

To punish Woodward for his independence, the mayor had the Board of Public Health abolished, thus depriving the outspoken Woodward of a job. Yet Woodward refused to give up. Following his brief term in Common Council, he helped to form the City party, which won a stunning but temporary victory over the machine in 1905.[67] Then in 1919, he was elected to the first of his seven consecutive terms as a Pennsylvania state senator. During his first term he was helpful in steering the 1919 home-rule charter for Philadelphia through the legislature, a measure that was designed by Woodward and others to cripple boss rule. It failed to do so, but Woodward went on fighting for good government from his seat in Harrisburg.[68]

Woodward and other reformers enjoyed solid support in Chestnut Hill and the rest of the 22nd Ward. Besides electing him again and again to public office, voters and political activists in the ward formed local units of various reform parties that emerged in Philadelphia during the Progressive Era. In 1905, well-to-do women such as Gertrude Woodward organized a women's ward committee of the City party. Three years later, Chestnut Hillers responded enthusiastically to the candidacy of Bayard Henry (a trustee of the Houston estate), who was elected to the Common Council on the City ticket.[69] Later residents of the 22nd Ward became active in the reformist Washington party and in the equally reformist Independent Republican movement. In 1919, for instance, Independent candidates in the ward won every race in the Republican primary.[70] When the new city charter was being discussed that same year, the G&CH Improvement Association supported the proposal and invited Dr. Woodward to speak on the question at a special meeting. Independent Republicans backed the charter reform strongly, but in future years were not always as well organized as the machine Republicans and frequently argued over candidates and strategy, as in 1921, when several independent candidates put themselves forward for a seat in a state constitutional convention.[71]

Given the strength of the Independent movement in the 22nd Ward, it is not surprising that the Republican machine sought to di-

lute its strength by dividing the ward into two or three smaller segments. Because the 22nd was the largest ward in the city, with an
estimated population of just over 70,000 in 1910, this proposal did
not sound unreasonable on its face, but because it was the machine
bosses who proposed division time and time again, the reform element
was dubious.[72]

The question of ward division was first proposed in 1906, but was
beaten down by the reformers, only to be brought up and defeated
again in 1914.[73] The next battle over division took place in 1921.
Among the division's strongest proponents was attorney Owen B.
Jenkins, the regular Republican candidate for state senate who had
been defeated by George Woodward in 1919. This time the Chestnut
Hill Businessmen's Association denounced the scheme. According to
its president, James McCrea, the machine had again petitioned for
division because "the gang wants more jobs. But wait until the election. We will show them we have no use for them in the Twenty-
second Ward. The only persons who want the ward divided are the
division leaders and the ward boss."[74] The G&CH Improvement Association agreed, and in a formal resolution added an appeal to historical and civic pride:

> Whereas the Township of Germantown, comprising the Twenty-second Ward
> has been a physical unit dating back to the original grant by William Penn in
> 1683 to Francis Daniel Pastorius and has been maintained to this day. Any
> change would tend to break its traditions and civic spirit and destroy the
> unanimity of the various agencies seeking the development of the Ward. . . .[75]

Such comments showed that there remained a large reservoir of
community feeling for the former German Township, as well as a
continuing sense of autonomy within the city of Philadelphia nearly
seventy years after political consolidation. These sentiments, combined with a determination to defeat machine attempts to dilute the
reform movement within the ward, were sufficient to combat renewed
attempts at division in 1926 and 1937. Not until 1958, after the political and demographic landscape had changed drastically, would
ward division succeed.[76] Although such opposition to ward division
reflected a strong sense of local identity, it also showed that leaders

in Germantown and Chestnut Hill believed that they had a duty to fight for better government for the whole city if they were going to do well themselves. In this respect, the dual identity of suburbanites in the 22nd Ward functioned to some degree for the betterment of both suburb and city.

Although the independent Republicans in the 22nd Ward, with support from the Improvement Association and the Businessmen's Association, were able to defeat ward division, both organizations began to decline in the early 1930s. Part of the decline may have stemmed from the aging leadership. Although they remained in charge of the organization, these leaders failed to recruit new and more energetic members. Nevertheless, they joined with several other local institutions in relief efforts during the depression and in war work thereafter.

Without any governmental agencies to help in the early years of the depression, churches, charities, and private individuals in the area did whatever they could. Late in 1930, several of the churches in Germantown, Mount Airy, and Chestnut Hill opened an employment department. Their idea was to match up the unemployed with available positions, most of them odd jobs of a temporary nature, such as fixing a roof or cleaning out someone's cellar. By the end of the month, they were swamped with more than 700 calls from men desperate for work.[77] Local businessmen, feeling the pinch of reduced purchases, launched an advertising campaign that urged residents to "Buy on the Hill."[78] At the same time, prominent Chestnut Hillers were active in a private relief campaign for the entire city, launched in November of 1930 by Horatio Gates Lloyd, a resident of Haverford. Chief among these was George Woodward, who contributed $50,000 toward the first goal of $5 million.[79]

In Chestnut Hill itself, Woodward and others whose wealth was not threatened by the economic catastrophe did much for relief. Woodward spent $5,000 to hire unemployed men to cut down dead trees along the Wissahickon Creek. When some of Woodward's tenants found themselves in financial trouble, he deferred and in some cases forgave their rents altogether. He also donated materials for some sixty-eight garden plots that were laid out beside the playground at the Water Tower Recreation Center, a relief scheme that was doubtless inspired by memories of victory gardens during World War I.[80] Another private make-work project in Chestnut Hill was undertaken by the independently wealthy artist Carroll Tyson, who commissioned a huge stone wall around his home at 8811 Towanda Street. He hired the Marcolina Brothers to undertake the work, with the stipulation that they should hire a new crew every three months in order to spread the jobs around as much as possible. The project took about two years, and helped to relieve some of the Hill's unemployed stonemasons.[81]

Continuing the work they began during World War I, the women of the Chestnut Hill Community Center redoubled their efforts to help needy families during the depression. They made hundreds of layettes for babies, collected and distributed used clothing, and sold various foods and crafts from their shop at 8419 Germantown Avenue, the profits going to several charities. They also raised money to buy coal for the unemployed, paid for medical care for the poor families on the Hill, and distributed large amounts of food. During the early years of the depression, for instance, they sent thousands of bags of flour each week to relief agencies in Philadelphia. It was the Community Center that supervised the food gardens program in Chestnut Hill, dispensing advice on gardening along with Dr. Woodward's fertilizer and seeds.[82]

When war broke out in Europe in 1939, Chestnut Hillers almost immediately began to gather clothes and sew surgical dressings for the beleaguered British. Some residents opened their homes to British children whose parents sent them abroad to escape the expected bombings and a possible German invasion. Residents also held various benefits to raise money for British war relief.[83] Once the United States entered the war in late 1941, Chestnut Hillers continued to work on relief projects, bought war bonds, gave blood to the Red Cross, planted hundreds of new victory gardens, and cooperated with the city's civil defense system.[84]

Such activities during the depression and World War II fit well with Chestnut Hillers' image of themselves as a progressive people who could marshal their reason, organizational abilities, and private

NRA
MEMBER
U.S.
WE DO OUR PART

Chestnut Hill
Title and Trust Company

w h e r e Gravers Lane crosses
Germantown Ave., Chestnut Hill

BANKING HOURS:
8.30 a. m. to 3 p. m.
Friday Evening, 6.30 to 8.30

An advertisement by the Chestnut Hill Title and Trust
announcing its support for the National Recovery Administration. This notice appeared in the *Germantown Telegraph*, 18 August 1933. GHS.

wealth to solve problems. But this approach to problems was not in
sympathy with Franklin Roosevelt's New Deal, which called for massive public assistance and unprecedented regulation of the American
economy.

At first frightened, local businessmen showed enthusiasm for the
National Recovery Administration (NRA) and its symbol, the Blue
Eagle. The Chestnut Hill Title and Trust Company proudly displayed
the Blue Eagle at the top of a large advertisement in the *Germantown
Telegraph*.[85] Even some of the Hill's frightened social and economic
elite, realizing that Herbert Hoover had failed to cope effectively with

the depression, wished Roosevelt the best during his first months in office.

Despite these initial good wishes for Roosevelt, most of Chestnut Hill's upper classes soon rallied to the standard of the Republican party and began denouncing Roosevelt's programs to regulate the economy as outright socialism. Then, as Roosevelt won one election after another, local Republicans grew more enraged. One of these was Dr. Woodward's son, George Woodward, Jr., who became furious at the mere mention of Roosevelt's name, so much so that family members studiously avoided all talk of politics at the dinner table.[86] A large number of local Republicans, including the younger Woodward, believed that Roosevelt, who had come from one of the most privileged families in America, was simply a traitor to his class.

Like many former Progressives, most upper-class Chestnut Hillers found that their notions of civic improvement and political reform did not go very far beyond private charity, or allow much room for even mild government regulation.[87] For this reason, as well as others, the more limited approach of Progressive reformers would continue to appeal to suburbanites in Chestnut Hill as they sought to preserve their privileged way of life in both city and suburb. Nevertheless, this circumscribed view of government and community would later prove a handicap in local attempts to deal with serious urban problems as they began to afflict their suburb in the city and surrounding communities several decades later.

7

COMMUNITY ORGANIZATION

Postwar Chestnut Hill

World War II and the immediate postwar period brought many changes to the suburb in the city, although some of them would not emerge entirely for a number of years. These included higher taxes, economic reforms, the subdivision of larger estates, the growth of automobile suburbs and drive-in shopping centers in adjoining Montgomery County, and the partial decay and subsequent revival of Chestnut Hill's own shopping district. In these respects Chestnut Hill became less isolated and in the process more likely to be affected by conditions in surrounding communities. Its semi-isolation on the borders of the city was coming more and more to an end, although it would take several decades for many residents to realize it and to begin facing its implications.

At the same time the identification of Chestnut Hillers with residents in nearby Mount Airy and Germantown began to erode as inhabitants of the Hill perceived that these communities were in decline. The decay of these other suburban neighborhoods within the city became symptomatic to many Chestnut Hillers of a more general decline in Philadelphia. Over the next four decades, mounting problems in the city below, combined with the rise of new automobile suburbs beyond Chestnut Hill, would erode though not destroy the dual identity with suburb and city that had characterized life in Chestnut Hill since the middle of the nineteenth century.

In response to these changes, many of them perceived as threats, civic-minded residents of Chestnut Hill organized themselves more effectively than ever before and paved the way for suburban quasi government a decade or two later. In the process, socially prominent residents continued to see themselves as talented and capable individuals who could employ reason, persistence, common sense, and local organization to solve problems in their community, much as progressive leaders had done a generation before. This self-confidence was reinforced by the fact that Chestnut Hill remained home to many leaders on the local and national level, some of whom were responsible for a new city charter in Philadelphia and an ambitious commitment to urban renewal in the City of Brotherly Love.

Many of the forces bringing change to Chestnut Hill in this postwar period were economic and demographic. For example, rising federal income taxes, increasing real estate taxes, and the disappearance of domestic servants all contributed to the subdivision of large estates on the Hill, and to the more intense development of these properties. Steeply graduated tax rates on the wealthy during World War II, for example, and relatively high taxes thereafter left less money for maintaining large properties than in the past. During the 1930s, the city of Philadelphia also changed the property tax assessments for large estates in Chestnut Hill, now defining them as residential properties rather than as undeveloped land, which had been their designation in the past, and raising their assessments accordingly.

At the same time, social and economic factors over several decades, culminating with the war itself, made servants more expensive and difficult to find. One factor was the decision to limit immigration severely in the early 1920s, resulting in a declining supply of recent arrivals, who had gone into domestic service in great numbers during the late nineteenth and early twentieth centuries. Ironically, these immigration restrictions had been urged by the very WASP establishment that depended upon a pool of cheap immigrant labor for its own way of life. New Deal labor legislation, such as federal minimum wage laws and the right to form labor unions, would also help to raise wage levels throughout the economy — including, indirectly, the remuneration of servants. But the new opportunities during and after the war were what truly began to decimate the servant class. Young female servants found that they could earn much higher wages in Philadelphia's wartime defense industries than they could scrubbing floors or preparing and serving meals in some Chestnut Hill home. They could now afford to live on their own and enjoy the accompanying personal freedom.

World War II meant military service for young male servants and the sons of older servants. After the war, these veterans could go to college or vocational school with all expenses paid by the G.I. Bill. This same legislation made them eligible for low-interest loans to start their own business or to buy a new house. Thus for many young servants, or the children of servants, the war provided undreamed opportunities. Above all, they did not have to return to Chestnut Hill and take up their old lives. One man, who was particularly bitter about how his parents had been treated as domestic servants, wrote the author that even being killed or maimed in battle was better than a servant's life in Chestnut Hill:

> My father and mother worked for several families after arriving from Ireland in 1911. My father stayed with [one Chestnut Hill family] for 47 years. The only relief he had, he often said, came during the years he spent in the army in the First World War. . . . I'm glad I left and took a few hits in World War II. Uncle Sam was a better employer.[1]

Another man, whose father had been a chauffeur for many years on the Hill, remembered that his father's employer never took the slightest interest in their family. Even when one of the young children died, the mistress of the household expected the chauffeur/father to bring the car around to the house within an hour of the dead boy's funeral.[2] Other servants, or the children of servants, recalled that some large households provided only one bathroom for a dozen or more servants and then complained if their domestics did not bathe every day.[3]

Such accounts would have come as a shock to many wealthy Chestnut Hillers, who wanted to believe that their servants were largely contented with their lot. Certain upper-class residents even hoped that local domestics might become something of a hereditary class in America whose descendants would be happy to work as servants for generations. Knowing of such attitudes, some men returning to the area after the war decided to settle in some community near Chestnut Hill, such as Flourtown or Ambler, where they would not be marked for life as the gardener's or chauffeur's son, no matter what they did in their own right.[4] "The servant problem," and especially the shortage of servants, became constant topics of polite conversation in Chestnut Hill during the war and for decades thereafter.

Several of Chestnut Hill's large estates began to undergo significant changes, including Henry Howard Houston's Druim Moir, now the home of his son, Samuel F. Houston; and the two adjoining estates, Stonehurst and Krisheim, that belonged to the elder Houston's daughters, Sallie Henry and Gertrude Woodward, respectively. In March 1942, just three months after Pearl Harbor, Samuel Houston wrote to his daughter, Eleanor Houston Smith, that he intended to tear off the tower and third floor of Druim Moir in order to reduce his tax burden and to make the house easier to dispose of after his death.[5] Despite protests from Eleanor about the impending shortages of building materials and increasing wartime labor costs, he completed his renovation plans that summer. Following Houston's death in 1952, his heirs gave Druim Moir to the Episcopal church as a home for retired clergy.[6]

Sallie Henry's mansion next door at Stonehurst had been demolished by her children after her death in 1938. None of them wanted to live in it or to continue paying the high property taxes. In the early 1950s they engaged the architect Oscar Stonorov to build a series of apartments and townhouses on the grounds.[7] Over at

Krisheim, whose grounds directly abutted the Stonehurst property, Gertude Woodward was furious when she realized what the Henry heirs were doing. She hated to see the destruction of so much open land, believing that it was a betrayal of her father's wish to maintain a rural atmosphere on the far West Side of Chestnut Hill.[8] Defending his family's actions, her nephew-in-law, Donald D. Dodge, tried to explain their decision within the context of new demographic realities: "Growth of populations surrounding great cities simply does not stand still; our whole manner of life has been changed by the automobile." Dodge went on to say that Henry Howard Houston himself, "being the practical man that he was," would have understood such changes and the need for alternative uses of the land.[9] Although she was never really happy about the resultant Cherokee development, Gertrude eventually reconciled herself to the inevitable. Following her death in 1961, the Woodward children gave Krisheim to the Presbyterian church for a conference center.[10]

As it turned out, all three estates belonging to the Houston/Henry/Woodward heirs were developed in ways that preserved some open land. This was particularly true at Krisheim, where no additional building occurred in front of the house or directly across McCallum Street near the stables and former vegetable gardens. The Cherokee development at Stonehurst meant dozens of new structures, but they were carefully sited within a wooded landscape that produced a park-like setting for the dwellings. At Druim Moir the grounds fronting the property remained open and undisturbed until the late 1950s, when Springside School was built along Cherokee Street, although much open lawn remained between the school and Druim Moir itself.

It was on the far East Side of Chestnut Hill, however, that postwar pressures to sell and develop large estates resulted in the greatest demographic changes for the community. In the early 1950s, the sale and development of the Randal Morgan estate alerted Chestnut Hillers as nothing else could have that the world of large country estates was coming to an end, and that they would have to confront the question of land development and land-use planning more seriously than ever before. Once the Morgan tract was developed, it added more than 2,000 individuals to the local population, it greatly increased

Aerial view of the Morgan Tract, 1955. West Willow Grove Ave. is on the left,
Stenton Ave. extends across the center of the photograph, and the tracks of the
Reading Railroad (Chestnut Hill-East line) are near the bottom. *Local.*

traffic congestion, and it introduced the first shopping center and
high-rise apartment building into the community. Chestnut Hillers
also found that they had to cope for the first time with powerful absentee landlords, individuals whose interests did not always coincide
with the locals' view of the community's welfare. A generation later,
in fact, the Morgan Tract development would become a major scene
of criminal activity in Chestnut Hill. In the many protracted attempts
to block the development of the tract, residents created a powerful
community organization that later formed the basis for a quasi government in Chestnut Hill.

What Chestnut Hillers called the Morgan Tract (and later Market
Square/Chestnut Hill Village) lay in the far southeastern corner of
the community. Although most of the eighty-five acres were on the

Chestnut Hill side of Stenton Avenue, about one-third of the property lay outside the city limits in adjacent Springfield Township of Montgomery County. The estate was bounded on the west by the Reading (SEPTA's Chestnut Hill-East) Railroad, on the south by Cresheim Valley Road, on the east by Pine Road, and on the north by Willow Grove Avenue. There was also a small parcel of land, known as the "dogleg," that extended slightly north of Willow Grove Avenue between the railroad tracks and Crittenden Street. During the Civil War, the lower part of the property had been the site of the Mower Hospital.

About 1900 the tract was purchased by Randal Morgan (1853–1926), an extremely wealthy man who had made a fortune in oil. He was also general counsel for the United Gas Improvement Company, a powerful and often despised Philadelphia utility. Morgan built an impressive house facing Willow Grove Avenue, devoting the rest of the grounds to formal gardens and a working farm. Called Wyndmoor, the estate's name eventually encompassed and replaced the older designation of Springfield Village, the small collection of shops and houses just east of Stenton Avenue. The whole residential section east of Stenton Avenue thus came to be known as Wyndmoor.

In 1950 the Morgan estate gave an option on the entire property to Temple University, which then planned to abandon its site in North Philadelphia and to build a new campus in Chestnut Hill. Upon learning of this intention, neighbors grew alarmed and entered into negotiations with Temple president Robert Johnson and others in order to work out a plan that would cause the least disruption to the residential neighborhood that bordered the Morgan Tract. In the process, residents established a group known as the East Chestnut Hill Neighbors. Its organizer was Joseph Pennington Straus (b. 1911), an attorney who then lived at 8210 Crittenden Street. Straus had grown up in a prominent family in West Philadelphia and had settled in Chestnut Hill twenty years earlier. After service in the navy during World War II, he returned to Chestnut Hill, where he became a community leader.

In the midst of the negotiations, Straus and the East Chestnut Hill group learned that Temple had changed its mind about building a campus in Chestnut Hill and had decided to remain in North Philadelphia. Recent federal and state legislation had provided a mechanism for public funds, as well as the power to condemn adjoining properties and thereby to obtain the land that Temple needed for expansion around the existing site on North Broad Street. Under these changed circumstances, the university decided in February 1954 to transfer its option on the Morgan Tract to Mayer I. Blum, a well-known Philadelphia builder and member of the Temple board. The fact that this arrangement looked like a flagrant conflict of interest did not seem to bother either Blum or the other board members.[11]

Blum's plan was to build an ambitious combination of six highrise apartment buildings, an unspecified number of single-dwelling houses, and a 50,000-square-foot shopping center. According to some estimates this plan, which never materialized, would have added some 5,000 people to the approximately 9,000 residents of Chestnut Hill in the 1950s — an increase of about 70 percent. Because the Morgan property was then zoned for R-I, a residential classification that required at least 10,000 square feet of land around each property, Blum would need a special zoning ordinance from the Philadelphia City Council. Blum knew that the council would be reluctant to approve his precise plans if the community put up stiff opposition. He accordingly approached the Chestnut Hill Community Association in hopes of quieting community fears and of gaining their assent not to oppose the project at city hall.[12]

The Chestnut Hill Community Association had been founded seven years before, in the fall of 1947, by a group of civic-minded residents who believed that other organizations were not as effective as they should have been in dealing with local problems. Its first presiding officer (then known as the chairman of the association) was Sidney B. Dexter (1896–1973). Dexter was a banker and member of Philadelphia's Committee of Seventy, in addition to being head of the city's Civil Service Commission for sixteen years.[13] According to Dexter, many of the early members had been active in the Germantown Community Council, established in 1933–1934, an organization that had superseded and would later replace the G&CH Improvement Association. Now they concluded "that Chestnut Hill was too remote from the center of the Germantown sphere of influence," an indication that Chestnut Hillers were beginning to disassociate themselves from Germantown early in the postwar period.

Ironically, Dexter's descriptions of the new organization's goals were remarkably similar to those of the now nearly defunct G&CH Improvement Association, renamed in the early 1940s as the Germantown, Mount Airy, and Chestnut Hill Improvement Association in a renewed effort to show that it was interested in the welfare of all three communities. These goals were "to coordinate the efforts of the community in securing the improvements which were so much desired by the residents and business people of the Hill."[14] It almost sounded as if Dexter had the older improvement association in mind as he and others launched their new group. Dexter was also an active member of the local businessmen's association, now called the Chestnut Hill and Mount Airy Businessmen's Association. Thus on the level of both ideas and individuals, the new Chestnut Hill Community Association was connected, however loosely, with its predecessors in community improvement, a record of persistence that has been equaled by few urban communities in the nation.

The Community Association soon became a well-respected organization, in part because it was led by socially prominent members of the Hill. Of the first sixteen chairmen, or presidents as they were later called, all but five were listed in the *Social Register*. Even the five who were not listed, all but one of them male, were prosperous or highly successful professionals. Ten of the sixteen were lawyers and two were solid local merchants. There was one physician, one hospital administrator, and one banker. The only woman to serve as head of the organization before 1980 had studied architecture but did not practice her profession. Twelve of the sixteen were Episcopalians, one was a Quaker, one was a Presbyterian, one was a Unitarian, and one was a Roman Catholic, who had been reared a Quaker, but had converted to his wife's faith. All these chairmen/presidents lived in the socially prestigious neighborhoods of North Chestnut Hill or the West Side. An examination of the names of those who served as board members before 1971 shows that nearly all of them resided in these same sections of the Hill. In both 1961 and 1971, for example, only one of approximately thirty board members lived on the East Side of Chestnut Hill.

These backgrounds were very similar to those of the past leaders of Chestnut Hill's improvement organizations and civic groups. Like their predecessors, they sought primarily to maintain a pleasant suburban lifestyle, as they and their social counterparts defined it, within the city of Philadelphia.[15]

The early Community Association was run by a self-perpetuating board, an executive council of four, and a chairman selected by the board. Any individual could join the association by paying dues of two dollars per year, but members did not have any voting privileges. Under this arrangement, the group obtained a number of improvements for the Hill, with a particular focus on the Water Tower Recreation Center.[16]

It was the threat of Blum's ambitious plans for developing the Morgan Tract, however, that gave far greater visibility and force to the Community Association than it had enjoyed during its first half dozen years or so. The association chairman Alexander Hemphill, then controller of the city of Philadelphia, appointed a special Morgan Tract Committee to deal with the crisis. Its coordinator was Joseph Pennington Straus, who also continued to head the East Chestnut Hill Neighbors. Other members of the committee were Walter Miller, a manufacturer and fellow member of the East Chestnut Hill group; John Bodine, a prominent Chestnut Hiller and Philadelphia lawyer; George Woodward, Jr., who was now managing the family properties in Chestnut Hill; and Richard Stevens, also a lawyer. Hemphill and the Morgan Tract Committee then held public meetings on 10 March and 12 May 1954 to inform residents about what was transpiring. Hundreds of citizens descended on the Water Tower Recreation Center for these assemblies, believing that they faced the greatest upheaval in their community since the end of the war. In the meantime, the Morgan Tract Committee had held several discussions with Blum and Temple president Johnson.[17]

As a result of these meetings and consultations, the Community Association tentatively agreed to support three high-rise apartment

Joseph Pennington Straus addresses a large meeting of the Chestnut Hill Community Association on the subject of the Morgan Tract development, c. 1954. *Local.*

buildings (half the number that Blum had planned), for a total of 1,240 dwelling units, and a 50,000-square-foot shopping center. The remaining tract would have to be developed for individual family residences, each with at least a half acre of land. To ensure that any agreement would be legally binding on Blum, or on anyone else who might buy the property from him, the association insisted on "covenants running with the land." Blum objected to this last provision because he feared that financing would be harder and more expensive to obtain, as lenders would worry that such covenants might make it difficult to sell the property if for some reason Blum defaulted on his loans. The result was an impasse. Blum became more and more frustrated and allowed his option on the Morgan property to expire in October 1954.[18]

More anxious than ever to dispose of the tract, Temple arranged to sell it in November 1954 to the Summit Construction Company, a subsidiary of Schafran Associates, whose central offices were in New York City. Now the community would have to deal with an absentee landlord who had no personal connections with either Philadelphia or Chestnut Hill. Just as worrisome were Summit's even more ambitious plans for developing the tract. They wanted to construct

The Market Square Shopping Center, 1970s. *Local.*

twelve eight-story apartment buildings that would house 1,250 families, in addition to a 100,000-square-foot shopping center and a 400,000-square-foot parking lot. Summit also insisted on placing the shopping center directly along Stenton Avenue, a plan that would obliterate the semirural atmosphere along the far east side of Chestnut Hill. It was also evident that such a large shopping center would be regional in character and not just a collection of shops to serve local residents.[19]

Needing local support for a zoning ordinance, Summit entered into negotiations with the Community Association's Morgan Tract Committee. The talks were protracted and dragged on throughout 1955, 1956, and 1957.[20] Finally, in May 1958, Summit Construction agreed to a compromise that included legally enforceable covenants "running with the land" that would be in effect for twenty-five years. The number of apartment units would be reduced slightly to 1,200 and the shopping center would be built, not on Stenton Avenue, but at the west end of the property along the railroad tracks. The center would be limited to 75,000 square feet, with a perimeter of trees and shrubs to screen it from Crittenden Street and Mermaid Lane. Flashing or protruding signs and drinking establishments were forbidden. At a mass meeting of some 800 Chestnut Hill residents on 12 May 1958, the Community Association approved this agreement overwhelmingly.[21] Construction did not begin, however, until the fall of 1961, when the first individual dwellings were started. Work on the only high-rise apartment building to be completed at the site, the present Morgan House, began the following autumn.[22]

This would not be the end of the protracted Morgan Tract dispute. But the role played by the Community Association had given that body a higher profile than ever before in the community. Once again, self-confident, well-educated, and professionally resourceful Chestnut Hill residents had persisted long enough to make a real impact on the development of their community. In this case, however, they were unable to block the development of the Morgan estate, their first preference, and had to settle instead for limiting the development.

Yet while such residents were negotiating over the Morgan property, other demographic forces, in Philadelphia as well as in communities in outlying Montgomery County, were beginning to subject Chestnut Hill to other pressures. Chief among these was the huge migration from the city of Philadelphia to surrounding suburbs after World War II. Although Philadelphia reached its peak population of nearly 2,100,000 in 1950, up from just over 1,900,000 in 1940, its rate of increase was only a little over 7 percent. This compared to an increase of over 28 percent in the four surrounding counties in Pennsylvania (Bucks, Chester, Delaware, and Montgomery), which now had a combined total of slightly more than 1,000,000 people.[23] Over the next four decades Philadelphia would actually lose population as the suburban counties grew even larger.

Until this postwar boom in construction beyond the city limits, Chestnut Hill had been surrounded on the north and east by relatively undeveloped land, some of it occupied by large estates, and some of it by farms and rural villages such as Barren Hill, Plymouth Meeting, and Spring Mill. In fact, so long as commuters had depended upon railroads instead of automobiles, Chestnut Hill remained a somewhat isolated enclave at the end of a commuter corridor in the northwest corner of Philadelphia. But now that postwar prosperity had put the automobile within reach of nearly everyone, the rural land around Chestnut Hill could be transformed into acre after acre of new dwell-

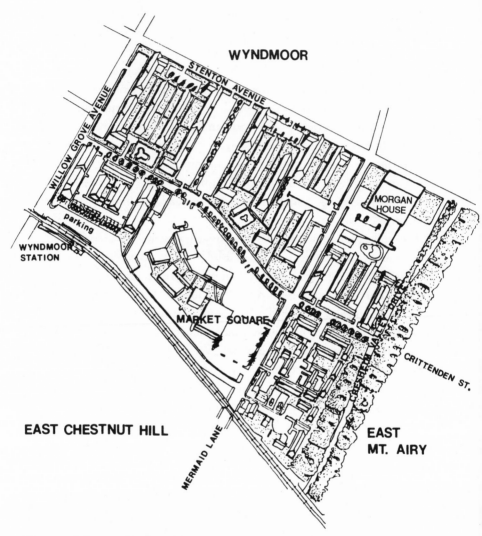

Diagram of the completed Market Square/Chestnut Hill Village development. The high-rise Morgan House is near the corner of Mermaid Lane and Stenton Ave. ERG.

ings. Many of the open, rolling vistas over the Whitemarsh Valley would disappear in the process. Automobile commuters on their way to and from the city, it was feared, would clog Chestnut Hill's quiet streets, and convenient parking at one-stop shopping centers in the new suburbs might even lure Chestnut Hillers away from stores on their own main street and touch off a spiraling commercial blight along Germantown Avenue. Such a fate had already befallen other suburban neighborhoods in the city, such as West Philadelphia and nearby Germantown.

For obvious reasons, the automobile would also help to undermine Chestnut Hill's connection to downtown Philadelphia. So long as the train was the dominant form of transportation, the downtown served as a giant terminal for travel, business, and pleasure. Now automobile owners in Chestnut Hill could point their vehicles in almost any direction and drive to work or shopping centers in neighboring suburbs as easily as, and perhaps even more conveniently than, taking the train downtown. They could drive door to door, on their own schedules and in the privacy of their own cars. The automobile thus became one of the prime factors in weakening the dual identity that Chestnut Hillers had felt with Philadelphia and their suburb in the city.

Not surprisingly, local newspapers alerted Chestnut Hillers nearly every week to the changes taking place in new developments all around the Hill. This was especially true of the *Herald*, a weekly publication that in 1946 began serving Mount Airy and Chestnut Hill as well as adjacent Springfield and Whitemarsh townships. One such subject of press notices in the early postwar period was an undertaking by the Houston estate to develop Upper Roxborough, a parcel of 1,000 acres that had been put in trust by Henry Howard Houston for his heirs. Between the two world wars, Samuel F. Houston, the principal trustee of the estate, had tried to develop these Roxborough lands in several ways, all of them failures to a large degree. In the 1920s he had tried to open the area to large estates such as those in the Gwynedd Valley, but wealthy and socially prominent Philadelphians had thought that the area was too close to mill towns such as Manayunk and Conshohocken ever to be fashionable. He did succeed in getting the Episcopal Diocese of Pennsylvania to begin a cathedral there, but it was never completed for a variety of reasons. Just before World War II he tried to sell land in the area for a new veterans hospital, but it was built near the University of Pennsylvania instead. After the war Houston tried to sell some of this land to the United Nations, then looking for a permanent headquarters, and a bit later to Temple University. Having failed in all these efforts, Houston and the estate decided to create a shopping center and surrounding residential area of modest homes on land that had once been a gentleman's farm called Andorra. The resultant Andorra development, begun in early 1950, became the first set of small houses and apartment complexes built in Upper Roxborough on Houston estate lands. In order to facilitate automobile transportation in the area, the estate pressed for an extension of Henry Avenue into Upper Roxborough, in addition to a bridge across the Wissahickon Creek at Cathedral Road that would provide easy access to Chestnut Hill. The Henry Avenue project would be completed, but the bridge would fall victim to opposition in Chestnut Hill (see chapter 8).[24]

With or without a new bridge to Chestnut Hill, Upper Roxborough would witness tremendous growth over the next two decades. But it was the two Montgomery County townships near Chestnut Hill, Springfield and Whitemarsh, that would experience the greatest growth during the 1950s and 1960s. In August 1953, for example, the *Herald* reported that a record number of building permits had been issued in Springfield Township the month before, amounting to the then impressive value of $442,000. School enrollments were rising apace, spurred by both the baby and the housing booms: in the fall of 1953 there were 280 more pupils enrolled in the township's school district, for a total of 2,596. In order to cope with the rising tide, the township had awarded contracts for a new high school the preceding February.[25]

In Whitemarsh Township the population was also rising steadily, up from 4,855 in 1940 to 5,977 in 1950 and to an estimated 7,620 in 1952, for an increase of 64 percent in just a dozen years. Like their neighbors in Springfield, Whitemarsh authorities were forced to build new schools. Even two-centuries-old St. Thomas's Episcopal Church at Whitemarsh had to expand its physical plant and parking facilities in 1953.[26]

In order to take advantage of potential shoppers in the new suburbs, investors raced to build shopping centers and department stores. In September 1952 the *Herald* announced that a shopping center had opened in the Springfield Township community of Oreland that included a drugstore, dry cleaner, and Acme supermarket. The article then went on to speculate that the new center posed a possible threat to Chestnut Hill merchants. Three years later, the newspaper reported the grand opening of another such facility in Springfield: the Flourtown Shopping Center at Bethlehem Pike and East Mill Road. Plans for a shopping center in Erdenheim, just east of Chestnut Hill at the corner of Stenton Avenue and Bell's Mill Road, were successfully opposed by residents of the area.[27] A little further afield, but within easy driving distance of the Hill, several major department stores had opened or expanded their suburban branches: Strawbridge and Clothier, as well as Wanamaker's, in Jenkintown; Gimbel's in Cheltenham; and Lord and Taylor on City Line Avenue.[28]

In Philadelphia, too, there were many signs of change during the postwar period. In 1951 a group of reformers that included a disproportionate number of Chestnut Hill residents obtained a new municipal charter that provided for a strong mayoral system, a smaller city council, and genuine civil service reform. The following year a slate of reform-minded Democrats swept out the Republican machine that had held Philadelphia in its grip for the better part of sixty-seven years. At the head of the ticket was Joseph S. Clark, Jr., born and reared in Chestnut Hill and a member of one of its most socially prestigious families. Also victorious was Richardson Dilworth, another Chestnut Hill resident of patrician background, who was elected as Philadelphia's district attorney. Dilworth would succeed Clark as mayor in 1955 when the latter won a seat in the United States Senate. Members of their administration included other Chestnut Hillers, such as lawyers Sidney Dexter and Shippen Lewis, both members of the mayor's new Civil Service Commission. Lennox L. Moak, a new-

Had Enough, Philadelphia?
Then Vote For

RICHARDSON DILWORTH
Democratic Candidate for Mayor

His background and career insure you the vision and determination
needed to bring to an end the too-little, too-late era of government
under which we Philadelphians suffer.

VOTE DEMOCRATIC .... ☒

ELECTION DAY — TUESDAY, NOVEMBER 4, 1947

An early campaign poster for Richardson Dilworth,
1947. *Local.*

comer to Chestnut Hill, was Clark's finance director.[29] There were
so many residents of Chestnut Hill in high places at city hall that it
would have been no exaggeration to call it a Chestnut Hill regime.

This predominance of Chestnut Hillers in Philadelphia's reform
movement is understandable, because the reformers themselves stood
in the Progressive tradition that had long attracted the kinds of businessmen and professionals who lived in the community.[30] Indeed Dr.
Woodward, a survivor from the Progressive Era, had chaired a committee in 1947 that began the process that led to charter reform four
years later.[31] At the same time, Chestnut Hill remained the most at-

tractive residential area in Philadelphia and continued to attract wealthy and well-educated residents who wanted to vote or hold office in the city, as well as already elected city officials.

Once elected, the reformers committed themselves to an ambitious plan for urban renewal that was drawn up by City Planning Commissioner Edmund Bacon. A scale model of these plans was exhibited at Chestnut Hill Academy in the spring of 1952 as part of a four-week program at the school to acquaint both students and the wider community with "the civic, physical, and cultural problems confronting today's metropolitan cities. . . ."[32] There visitors could revel in vistas of shiny glass and chrome office towers and efficient new parkways. Such plans, combined with the excitement of Clark's reform movement, could only have encouraged the men and women of Chestnut Hill to plan for their own future.

Chestnut Hillers may have also been encouraged by knowing that several other past or present residents of the community were or had been in the forefront of local and national events. These included Republican Hugh Scott, who had served for many years as the area's U.S. congressman and then was elected to the U.S. Senate in 1958. With former mayor Joseph S. Clark also in the Senate, locals could boast that both of Pennsylvania's senators hailed from their little suburb in the city. George Woodward's son Stanley Woodward had made a national reputation for himself by serving as assistant chief of protocol for President Roosevelt, as chief of protocol for President Truman, and from 1950 to 1953 as the U.S. ambassador to Canada.[33] Thomas Gates, Jr., who had grown up in Chestnut Hill, became secretary of defense under President Eisenhower. Chestnut Hillers were proud, too, that the University of Pennsylvania had chosen a house at 8212 St. Martin's Lane for its presidents. Among these were Harold Stassen, whom Americans were already coming to know as a perennial Republican candidate for the national presidency. Thatcher Longstreth, whom Philadelphians would soon recognize as a Republican mayoral candidate and later as a city councilman, also moved to Chestnut Hill in the 1950s. It was in the 1950s, too, that the Episcopal Diocese of Pennsylvania selected St. Martin's Lane as home for its bishops when it purchased number 7737.[34]

Despite these examples of local leadership, Chestnut Hill residents awakened slowly to the challenges and opportunities posed by the postwar era. Familiar as they were with the look and feel of Chestnut Hill, it did not occur to most that what earlier generations had created and sustained on the Hill might be affected by recent cultural and demographic currents. Two decades of national emergency, first the Great Depression and then World War II, had probably distracted them from local civic groups. By the time the war had ended, the generation that had created and managed the civic organizations that were founded early in the century had retired or died. As in most communities throughout the nation, it was the generation that had fought the war and who were now in their late twenties and early thirties who would step forth to lead Chestnut Hill.

More than anyone else, it was Lloyd P. Wells (b. 1921), a newcomer to the Hill and a very controversial figure, who aroused residents and organized them to face many of their postwar problems. Wells had been born in St. Louis, Missouri, to a wealthy and socially prominent family that could trace its American roots to early New England. Although he had the advantages of family wealth and high social status, Wells suffered from severe dyslexia as a child, and even as an adult found it difficult to read and write. Education proved such an obstacle that he was unable to graduate from high school, although he later managed to earn a certificate in business from the University of Pennsylvania's Wharton School. As if in compensation, Wells possessed an aptitude for mechanical devices of all kinds. During World War II he served as an airline pilot with Northeast Airlines, carrying military personnel and high-priority equipment across the North Atlantic. After the war he married Jean Ballard of Chestnut Hill and came to live in the community in 1947.[35]

Without a college degree, Wells could not hope to enter such professions as law, banking, medicine, or corporate management. Faced with the prospect of making a living, he decided to utilize his mechanical aptitude by joining with two other men to open a hardware store in Chestnut Hill. They opened their store, Hill Hardware, in 1948 at 8615 Germantown Avenue, just south of the avenue's historic junction with Bethlehem Pike.[36]

Lloyd P. Wells (left) in a typical pose along Chestnut
Hill streets, 1969. *Local.*

Wells's early experiences in business awakened him to a number of problems facing Chestnut Hill at the time. The most urgent, according to him, was parking. Increasingly heavy traffic on Germantown Avenue and the difficulty of finding a parking space near the store threatened to destroy his business almost as soon as it had opened. The solution, it seemed to Wells, lay in the unused backyards behind the business establishments on both sides of the avenue. By joining them together, merchants could create off-street parking lots that would allow their customers more convenient access to their stores. In his own words, it was a case of "enlightened self-interest" that would benefit the merchants in particular and ultimately the whole community.[37]

Wells took his parking idea to what he saw as the logical forum, the Chestnut Hill and Mount Airy Businessmen's Association, a merger of the old Chestnut Hill group and its counterpart in Mount Airy. Although the association had been involved in civic affairs for thirty or forty years, it had become less active. Dominated by a group of older businessmen, it was largely content to sponsor such noncontroversial activities as the Hill's Fourth of July celebration and various window display contests. Wells and several young acquaintances, including Logan Bullitt of the Dorothy Bullitt dress shop, Jack Warner of Warner Shoes, and Bill MacDonald of MacDonald's Cleaners, decided to push the off-street parking scheme. Among the older generation, they were able to enlist Russell Ferrier, manager of the Chestnut Hill branch of the Broad Street Trust (now part of Continental Bank). As might be predicted, they made little impression on the Businessmen's Association or on fellow merchants, who, unwilling to give up control of their property, refused to cede their backyards to a joint parking venture.[38]

In the fall of 1951, Wells approached the newly elected mayor of Philadelphia, Joseph S. Clark, Jr., a political reformer and lifelong resident of Chestnut Hill (see also chapter 8). Hoping that Clark's commitment to municipal improvement might inspire him to help with the Hill's parking and traffic problems, Wells discussed the issue when he chanced to meet the mayor one day at the Philadelphia Club downtown. Although Clark admitted the validity of Wells's arguments, the mayor told him that it would be politically "inexpedient" for him to invest city resources in a small, privileged, and predominantly Republican community such as Chestnut Hill. Wells, like many residents in the past, was discovering that Chestnut Hillers could not rely upon Philadelphia's city government to solve the problems of the suburb in the city.

In 1953, the frustrated Wells and his young associates in the Businessmen's Association decided to contest the nominating committee's recommendations and attempt to take over the association's board. Although the rebels campaigned vigorously for votes among the organization's 150 or so members, they lost their bid to overturn the old guard by a large margin. But rather than give up altogether, the defeated slate met the next day in the conference room of the Broad Street Trust. After several hours of excited discussion, they decided to form an independent organization, the Chestnut Hill Development Group. This group would eventually replace the Businessmen's Association entirely and become the springboard for many other community organizations over the next three decades.[39] Although the older Businessmen's Association continues to exist on paper at the time of this writing, it is completely moribund as a functioning group in the community. Partly in recognition of this fact, the Development Group officially changed its name in 1990 to the Chestnut Hill Business Association.

By the time that they had formed the Development Group, Wells and the others were coming to realize that Chestnut Hill needed to face far more than parking problems if it were going to compete with the shopping centers being built all around it.[40] Such economic and demographic threats from the new suburbs were already generating a body of literature that criticized the suburban way of life. The reaction of Wells and most other Chestnut Hillers, however, was not to join the chorus of condemnation, but instead to try to imitate some of the advantages of the newer automobile suburbs.[41] Thus instead of identifying with the many ways in which the postwar suburbs were threatening cities such as Philadelphia, Chestnut Hill began to associate itself in certain regards with the newer suburbs outside the city. From a prosperous older suburb on the edge of the city, this

Aerial view of Germantown Ave., which Lloyd Wells and the Development
Group wished to transform into a "horizontal department store." View looking
northeast, with the forks of Germantown Ave. and Bethlehem Pike in the upper
left corner. Photo 1962. CHHS.

reaction was understandable, if not predictable. Over the next three
decades, many residents of Chestnut Hill would identify themselves
so strongly with the newer suburbs that they would propose to secede
from the city altogether.

Among the immediate problems that Wells and others faced on
the Hill was the deteriorating condition of many local businesses. In
the early 1950s, for example, about 30 percent of the available floor
space in the business district along Germantown Avenue was vacant.
Low commercial rents, only five cents per square foot in some cases,
left little incentive for landlords to improve properties. Many shop
facades were marred by neon signs, some seventeen altogether between Southhampton and Rex avenues, several of which were over
ten feet high. Architecturally, the stores presented a jumble of styles

One of the community parking lots just off Germantown Ave. *Local.*

and ages: authentic colonial and Victorian, twentieth-century art deco, and plain, functional designs from recent decades. Worse yet, many of the original facades had been defaced in futile efforts over the years to keep up with the latest fashions in commercial decoration. Under the circumstances, Wells and others believed that Chestnut Hill's business district looked as dilapidated as those in West Philadelphia or certain portions of Germantown. Wells feared that this "blight" might spread to residential areas immediately beyond the commercial district. Residential property values would then begin to fall, many homeowners would leave for the newer suburbs, and Chestnut Hill would decay still further, eventually losing its semirural character and ceasing to be a suburb in the city of Philadelphia.[42]

Drawing upon his familiarity with Nantucket and Martha's Vineyard in Massachusetts and Palm Beach in Florida, with their uniform architectural styles and compact, one-stop shopping, Wells conceived of Chestnut Hill's commercial district along Germantown Avenue as a cooperative "horizontal department store." Essential to this concept, Wells believed, were sufficient off-street parking, harmonious

The Masonic Building, originally the Knights of Pythias Hall, at 8427 Germantown Ave. Constructed in 1889. Photo from early twentieth century. *Local.*

Masonic Building in the 1950s, before its "colonial" renovation. Notice that the Romanesque arch has already
disappeared from the left side of the building. *Local.*

Masonic Building after 1960, when it was remodeled in
the colonial style. *Local.*

architectural facades, trees and other landscaping, joint advertising,
and cooperative extension of credit, all of which would market the
whole shopping district rather than individual stores. Above all, merchants would have to stop competing with one another, Wells insisted, and learn to cooperate for the good of all. In the process, they
and everyone else in the community would profit.[43]

As the "coordinator" of the fledgling Development Group, Wells
began to appoint committees to work on the various areas of concern.
Because he did not want to waste time arguing over means and ends,
he openly appointed individuals to these working groups who already
agreed with him. At the same time, he consulted community professionals and sought the advice of various groups in Germantown and
elsewhere in Philadelphia, including the Germantown Community

The Chestnut Hill Hotel, 8229 Germantown Ave., soon after its completion in 1894. CHHS.

Council (a significant link to older civic organizations in the area), the Germantown Historical Society, and the Citizens' Council on City Planning.[44]

On the parking question, Wells continued to talk to property owners adjacent to his hardware store. When some of them still refused to join their backyards, Wells himself purchased a strategically located lot at the northeast corner of Germantown and Evergreen avenues in December 1952 and contributed it, together with Hill Hardware's backyard, to the parking project.[45] Two months later, in February 1953, a Parking Company was incorporated, with Russell Ferrier as its president and Wells as one of its board members. In June of that year the first parking lot opened, extending along the rear of several establishments and beginning just around the northeast corner from Evergreen and Germantown avenues. The parking lot was an immediate success; by May 1955 over 100,000 patrons had

The Chestnut Hill Hotel after its renovation along colonial lines in 1957–58. *Local.*

made use of it. This success began to feed upon itself, and eventually there were eight lots in the system, each piece of property being leased to the Parking Company for a token fee of one dollar per annum. By the late 1980s, the lots were serving over half a million customers each year.[46]

On the question of a uniform architectural style for the shopping district, Wells decided that it would be colonial.[47] He was influenced in this by the Germantown Historical Society, which was then hoping to restore the area around Market Square in the colonial style. Wells also realized that this was a style that would appeal to Chestnut Hillers, many of whom were proud of their early American roots. He further argued that some of the shops inhabited genuine colonial structures — though they were a distinct minority. Besides, the eighteenth-century motifs were relatively clean and simple, thereby making it easy for merchants to remodel their facades into something vaguely colonial. Finally, Wells believed that it would remain a rel-

Robertson's Flowers, 8501–8507 Germantown Ave., during its remodeling in 1952. CHHS.

atively permanent style — unlike the latest contemporary design — that would not change and thus require proprietors to remodel their store fronts every decade or so in order to keep up with current trends.

One could of course object that most of the renovations were far from authentic, with some merchants merely placing fake dividers (in order to simulate small panes of glass) in their plate glass windows and hanging a painted wooden sign outside. Some of the "colonializations" even destroyed the integrity of certain buildings, producing a facade that looked far worse than what had been there before. An example of this is a formerly attractive Romanesque/Gothic-style commercial building at 8427 Germantown Avenue, built in 1889 and belonging to the Masonic Lodge. Early photographs show a massive rounded stone arch on the north side of the building. On the second story there were Romanesque and Gothic stained glass windows. Its

Robertson's Flowers after remodeling. CHHS.

renovation in the colonial style, achieved in 1960 by making all the windows rectilinear and then dividing them into small panes of glass, has left the building looking cold and somewhat top-heavy.[48]

Equally inappropriate was the renovation of the Chestnut Hill Hotel. Built in 1894, it was originally designed in an eclectic Victorian style with Romanesque highlights. Nearly all these features were destroyed in 1957–1958, when an awkward two-story-high portico and columns were placed across the front of the building.[49] Above the doorway the renovators erected a large scrolled pediment that no eighteenth-century builder or architect would have contemplated. The result is a hotel facade that looks stark, artificial, and out of place in a community that had long prided itself on tastefully designed structures. Fortunately, there was no attempt to alter the facade of the Streeper drug store building (now the site of the Batten and Lunger Pharmacy) on the southwest corner of Germantown and Evergreen avenues. Erected in 1891–1892, it is a superb example of the picturesque Gothic Revival style, with its steeply pitched roof line and fancy stucco and half-timbering on the massive gable ends.[50]

The colonial renovations understandably worked best with the commercial district's eighteenth- and early nineteenth-century structures, with its Colonial Revival edifices from the early twentieth century, and with other buildings of plain design. To be fair, one should admit that few if any merchants would have been willing to spend the funds necessary to restore each establishment to its original style. Nor would it have been easy to work out guidelines about which structures should be rendered in the eighteenth-century manner and which should be restored more accurately to their original motifs.

In any case, Wells promoted his plan for uniform colonial facades in much the same way as he did all the Development Group's programs — by arranging for an initial and well-publicized success, which then encouraged others to do likewise. In this regard he made effective use of the *Herald*, the principal weekly newspaper then serving Chestnut Hill. He obtained the full cooperation of its publisher, Thomas Birch, by submitting articles himself, thoroughly briefing Birch on everything that was undertaken, and directing a great deal of local advertising to the newspaper. For his part, Birch ran front-page photographs of newly restored facades, often showing before and after views of the same building side by side. These images gave valuable publicity to the cooperating merchants, impressed the public at large, and caused other proprietors to renovate.

The most appealing of the early colonial renovations was undertaken in 1952 by George Robertson and Sons, florists, whose shop on the northeast corner of Germantown and Highland avenues had once housed a late-eighteenth-century inn and stagecoach stop. That same year De Palma's furniture store announced that it would renovate in the colonial style. Over the next decade, enough other establishments cooperated with the Development Group's remodeling plans that the "restoration" of the Chestnut Hill shopping district was declared complete in 1961. To celebrate this event, merchants staged a colorful parade on 20 April, with most of the marchers attired in period costume.[51]

Wells used the *Herald* in the same way to persuade merchants to

Planting a ginkgo tree in front of the Gulf Oil station at the corner of German-town Ave. and Bethlehem Pike in the mid–1950s. Left to right: Joseph Pirell, Russell Medinger, and Mary Ann Stalb. *Local.*

plant ginkgo trees in front of their properties. These articles featured photographs of store owners standing proudly beside a newly planted specimen, sometimes with a shovel in hand. Each tree cost the merchant thirty-three dollars, with planting being supervised by a well-known Chestnut Hill florist, Russell Medinger. The Development Group also began a cooperative advertising campaign on WFLN, Philadelphia's classical music station. The commercials invited listeners over and over again to visit "the 100 extraordinary shops of Chestnut Hill."[52]

Yet many of Wells's plans for greater cooperation within the community would prove elusive. Although the Development Group had made a good beginning in this direction by 1955, there were many merchants who ridiculed their plans as too visionary, opposed such projects out of sheer stubbornness or, in some cases, resisted Wells and his followers because they felt that their own authority was being threatened by younger men in the community. By his own admission, Wells was often outspoken and undiplomatic in his crusades for local improvement. Some critics described his tactics as ruthless and totalitarian.[53] Certain merchants took such a dislike to Wells that they would cross the street if they saw him coming. Feeling both angry and wronged, Wells resigned as coordinator of the Development Group in early 1956 and left for Florida for a year with his wife and three children. As it turned out, this was the first of Wells's three resignations from Chestnut Hill's civic life.

Like the improvement associations and other community groups before them, the organizations created by Wells and others after World War II focused almost wholly on solving problems in Chestnut Hill. The organizers' major goal was to preserve and improve life on the Hill as defined by its more prosperous residents. In focusing on Chestnut Hill as a suburb in the city while continuing to work in Philadelphia and to participate in the city's culture and politics, they reinforced their dual identity with city and suburb.

8

COMMUNITY REORGANIZATION

Suburban Quasi Government

The Chestnut Hill Community Association and the Chestnut Hill Development Group had both emerged by the mid-1950s as the Hill's most important organizations. While the Development Group had led a renewal of the Hill's commercial district, the Community Association had undertaken complex and protracted negotiations over the Morgan Tract development. During the next two decades, both organizations retained their influence in Chestnut Hill, but the persistent activities of the Community Association in particular spawned several other institutions and formed the basis for Chestnut Hill's emerging quasi government.

Like earlier community organizations, Chestnut Hill's quasi government worked mainly to preserve and protect a pleasant way of life on the Hill. Despite some increasing awareness that conditions elsewhere in the city affected the quality of life in Chestnut Hill, most residents hoped that they could continue their dual identities with city and suburb and reap the economic rewards of living in a large metropolitan area without having to experience the less attractive side of urban life.

One is tempted to connect this renewed civic activism on the Hill to a national movement of neighborhood organizations during the 1960s and 1970s, which was spawned in part by the Economic Opportunity Act of 1964, which called for community action groups. Despite this wider atmosphere of civic activism, Chestnut Hill's quasi government would appear to be an indigenous movement. It grew most immediately out of the Community Association that was formed in 1947 and took on renewed life in the mid-1950s over the Morgan Tract dispute. There is no evidence in the minutes of the Community Association or in Chestnut Hill's local newspapers that the founders and subsequent leaders of the Hill's quasi government were directly influenced by a national impulse toward neighborhood organization.[1] Rather, the powerful community organizations that arose in Chestnut Hill during the postwar period would seem to have emerged from a continuing sense of being a suburb in the city, combined with the initiative and skills of its successful residents. It is possible, of course, that Chestnut Hill's quasi government was energized in a more general way by the spirit of community activism that swept the United States during the 1960s.

The word "quasi" is used here in its literal sense to mean "having a likeness to." Thus quasi government in Chestnut Hill is defined as a set of local institutions that function somewhat like government. Although employed for the first time in the late 1960s to describe what had already come to exist in Chestnut Hill, quasi government had actually evolved over many decades, and through a succession of organizations.

Community leaders in the postwar period appeared largely ignorant of earlier precedents, but it is obvious to the historian that the most recent organizers dealt with being a suburb in the city in much the same ways as their predecessors had. Weak local government and a tradition of privatism in the eighteenth and early nineteenth centuries had forced Chestnut Hillers to create a series of institutions, such as a fire company, burial ground, library, and schools. After the city/county consolidation of 1854, local residents had discovered that they could not depend upon the municipality for a waterworks or paved roads — at least in the beginning. In the late nineteenth and early twentieth centuries, Chestnut Hillers had created improvement associations, first to raise funds and provide their own public works and then to put pressure on the city to make repairs and improvements.

The efforts of the Germantown and Chestnut Hill Improvement Association in particular had reflected the main tenets of the Progressive Era, with its emphasis upon organization, efficiency, and political reform. These activities, supplemented by the undertakings of the Chestnut Hill Businessmen's Association and especially of the Community Center, could also be seen as manifestations of the organic city concept, which held that very different neighborhoods, each focusing on its own well-being, were essential to the city's welfare. Such sentiments continued to hold sway in Chestnut Hill during the 1950s, 1960s, and 1970s as socially prominent and successful residents led and staffed local civic organizations. These individuals came overwhelmingly from North Chestnut Hill and the West Side. They were also largely male at first, although volunteer work by women contributed greatly to the success of civic activities.

It was these residents who launched Chestnut Hill's quasi government in earnest about 1957 with a restructuring of the Chestnut Hill Community Association. This movement was led by Joseph Pennington Straus and the redoubtable Lloyd Wells.

In 1957 Wells returned to Chestnut Hill and his various civic activities. As the founder and head of the Development Group, he had been concerned about the Morgan Tract Development. His earlier difficulties in trying to convince residents that they should cooperate for the good of the entire community had set him to thinking about how he might create a forum where problems could be solved as selflessly as possible. His answer was to transform the governing body of the Community Association, then made up of a small, self-perpetuating board. He would replace it with a thirty-member board, two-thirds of whom would be the heads of nonprofit institutions on the Hill. In theory, these directors of hospitals, schools, churches, and the like spent much of their time trying to promote the well-being of everyone in their institutions rather than working for profit or for undue personal gain. They and their institutions also stood to benefit from policies that promoted the welfare of the entire community. Although no one could expect them or their institutions to be perfectly altruistic, Wells believed that they would be less self-serving than individual residents or businesspeople.[2]

This concept of institutional representation on the Community Association board may have been inspired by the Germantown Community Council, which was essentially a clearing house for local organizations. If so, neither Wells nor anyone else in Chestnut Hill avowed that the idea of institutional representation had come from the Germantown group. Yet Wells has been known to borrow ideas from many sources, and it is not unreasonable to suppose that he had the Germantown Community Council in mind when he set out to restructure Chestnut Hill's Community Association.

In any case, Wells presented his idea in the spring of 1957 to Straus, who was then chairman of the Community Association. Straus approved the plan warmly, maintaining that the new structure would allow the organization to confront virtually any problem facing the community:

> The new plan will find the Association interesting itself in every phase of community life. . . . To my thinking this will give the Community Association a great deal more standing, and greater usefulness. . . . We'll be able to receive all the problems facing the community, to discuss them and to act upon them. We will be able to serve as a sounding board for community complaints and activities.[3]

In order to pursue its new means and ends, the Community Association obtained a corporate charter and drew up a set of bylaws. The latter were drafted by Straus and formally approved by the membership in December 1959.[4] The bylaws allowed "any individual or organization interested in the welfare of Chestnut Hill" to join the association, whether residing in the community or not. The body was originally governed by two groups of directors. The first group, later dubbed the board of presidents, comprised twenty persons, "each of whom . . . is the principal officer of a non-profit organization having its principal activity in Chestnut Hill." The other group of directors, numbering ten in all, would be elected "at large" from among the association's membership. Officers would consist of a president (instead of the former chairman), vice-president, secretary, and treasurer, all to be elected by the combined board of directors, who had the authority to make decisions for the association between regular meetings. In 1967 the bylaws were amended to allow for a single board of fifty directors, only half of whom had to be from nonprofit organizations. In 1971 the bylaws were amended again to allow for seven student representatives from high schools and colleges in the community, an obvious bow to the nationwide trend of inviting young people to represent themselves in a variety of organizations and institutions.[5]

The original objectives of the association, as set forth in the certificate of incorporation, were modest and emphasized research and education:

> to educate the residents of that section of Philadelphia known as Chestnut
> Hill, and its environs, in subjects useful to the individual and beneficial to the
> community; to lessen the burdens of government; to lessen neighborhood ten-
> sions; to combat community deterioration; to engage in non-partisan analysis
> and research and to make the results thereof available to the public, including
> research in land use planning and development, and to inform the public of
> the results of such expert advice; to educate the citizens of their civic respon-
> sibilities, and to keep them informed of all activities of religious, educational,
> social and patriotic organizations active in the Chestnut Hill Community; to
> provide awards for outstanding citizens and organizations contributing to the
> leadership and growth of the Chestnut Hill community; and to initiate and as-
> sist charitable and educational institutions in the Chestnut Hill area.[6]

As it turned out, the reformed Community Association and its committees would use tactics that were remarkably similar to those of the old Germantown and Chestnut Hill Improvement Association and its predecessor, the Chestnut Hill Improvement Association. Like the more recent of these two bodies, which had not collapsed

entirely until the early 1950s, the Community Association often functioned as a lobbying group to pressure the Philadelphia City government and its various agencies. But like the much older Chestnut Hill
Improvement Association, it soon began to raise its own funds in order to undertake a variety of projects. When asked by the author,
neither Straus nor Wells could recall that they had ever heard of the
two improvement associations. But similar tactics could well be explained by similar circumstances; like their predecessors, they had to
deal with the reality of being a suburb in the city.

Although unaware of past parallels, these reformers of the Chestnut Hill Community Association realized that communicating with
their public was essential to success. Leaders of the G&CH Improvement Association had known this earlier in the century, and Wells
had made effective use of the *Herald* to promote his concept of a horizontal shopping center along Germantown Avenue. But Wells's
happy association with the *Herald* came to an end when the newspaper
was sold in 1952 to a regional syndicate called the Weekly Review
Publishing Company. At first, Wells enjoyed good relations with the
new editorial staff, who happily continued the old pattern of supporting the Development Group's projects in exchange for stories and
advertising from local merchants. However, the arrangement broke
down around 1954 when Wells learned from City Councilwoman
Constance Dallas, a Democrat, a Chestnut Hill resident, and the first
woman ever elected to council, that the *Herald* refused to cover her
campaign for reelection. As it turned out, the *Herald*'s publisher was
a very partisan Republican who did not want to give Democratic
candidates any more coverage than he had to. This became even more
evident in 1956 when the *Herald* filled its pages with glowing accounts
of President Eisenhower's campaign for reelection while barely men-
tioning the existence of his Democratic challenger, Adlai Stevenson.[7]

Although Wells was then a Republican himself, he was both angry
and indignant at the *Herald's* lack of community spirit in refusing to
provide coverage for a local resident's political campaign. He decided
that he and other community leaders should start their own newspaper. They called their monthly publication the *Chestnut Hill Cymbal,*
the inaugural edition of which appeared in December 1955. In this

first issue, the publication board, which included both Wells and Straus, proposed to open their newspaper to all views. Controversy would not be avoided, "but rather sought in the belief that constructive argument is a vital factor in achieving broader comprehension."[8]

The new newspaper was written and edited by a volunteer staff, all amateurs in the business of running a newspaper, who wrote essay-type articles on a variety of community subjects. After a year and a half of publication, however, the *Cymbal* expired in June 1957, a victim of the *Herald*'s continuing appeal as a local newspaper, the lack of strong financial support, the inexperience of its publication board, and Wells's own temporary departure from Chestnut Hill in early 1956.[9]

The decision to reform the Community Association, however, reignited interest in a community newspaper. It was Wells who again proposed the idea. The question of whether the Community Association should sponsor a newspaper was debated heatedly before the board decided to adopt the project in December 1957. The paper's name would be the *Chestnut Hill Local,* referring to both the commuter's familiar name for the two local train lines and the fact that it would be Chestnut Hill's local newspaper. During the first few years, the *Local* struggled to survive with the same sort of volunteer staff, mostly female, who had run the *Cymbal.* Even after the *Local*'s finances were strong enough to allow a paid editorial staff, almost all its editors and writers were women. According to those associated with the newspaper then and later, this was because the pay was so low that only married women whose husbands made good salaries could afford to work on the *Local.* These women were attracted to the newspaper because of the opportunity that it gave them to use their intelligence, education, and skills, and to have a positive voice in the community at a time when few positions of power and influence were open to women.[10] Ellen Newbold (later the second Mrs. Lloyd Wells) became the *Local*'s first full-time editor in 1961. She was succeeded in 1979 by Marie Reinhart Jones, the present editor.

Because the *Local* was owned by the Community Association, and thus by all its members, the question of just who was its publisher and who controlled editorial policy would become thorny issues in

the future, particularly after the *Local* became a powerful instrument
of public opinion. Some of the most protracted and passionate civic
battles in Chestnut Hill would revolve around control of the *Local*.[11]

As the *Local* was struggling to establish itself, the Community Association was busy dealing with numerous issues. In order to maintain
an ongoing examination and discussion of various problems, the association created numerous standing committees. By 1970 these included committees on aesthetics, conservation, land use planning,
maintenance, parking, pollution, station grounds, traffic, transportation, zoning, cultural affairs, education, mental health, political
action, recreation, religion, and senior citizens. Later these and succeeding committees were grouped under three divisions, each headed
by a vice-president: the physical division, the operational division,
and the social division. Besides these Community Association committees, there were several independent organizations, such as the
Development Group, Parking Company, the Chestnut Hill Realty
Trust, and the Chestnut Hill Historical Society. To ensure that these
groups worked in harmony with the Community Association, Wells
proposed a system of interlocking directorates. As implemented, this
meant that there were representatives of each independent organization on the Community Association board. The board also chose
several directors to serve on the boards of the independent organizations, such as the Development Group or the Historical Society.[12]

Given the continuing concerns over the Morgan Tract, it is not
surprising that the Land Use Planning Committee was one of the
most active from the beginning. There was a consensus that the survival of Chestnut Hill as a suburban neighborhood depended upon
more effective control over real estate development. In the very first
issue of the *Local*, for example, an editorial warned:

> Chestnut Hill, . . . which is within the city limits, lies close to congested sec-
> tions of Philadelphia and is already heavily populated. We are, therefore, con-
> tinually threatened by "Urban Blight," the downgrading of a community
> caused by the uncontrolled and unplanned extension of a great metropolis. It
> is our purpose to foster the continuation of the work which has already been
> done by such groups as the Morgan Tract Committee of the Chestnut Hill
> Community Association and the Chestnut Hill Development Group, to fore-

CHESTNUT HILL COMMUNITY ASSOCIATION
51 non-profit institutions

Interlocking Directorates

C.H. Development Group

C.H. Historical Society

C.H. Music Association

C.H. Parking Foundation

Chestnut Hill Local | C.H. Community Fund | C.H. Preservation and Development Fund

Staff
A Quasi Government Responsible to all of the People

Operational

Annual Meeting

Art and Design

Aspinwall Fund

Awards

Bird In-Hand

Budget

By-Laws

Legal

Local Management

Long Range Planning

Membership

Nominating

Physical

Aesthetics

Land Use Planning

Maintenance

Parks

Railroad-Station Grounds

Street Trees

Traffic and Transportation

Zoning

Social

Blood Availability

Community Gardens

Crime Prevention

Education

Health

Pastorious Park Concerts

Political Information

Public Safety

Recreation

Religion

Senior Citizens

Youth

Organizational chart, Chestnut Hill Community Association, 1990. ERG.

stall such deterioration in Chestnut Hill, and to preserve and better our community as a distinct and distinctive residential and commercial center.[13]

Most of all, Chestnut Hillers worried about what was happening directly south of them in Germantown. It, too, had been a suburb in the city, but was now undermined in several ways: by excessive development, by the decay of its aging housing stock, by racial tensions, and by the flight of many prosperous residents into Chestnut Hill itself, or into suburban communities outside the municipality. In the words of another early editorial from the *Local*:

> Many years ago Germantown, Mount Airy and Chestnut Hill were distinct suburbs of Philadelphia[,] as Ambler is today. These areas were vacation spots where people of wealth spent their summers in green country towns. As Philadelphia grew, Germantown and Mount Airy were swallowed up and lost not only their green environment, but also much of their general attractiveness, and many of the former residents moved farther afield.
>
> Now Chestnut Hill remains as the last bastion of the "Green Country Towns" within the city limits. *The Chestnut Hill Local* is frankly and, we believe, justifiably, concerned about succumbing to the fate suffered by our southern neighbors. . . .
>
> There is an old and very trite saying that "Home is where the heart is." If we are not careful, our hearts may lie in Chestnut Hill, but our homes may be elsewhere.[14]

The editorial writer might have added, but did not, that local residents had been worried about changes in Germantown and Mount Airy for over a decade. The decision to leave the Germantown Community Council in 1947 and to form a separate Chestnut Hill Community Association, in addition to the abandonment of the Chestnut Hill and Mount Airy Businessmen's Association in favor of a development group that would serve Chestnut Hill alone, were both signs of a rising isolationist mentality on the Hill.

A concentration on land use and real estate development, which had begun with the Morgan Tract controversy, was also a new departure for community organizations in Chestnut Hill. Until the postwar period, the existence of attractive housing and pleasant neighborhoods elsewhere in Philadelphia, combined with the rural nature of much of adjoining Montgomery County, meant that Chestnut Hillers could afford to leave the question of land development to market forces. Now they felt compelled to try to oversee it themselves.

Several factors promised to make this task a difficult one. First, because Chestnut Hill remained within the city of Philadelphia, it would have to work with the zoning regulations of the larger municipality, unlike suburbs outside the city, such as those on the Main Line, which could formulate and apply their own zoning and development directives. Second, intense building in the new suburbs around Chestnut Hill, along with the increasing success of its own commercial district, was resulting in rising land values and property taxes on the Hill, with concomitant pressures and inducements to build on every available piece of land. Finally, local residents and institutions themselves could not always agree on proper land use, leading to much division within the community itself. These factors gained momentum over the years and would not be felt in their greatest force for another two or three decades.

Under the circumstances, the first new group established by the Community Association was a Land Use Planning Committee (LUPC), formed in April 1958 — even while a new charter and bylaws were being drawn up and debated by the parent organization. The LUPC was a direct descendant of the Morgan Tract Committee, which had been the first local group to concern itself extensively with land use in the community.[15] It would remain the most important committee of the Community Association despite its mixed record of success and failure over the years.

One of the Land Use Planning Committee's first assignments was to draw up a long-range plan for Chestnut Hill. In April 1960 they asked for assistance from the Philadelphia Planning Commission, which agreed in August to help.[16] This collaboration between local planners and city hall led to considerable friction in Chestnut Hill, as various interest groups grew suspicious of the LUPC's motives and authority. Among the most alarmed were residents of the East Side, who were angered by the LUPC's opposition to renting apartments on the upper floors of homes in the area, a common practice on the East Side even though zoning regulations forbade it. East Side residents were also incensed at a proposal by the Development Group to extend the commercial district "laterally" for a block or so on either side of Germantown Avenue in places where it seemed feasible. In order to make themselves heard, inhabitants formed the Mid-Chestnut Hill Residents Association, which reached a peak of about 500 members.

Doubtless contributing to their irritation was the knowledge that so many of the Community Association's leaders were socially prominent residents from the West Side and North Chestnut Hill. In 1961, for example, the earliest year for which figures were available, an analysis of the board of directors of the Community Association revealed that only one of the twenty-four directors who lived in Chestnut Hill had an East Side address. Ten years later, in 1971, the figures were virtually the same, when only one of the thirty-three board members from the Hill lived on the East Side.[17] Suspicions raised by this domination of the board by inhabitants from the wealthier sections of the Hill erupted at a meeting of the Mid-Chestnut Hill group in September 1959, where a number of the assembled wanted to know how much Lloyd Wells was being paid as the executive director of the Community Association and "who was paying him." Such socio-economic clashes would continue for decades and sometimes thwart community cooperation.[18]

Despite such clashes, the community managed to agree on general zoning revisions for Chestnut Hill. As a tool for urban planning, zoning had not existed in Philadelphia at all until the early 1930s. At that time most of Chestnut Hill received the highest residential and commercial classifications.[19] But the R-1 category required only a minimum of 10,000 square feet for each residential lot, a figure that would do nothing to keep large estates from being divided and developed. Most of the northeastern quadrant of Chestnut Hill received an R-2 designation, which allowed for small businesses and institutional use. The LUPC therefore decided in late 1963 to ask city council to upgrade the entire northeastern section of the Hill to R-1, with exceptions for institutions, such as the hospital and Chestnut Hill College, that already existed in the area. Although it took ten years for the council to act, the rezoning was accomplished in September 1973.[20]

In the meantime, however, the LUPC (and its parent organization, the Chestnut Hill Community Association) suffered several defeats. One of these, in the early 1960s, involved an eleven-story apartment building in the 200 block of West Evergreen Avenue that was eventually named Hill House. The LUPC opposed it from the start, believing that it was inappropriate for a community made up largely of single dwellings, twins, and a few modest row houses. They also feared that such a high-rise facility would contribute to traffic congestion. In July 1963 they hired legal counsel to represent them before Philadelphia's Zoning Board of Adjustment. When the board decided in favor of the developer, the LUPC and the Community Association appealed to the Court of Common Pleas in Philadelphia. When the judge also ruled in favor of the developers, the LUPC and the Community Association petitioned Pennsylvania's highest court to hear an appeal. Only when the high court refused to take the case did the local planners concede defeat, having marshaled the considerable wealth and talent of Chestnut Hill in their crusade. In the long run, Hill House turned out to be a favorite spot for more affluent elderly residents of the Hill, many of whom did not drive cars. Given this outcome, the time and resources of the LUPC and the Community Association do not seem to have been well spent.[21]

At the same time that the battle over Hill House was unfolding, the LUPC and the Community Association also failed to guide the development of a property in North Chestnut Hill called the Volkmar estate. Known as Greystock, the property had belonged to George C. Thomas in the nineteenth century and most recently to his aged daughter, Mrs. W. Schuyler Volkmar. The tract, which commanded a view of the valley below, bordered Norwood Avenue on the east, Sunset Avenue on the north, Germantown Avenue on the west, and the Chestnut Hill Presbyterian Church on the south.[22] The initial alarm was sounded by the North Chestnut Hill Association, an organization of residents that had been founded back in May 1944.[23] Adding to their concern over development of the property may have been the fact that their group had been founded in Mrs. Volkmar's barn and had continued to meet there for many years. Before anything could be done, the property was sold to a developer.[24] Reflect-

ing on this alleged loss, an editorial in the *Chestnut Hill Local* proposed
that there were some lessons that the community could learn from
the Volkmar tract:

> There is an easily read lesson written into the Volkmar Estate case, settled
> last week by an independent buyer. The big question mark is whether Chest-
> nut Hill will have the wit to mark, learn and digest it.
>
> The lesson, we believe, is this: If we are to maintain control over the
> growth of Chestnut Hill or be smashed by it, we must activate, put teeth in,
> [and] delineate the Chestnut Hill Land Company. . . .
>
> It is unrealistic to hope that the great estates will remain open tracts of
> land. We should have learned that lesson when Temple University sold out to
> the Summit Construction Co. It is pessimistic, however, to think that nothing
> can be done. It is creative thinking to plan for attractive development of our
> open spaces.[25]

Once again, the community may have overreacted. Several expensive and attractive single dwellings were built on the Volkmar
property that in no way marred the appearance of North Chestnut
Hill or degraded the housing stock of the community in general. Still
reeling from the sting of the Morgan Tract development, editors and
residents alike tended to respond negatively to the disappearance of
any open land, regardless of how responsibly and attractively it might
be developed.

The Chestnut Hill Land Company, to which the editorial referred,
had been created to provide funds with which the community might
purchase properties on the Hill before they fell into the hands of outside interests such as Summit Construction Company. By developing
the properties themselves, or by selling them to others who would
agree to develop them in ways deemed suitable by the LUPC and the
Community Association, the Land Company could ensure that the
properties were not marred by excessive or inappropriate building.

Although the Land Company did not make much progress, its
successor, the Chestnut Hill Realty Trust, did somewhat better.
Founded in September 1965 by the ubiquitous Lloyd Wells, its stated
purpose was "to assist the community in its struggle to achieve an
orderly and enlightened pattern of land use development."[26] By April
1967 it listed eighty-one stockholders who had raised $165,000 at

$100 a share. As a private corporation made up of local citizens, the Realty Trust did not have any official connection with the Community Association, but it would work closely with the organization in the years just ahead to develop real estate on the Hill.

The Realty Trust's first successful project was the purchase and renovation of the Allen Garage, near the northwest corner of West Highland and Germantown avenues. By 1968 it had transformed the garage into a bright complex of shops, most of which opened onto an interior courtyard. The miniature shopping center also included a restaurant called 21 West. A decade later the Realty Trust would develop another successful shopping complex at the forks of Germantown Avenue and Bethlehem Pike.[27]

Yet another organization that emerged from the community's increasing efforts to direct local real estate development was the Chestnut Hill Historical Society. Like so many recent organizations on the Hill, it was born out of a perceived crisis, this time the threatened destruction in 1966 of the third floor of the VFW building at 8217–19 Germantown Avenue. The veterans organization had decided to take this action because it could not afford to make needed repairs on the upper story. But the structure, built in 1859, was one of the Hill's few good examples of Greek Revival architecture. To Anne Spaeth and Nancy Hubby, both new residents of the community, the demolition of its upper story would be a great loss. Enlisting the aid of Shirley Hanson, another recent arrival in the neighborhood, the three women wrote letters to the newspapers, circulated petitions, and within a short time raised $30,000 to save the third floor and restore the building's exterior.[28]

With this success behind them, Spaeth, Hubby, and Hanson, with the support of Wells and the Community Association, launched the Chestnut Hill Historical Society in May 1967.[29] In some ways this was not an entirely new venture for Chestnut Hill, because many of its residents had belonged to and supported the Germantown Historical Society, founded in 1900 as the Site and Relic Society. The Germantown group had designated the former German Township, which included Germantown, Mount Airy, and Chestnut Hill, as its domain for study and collection of archival materials. It had also

Two of the founders of the Chestnut Hill Historical Society, Nancy Hubby (left) and Shirley Hanson (right), receive the 1986 Chestnut Hill Award from Judy Thomas. *Local.*

taken an interest in architecture throughout the region, making several surveys that included Chestnut Hill. The founding of a separate Chestnut Hill Historical Society was thus another sign of how residents of the Hill were detaching themselves emotionally from Germantown.

In other respects, however, the establishment of the Chestnut Hill Historical Society represented a new and greater level of interest in the preservation of historic buildings, an effort that paralleled similar preservation movements around the country.[30] In Philadelphia, the historic preservation movement had made a modest beginning in the late 1920s with a survey of the city historical district undertaken by the Civic Club and the Philadelphia chapter of the American Institute of Architects. During the New Deal of the 1930s, federal grants had allowed a more extensive documentation of Philadelphia buildings, as well as the first restorations in the historic district downtown. After World War II, the city's commitment to urban renewal and the restoration and renovation of the Independence Hall area by the National Park Service focused more attention than ever before on historic preservation.[31]

Joining this trend toward the documentation and preservation of historic structures, the newly founded Chestnut Hill Historical Society set to work immediately on an architectural survey of Chestnut Hill and adjacent Wyndmoor. Believing that time was an all-important factor in preserving the architectural character of the community, they mobilized a group of amateur volunteers who completed their task in eight months. To supervise the work, the Historical Society hired the city planning firm of Willard S. Detweiler, Jr. Becoming more and more caught up in the project, Detweiler offered to write and publish an illustrated volume on the history of Chestnut Hill architecture that appeared in 1969.[32]

As with the *Chestnut Hill Local,* much of the work of the Historical Society has been undertaken by women in the community. Its founders were all women, its executive directors have all been women, and virtually all the volunteers who researched the architectural survey were women. According to Shirley Hanson, one of the founders of the Historical Society, she and her associates were young married women with college degrees, unlike most of their female counterparts in earlier generations on the Hill, who did not go to college. They discovered that the cause of historic preservation was an ideal outlet for their creative energies. They had homes and small children to care for, and they could work at preservation projects on their own schedules. As women from upper- and upper-middle-class families, they had grown up in households where women were taught that they had a duty to help care for the wider community. For Hanson, these early experiences as a volunteer led her to earn a master's degree in urban planning and to a career as a planning consultant. Compared to the early twentieth century, when volunteer activities became an end in themselves for women, they were now becoming the first steps to careers, at least for some.

Over the next two decades, the women of the Historical Society, which included men on its governing board, would become active participants in Chestnut Hill's quasi government and do much to preserve the historical character of the suburb in the city.[33] But, like the Community Association and other institutions of quasi government, its members and leadership would come almost entirely from North Chestnut Hill and the West Side, where education and social inclinations made for an interest in architectural preservation. Although men and women from the East Side have also expressed an interest in the Hill's past through letters to the newspaper and attendance at historical lectures, they have thus far not found positions on the Historical Society's self-perpetuating board.[34]

In addition to growing concerns over historic preservation, the leaders of Chestnut Hill's quasi government grew alarmed over the increase in automobile traffic through Chestnut hill during the post–World War II period. Although automobiles had first appeared on the Hill early in the twentieth century, they were confined in the early decades to the wealthiest inhabitants. Even many of these residents continued to use one of the two train lines to commute to and from work each day. Thus despite the advent of automobiles, the Hill continued to be a railroad suburb throughout the first half of the twentieth century. After World War II, however, widespread prosperity permitted local artisans, shop clerks, and even the better-paid domestic servants to own cars. The emergence of automobile suburbs north and east of Chestnut Hill also brought more motor vehicles into its streets.[35]

In considering the matter of traffic on the Hill, however, individuals as well as organizations were often of two minds. On the one hand, the idea of major traffic arteries in or around the community seemed a sensible way to ease the congestion on older and narrower streets, such as Germantown Avenue. On the other hand, new "through routes" threatened to destroy Chestnut Hill's semi-isolation from surrounding communities and attract even more traffic from commuters from the newer automobile suburbs in Whitemarsh and Springfield townships driving through the Hill on their way to and from the city. In order to study these problems and make recommendations, the Community Association created a standing committee on traffic.

Plans to construct highways linking Chestnut Hill more closely to surrounding communities went back for decades in some cases. This certainly was true of the recurring schemes to construct a direct route between Chestnut Hill and the suburbs of Philadelphia's Main Line, which lay due west of Chestnut Hill. The earliest public notice of such a route appeared in an article in the *Germantown Guide* on 14 June 1890. Even then, according to the *Guide,* the purpose of the highway was partly to open land for development.[36]

Given the holdings of Henry Howard Houston on the Roxborough side of the Wissahickon, it is probable that Houston himself had a hand in promoting this undertaking. Although nothing came of this earliest proposal, the fact that the Houston estate renewed the campaign for the Main Line route in 1907 adds credence to speculations that the idea may have originated with Houston.

Nothing substantial came of the proposal in the late nineteenth and early twentieth centuries, and it lay dormant until the mid-1920s, when the Philadelphia City Council gave serious consideration to the project. In February 1927, the council passed the necessary legislation and appropriated $1 million for construction. According to maps drawn up at the time, the road would enter Chestnut Hill's West Side at the corner of Gravers and St. Martin's lanes. From there it would proceed east through the middle of Pastorius Park. The depression came before construction could begin, and little was heard of the intersuburban route until 1937, when the Chestnut Hill and Mount Airy Businessmen's Association appointed a committee to study the proposal once again. But the continuing depression and then World War II meant that there was little possibility of executing the route during the next decade.

After the war, the Houston estate began pressuring the city government to revive the Chestnut Hill–Main Line route. By then the Businessmen's Association had reversed itself, fearing the additional traffic that the route would create in Chestnut Hill and stating in November 1953 that it "utterly opposed" the construction. Two years later, Charles Woodward, an heir to the Houston estate, came out publicly against the route. The Community Association also went on record in 1955 as opposing it. Bowing to such local pressure, the city dropped it from the six-year plan in 1955, and it was never seriously reconsidered. As a result, Chestnut Hill and the Main Line remained separated by both the Wissahickon Creek and the Schuykill River. Anyone wishing to drive between the two would continue to take an indirect and convoluted path that led either through Mount Airy and Manayunk to the south or through Conshohocken to the north.[37]

Another ambitious highway plan involved in the extension of Lincoln Drive (which already connected Mount Airy and Germantown to downtown Philadelphia) into the heart of Chestnut Hill, where it would intersect with Bethlehem Pike. This idea also extended back for more than half a century to 1891, when the Fairmount Park Commission drew up initial plans for the road. However, nothing serious was done about bringing the route into Chestnut Hill until the late 1920s, when the necessary surveys were done and curbings were constructed between Allen's Lane and Cresheim Creek, where a bridge would be constructed to take it across to the Hill. In this case, too, the depression probably interrupted further work. Meanwhile, Dr. Woodward had begun to have second thoughts about the Lincoln Drive extension. Although he had originally supported its continuation into Pastorius Park, where it would intersect with the east-west route to the Main Line, he now realized that heavy automobile traffic would interrupt the quiet of his Cotswold Village on the edge of the park. In late 1938 he sent a letter to the G&CH Improvement Association opposing the extension.[38]

After World War II, when the Lincoln Drive project was revived by the city, there was some initial support for it in Chestnut Hill. On a television program in September 1952, for example, Lloyd Wells called upon the city to complete the Lincoln Drive extension as soon as possible. As he put it, the old prerevolutionary roads in the area were "strangling business and causing great economic losses."[39] In January 1953 the 22nd Ward Planning Committee, of which Wells was a member, also pressed for the completion of the Lincoln Drive project. Within several years, Wells had changed his mind and joined the Community Association in opposing the extension into the Hill. By late 1962 the project was abandoned by the city for good.[40] In November of that year the *Chestnut Hill Local* summed up the whole problem with Lincoln Drive by saying, "A wide Avenue in this area heavily loaded with traffic would have spelled its ultimate deterioration."[41]

Although the Lincoln Drive extension and the Chestnut Hill–Main Line highway were successfully blocked by community opposition, there still remained the problem of how to ease the traffic flow on Germantown Avenue, which remained the only direct route through the Hill. The eventual solution was a series of street and road improvements that were designed to divert traffic around the edges of the community. This was accomplished by widening Cresheim Valley Drive on the southern boundary of the Hill, thereby providing a convenient link between Stenton Avenue on the eastern boundary of the community and Lincoln Drive to the south (via Emlen Street in Mount Airy). Stenton Avenue was also widened into two lanes in either direction in order to accommodate increased usage around the Morgan Tract project and to funnel traffic from East Mount Airy along the eastern edge of the Hill. This project included an improved intersection at Bethlehem Pike, Stenton Avenue, and Paper Mill Road. The creation of the Route 309 Expressway in Springfield Township also lessened congestion in the old Bethlehem Pike into Chestnut Hill. Finally, the extension of Henry Avenue through Roxborough, just across the Wissahickon Creek, provided another relatively fast route into center city. Thus by the late 1960s a loop of improved thoroughfares had deflected much traffic from local streets. This was accomplished at the expense of surrounding communities, such as Roxborough, Mount Airy, and Oreland, which had to endure traffic that otherwise might have gone through the Hill. Once again, Chestnut Hillers' wealth, persistence, professional skills, and influence at city hall had resulted in preferential treatment from municipal authorities.[42]

In addition to tackling problems of traffic and land use, Chestnut Hill's evolving quasi government sought to deal with an array of social difficulties, many of which had deep roots in the community's past. This social activism may also have been stimulated by such national phenomena as the civil rights and ecumenical movements and the general reformist atmosphere of the 1960s, although there is no direct evidence of this connection.

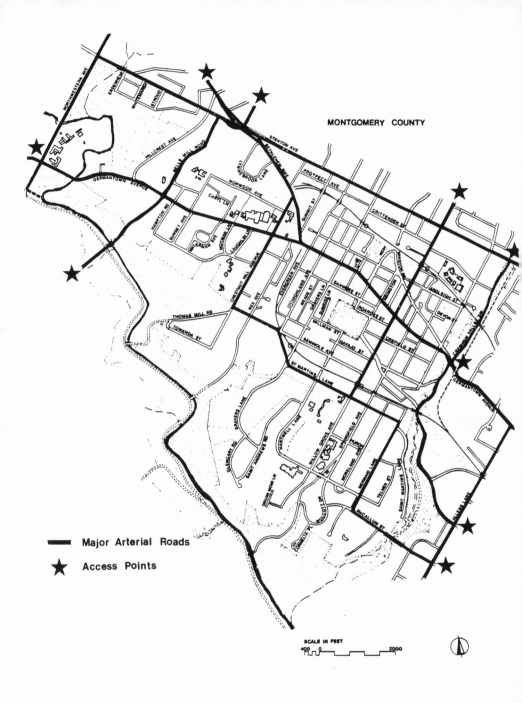

Road network showing major thoroughfares around and through Chestnut Hill, 1982. ERG.

The Orange Ell, the Chestnut Hill Community Association's youth center. Photo 1966. CHHS.

Among these social initiatives were the attempts by the Community Association's Community Relations Committee to create a social center where local youth could congregate in the evenings and especially on weekends. Between 1964 and 1970, the Community Association spent approximately $35,000 on this project. Its first teen facility was called The Orange Ell and was located at 8434 Germantown Avenue, the former Joslin's Hall and later the headquarters of the Community Association and the *Chestnut Hill Local*. Its successor, known as The Loophole, was further down the Hill in the 7900 block of Germantown Avenue. This second facility was owned by a nonprofit organization called Teenagers Incorporated. But both centers drew more youngsters from outside the local community than from Chestnut Hill itself. Neighbors at both locations objected to the noise on evenings and weekends. As a result, the Community Association abandoned the project in January 1971.[43]

Another social initiative was the Community Association's Religion Committee's attempt to encourage the ecumenical movement that was sweeping the United States. The Vatican II Council (1962–1965), which encouraged understanding and dialogue between Roman Catholics and other religious groups, did much to open the way to a better relationship among churches.

As with so many other projects, Lloyd Wells was in the forefront of this movement for religious understanding on the Hill. He not only believed that it was the right thing to do, but he also feared that the gulf between the largely Catholic East Side and the largely Protestant West Side and North Chestnut Hill would have to be breached if quasi government were to work effectively. Wells accordingly made sure that Catholics on the Hill were nominated to serve on the Community Association board. Among them was Sister Grace Miriam, S.S.J., then principal of Our Mother of Consolation parish school. Through Sister Grace Miriam, Wells learned of the need for more classroom space at the school. In response, he arranged to have neighboring St. Paul's Episcopal Church open its Sunday school rooms and auditorium for use during the week by the OMC parish school.[44]

Another important participant in Chestnut Hill's ecumenical movement was the Reverend John Casey, O.S.A. The jovial Irish-American priest was a rabid sports fan and became such a constant spectator at Philadelphia Flyers hockey games that the players made him their unofficial chaplain. A talented amateur musician, the priest was always happy to sit down at a piano and play a few show tunes. Accompanying him everywhere was his three-legged Boston terrier, Bugsie.

Father Casey realized soon after arriving in Chestnut Hill in 1963 that there were strained relations among the local churches. "There was a very bad feeling between the Protestant churches and the Catholic church," he recalled. "There was no communication between the churches. The clergy had nothing to do with each other."[45] Determined to improve the situation, the new priest decided to invite all the clergy in Chestnut Hill to a meeting. It was so successful that they agreed to take turns hosting an informal luncheon once a month. They also decided to join forces to conduct various activities, including a

joint Thanksgiving service. In September 1967, Father Casey invited
the entire community to an open house at OMC.[46] The *Chestnut Hill
Local* became a helpful ally in this process, running stories about improving relations among the churches.[47]

It had become clear to Wells and others in the Community Association that educational divisions on the Hill continued to work
against a sense of community spirit. A chronic lack of funds and constant teachers' strikes in the Philadelphia public school system also
alarmed Chestnut Hill's quasi government. As early as 1960, the
Community Association's Education Committee proposed to begin
helping the Jenks Public School. In addition to assisting the school
with various fund-raising drives, the Education Committee urged
state and local legislators to vote more monies for schools, even if it
meant raising taxes. In the early 1970s the committee, under the
leadership of Dr. George Spaeth, went much further to propose a
community-wide "alternative school." Like the Philadelphia School
District's Parkway School, which made use of various institutional
facilities around the city, the Hill's new experiment would be a
"school without walls." Credit for its courses would be given, through
prior agreements, by such area institutions as Germantown Friends
School and Penn Charter School. The committee also proposed that
Chestnut Hill's Jenks School offer courses once a week on the en-
vironment and the creative arts. Neither of these proposals was implemented, although the idea of making Jenks into a more attractive
alternative school would eventually bear fruit in the early 1980s.[48]

Far more sensitive was the question of racial integration, a topic
of increasing concern all over the nation. For Chestnut Hillers, some
of whom unfairly blamed all of neighboring Germantown's troubles
on a rising black population, integration was an unwelcome subject.
Wells confronted the issue at a Community Association meeting in
early 1961, urging the group to foster integration on the Hill. His
remarks were met with such hostility by certain members of the board
that he resigned as executive secretary of the association.

Wells's decision four years later to return to active participation
in civic affairs on the Hill was prompted in part by a racial incident
in the community. It involved two black couples who were refused

seats in a local restaurant. One of the women was the director of the
Chestnut Hill branch of the Free Library. Her husband was a respected attorney with a degree from Harvard Law School. Upon
hearing their story, Wells was furious. He decided that the Community Association would have to take a more active role in promoting race relations.

Beginning in the mid-1960s, there were some signs of constructive
action in Chestnut Hill on the subject of race. In 1965 the Community
Association held discussions on integration with its Mount Airy
neighbors.[49] There was a quiet decision in the mid-1960s at Springside School, initiated by headmistress Eleanor Potter and approved
by the school's board, to recruit and admit the institution's first black
students. By 1990 just over 20 percent of the students came from
minority groups.[50]

In early 1967 several Chestnut Hill churches joined with religious
groups in Germantown to sponsor a six-week seminar entitled "Black
Power–White Power." Later that year, Episcopal Bishop Robert
DeWitt, who was in the forefront of Phildelphia's civil rights movement, challenged parishioners at St. Martin-in-the-Fields to open
themselves up to men and women of all backgrounds and races. In
1968 the Chestnut Hill Development Group announced that it would
help to establish a fund in memory of the recently assassinated Dr.
Martin Luther King, Jr., to help young "Negroes" in North Philadelphia to start their own businesses.[51] Throughout the 1960s and
early 1970s, the *Chestnut Hill Local,* under its editor, Ellen Newbold
(Wells), did much to promote improved race relations.[52]

In order to deal more aggressively with such social problems,
Lloyd Wells had decided to establish a local political party and then
to take control of the Community Association. With about thirty others, he founded the Greene party — a conscious reference to William
Penn's "Greene Country Towne." By 1969 they had won control of
the Community Association, and Wells was elected its president for
two years. Wells dubbed Greene party opponents the "White party,"
a label that many in the so-called opposition rejected and despised.[53]

The Greene party set forth its activist philosophy in the *Chestnut
Hill Local* on 9 March 1972. In the area of education, the party would

try to provide better resources while trying to break down some of the divisions that separated the various school populations on the Hill. To achieve this, they would encourage "the private and parochial schools in the community to share their facilities and resources more actively. . . ." In order to promote greater harmony among the churches, they would urge religious leaders to offer "their particular talents to community activities."[54] A year earlier, Wells had suggested that Chestnut Hill could not afford to take an isolationist stance toward problems, but would have to seek cooperation with surrounding communities.[55]

In a referendum in which the entire Community Association membership was invited to vote, the bylaws were amended in 1972 to provide for the election of all directors by the membership. The next year, the Community Association established a network of block captains who would serve to channel information back and forth between the association and the neighborhoods. The idea was somewhat similar to the old G&CH Improvement Association's Auxiliary Committee, but there is no evidence that the earlier model inspired the later one.[56]

In an effort to dramatize the quasi-governmental nature of their undertaking, the Community Association decided in 1974 to call its annual membership dues a "quasi tax." But in order not to exclude younger or less prosperous residents of the Hill, an amendment to the bylaws set the minimum "tax" at just one dollar. Anyone over age fourteen could pay the minimum amount and enjoy the "privilege of voting and participating in all benefits and activities of the Community Association." As it turned out, most everyone continued to pay the prevailing membership dues, which also entitled one to receive the *Chestnut Hill Local* each week.[57]

In order to raise additional money for charitable purposes, the Greene party proposed a Chestnut Hill Community Fund that would receive tax-deductible contributions. The fund was established in 1972, and contributions totaled nearly $19,000 by 1975 and just over $40,000 in 1990. It was also in 1975 that Dorothy Y. Sheffield proposed that the association approve a thrift shop, eventually called Bird In Hand. Its purpose was to raise additional revenues for the fund, es-

A portion of the Top of the Hill area (Germantown Ave. and Bethlehem Pike) before its redevelopment by the Realty Trust. Photo c. early 1950s. *Local.*

pecially for tree planting and landscaping around the Hill. Located in the Community Center building and staffed by local women, the shop would prove very successful in the years ahead. In 1988 Bird in Hand contributed $55,000 to the Community Fund.[58]

With so many new activities, it became apparent that the Community Association needed a full-time manager. The board began to discuss the idea early in 1970 but did not create such a position until 1977, when the board chose Jeanne Scott to be its first community manager. Her duties included the administration of all employees and properties of the Community Association. She was also to act as a liaison between the association and such other community organs as the *Chestnut Hill Local,* the Realty Trust, the Development Group, and the Parking Foundation (the former Parking Company). In addition, she would administer the Chestnut Hill Community Fund, help to develop projects and long-range plans for the community, and assist

Top of the Hill after its redevelopment by the Realty Trust. Notice that the Acme Supermarket has been replaced by the arcade of shops in center right of scene. Photo c. 1976. *Local.*

in attracting volunteer support for the association's various activities. If Chestnut Hill had been an independent political entity, she might have been called a city or town manager, and in many respects that is the role that she and her successors would play.[59]

During this period, the Community Association continued to try to monitor real estate development on the Hill. In 1972 it began a battle with Bell Telephone, which wanted to demolish the neighboring Hill Theater at 8324 Germantown Avenue in order to expand its regional office. Although the association failed to keep Bell from removing the movie house, it did force the company to scale down its new building from five stories to three and to adopt a neoclassical facade that was more in keeping with its original building next door and with the architectural flavor of Germantown Avenue.[60]

Far more successful was the Community Association's cooperative venture with the Realty Trust in developing the Top of the Hill site, a property that was situated just above the intersection of Germantown Avenue and Bethlehem Pike. It was here that the number 23 trolley ended its long run up from South Philadelphia and made its turn around on a circular track that local residents had long called "the loop." The plot also contained an unattractive trolley station with snack bar, the Grove Diner, and a modest-sized Acme Supermarket. The Realty Trust acquired the properties in 1973 for $360,000 and chose the firm of LETR Associates to develop the site. Initial plans called for a multiuse facility that included apartments and commercial establishments. After long and often heated debates between the community and developers, an L-shaped arcade of shops was built to frame the trolley loop. A green space between the shops and the trolley tracks was landscaped with trees, shrubs, and a wood-rail fence.[61]

The Greene party and the Community Association worked to maintain and enhance Chestnut Hill's appearance as a "Greene Country Towne." In 1974 the Parks Committee drew up an ambitious scheme that included the replanting and restoration of Pastorius Park, relandscaping of the Water Tower Recreation Center, improving the Jenks School playground, and repairing and beautifying the Hill's railroad stations. It also supported the creation of Buckley Park at the intersection of Germantown Avenue and Hartwell Lane, named for a young local man who had been killed in the Vietnam War. Yet another proposal was to link Pastorius Park and the Water Tower Recreation Center with a green walkway along Hartwell Lane. The last project had not been realized at the time of this writing, but the others were carried out over a period of years.

In 1975 the Community Association purchased a maintenance truck in order to plow snow, haul leaves and debris, and perform other jobs around the Hill that the city of Philadelphia or other constituted authorities declined to do. Although no one seemed to realize it, this action echoed the efforts of the Chestnut Hill Improvement Association back in the 1880s, when it had undertaken to pave and maintain local streets.

Finally, the association created the position of ombudsman in 1970. As was true for Jacob Bockius of the former G&CH Improvement Association, it was the ombudsman's job to receive complaints and to refer them to the proper person or agency. After 1977 the ombudsman's job was taken over by the community manager.[62]

Community volunteers clean up Pastorius Park in the spring of 1986. *Local.*

Although the Community Association was active in a number of areas during the Greene party years, many area residents then and later contended that the credit for community accomplishments cannot be claimed by the Greenes alone, but must be shared with the entire association and its many volunteers. Others have charged that the Greene party was destructive in that it created a spirit of divisiveness. This charge of divisiveness would be used many times in the future in a community that professed to value a professional, nonpartisan stance toward local problems, a stance that echoed the reformist ideas of George Woodward and other Progressive Era leaders on the Hill two generations earlier.

Still other critics have charged that the Greene party took on far more issues than it could ever hope to resolve, and that under Well's leadership it tended to move from one problem to another without dealing thoroughly with any one of them. Then there were those who asserted that the Greene party was merely an organization created by Wells for his own aggrandizement.[63] It is clear that Chestnut Hill's quasi government reached a new level of activity during the early and mid-1970s. It is also clear that there was a mounting opposition to this activism, particularly to social activism.

Beyond the specific criticisms aimed at Wells and the Greene party, Chestnut Hill's quasi government suffered from serious limitations. Despite attempts to create a well-integrated and effective system, it remained unofficial and diffuse. There was no one charter or constitution that defined and empowered the various institutions that were involved with quasi government. Because the interlocking directorates were purely voluntary, there was nothing to keep the Historical Society, the Parking Foundation, or the Development Group from abandoning them, or from making decisions independently of and even at cross-purposes to the Community Association. Because the Community Association itself was not an official government institution, no legal or constitutional machinery could require it to continue functioning on a high level year after year. The effectiveness of the Community Association and its various committees, as well as of such independent institutions as the Historical Society, depended largely upon the energy, resourcefulness, and commitment of a handful of volunteer leaders. Thus Chestnut Hill's quasi government had an ad hoc quality that could never be overcome entirely. Finally, the lack of clear lines of authority and the need to work through legally constituted municipal agencies, such as Philadelphia's Zoning Board, led to quarreling and confusion—without any umpires, such as a superior court or a constitutional balance of powers.

Reflecting on many of these problems and reeling from constant criticism, the Greene party decided to disband in May 1975, with most of its members concluding that the intense controversy surrounding its existence had made it "counterproductive."[64] Yet Wells was not willing to give up, and during the Community Association elections in early 1976 he made a strenuous effort to salvage the Greene party platform, if not the party itself. He took out full-page advertisements in the *Local* in which he insisted that there were two diametrically opposed philosophies from which to choose in selecting candidates. His group believed in "open[,] broad based participation of all citizens, regardless of rank, race, religion, class, or ethnic background." The opposition, he contended, stood for "a comparatively closed policy[-]making procedure conducted by 'experts' or by the 'influential' at the executive level[,] . . . conforming basically to the pattern of a corporation's board of directors." When it came to discussing controversial issues in the community, his group believed in "telling it like it is," whereas the opposition, in Wells's opinion, favored "supervised speech and press."[65] Opponents charged that Wells himself had not lived up to this philosophy and had actually tried to run the Community Association as if it were a closed corporation, with little tolerance for dissent.

Despite his strenuous campaign efforts, Wells's candidates were defeated by a narrow margin in the Community Association elections in late March of 1976, which saw a record turnout of 1,891 members. Disappointed and angry at the defeat and at the mounting criticism against him, Wells left civic life on the Hill for a third time. Moving to Maine with his wife, Wells has never returned to live in Chestnut Hill, although he has made frequent visits to friends and old supporters.[66] A less activist Community Association would now be in charge of quasi government for the suburb in the city.

With or without Wells, Chestnut Hill's quasi government would devote itself primarily to preserving and extending a pleasant and privileged way of life in their suburb in the city. Like local civic groups in the past, the Community Association and its ancillary organizations were run for the most part by wealthy and prominent members of the community, who drew upon their professional skills, private finances, social connections, and personal self-confidence to achieve their goals. Believing that they did not have to settle for any less than the best, they persisted in their civic efforts year after year despite some disagreements on ends and means and some variations in their level of activity. In this sense, they were not too much different from their Progressive counterparts at the beginning of the century.

9

CONFLICTING IDENTITIES

City, Suburb, and Region

During the three decades after World War II, Chestnut Hill's leaders had severed their once close ties to Germantown and Mount Airy, creating a set of purely local institutions that resulted in a quasi government for the Hill. Yet the activist Chestnut Hill Community Association had concerned itself with some issues, such as public education and race relations, that affected the entire city, albeit as these problems bore upon life in Chestnut Hill. For more than a decade following the defeat of the Greene party platform in early 1976, however, the Community Association would show a reluctance to confront metropolitan-wide issues, or even to take a forceful role with local problems. Part of this lower profile stemmed from the association's relatively conservative leadership, which paralleled a more conservative mood in the nation at large, although there is no direct evidence that this national trend affected the local climate. At the same time, Chestnut Hill's tendency to turn inward during this period was a reaction to rising crime rates and physical deterioration in those areas of the city closest to Chestnut Hill, namely Germantown and Mount Airy.

This less active and more isolated stance by Chestnut Hill's quasi government was unfortunate for many reasons. In addition to mounting problems in nearby areas of the city, the Hill itself faced a multitude of forces that threatened the semirural atmosphere that had characterized it as a suburb in the city. One was the very success of Chestnut Hill's "extraordinary shops." In addition to generating increasing traffic along Germantown Avenue, the shops' success led to rising land values and rents, which in turn were forcing local enterprises out of business. Taking their place were national and regional chain stores whose absentee owners, it was feared, would not always act in the local interest. In addition, the expansion of institutions such as Chestnut Hill Hospital put increasing pressure on open spaces. Because the hospital was well respected in the community, residents faced the dilemma of choosing between two positive ends: better health care and the preservation of open spaces. Chestnut Hillers wanted to preserve their way of life, but there were increasing debates over just what that way of life should be, or how local organizations could go about protecting and extending it.

In focusing on Chestnut Hill's relations with the rest of Philadelphia, this debate had often ignored what was happening beyond the city limits. In the 1950s merchants in Chestnut Hill had awakened to the challenges of new shopping centers and had responded with a campaign to improve the Hill's shopping district. Development in the suburbs of adjoining Montgomery County had continued over the years, and by the late 1970s most of the land immediately north and east of Chestnut Hill had been developed. In 1980, for example, the two nearby townships of Springfield and Whitemarsh had reached stable populations of around 20,000 and 15,000, respectively.[1] The 1990 census showed little change in these figures.[2] The shopping malls in these communities continued to attract Chestnut Hill residents, and some inhabitants of the newer suburbs in Montgomery County shopped in Chestnut Hill. Census figures also showed that 25 percent of Chestnut Hill residents were commuting to jobs in the

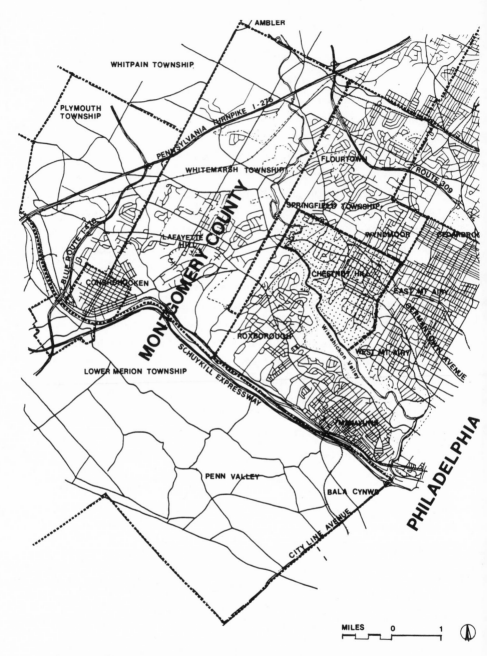

Chestnut Hill in relation to surrounding communities. ERG.

Despite a large decline in riders, the daily commute downtown by train remains a familiar part of Chestnut Hill life. *Local.*

surrounding counties — as many, in fact, as were commuting from the Hill to Philadelphia.

More than anything else, it was the ubiquitous automobile and the decline of the commuter railroad that had made these new patterns possible. With a car at their disposal, Hillers could now travel in any direction. Instead of the old identity with suburb and city, residents could just as easily attach themselves to the newer communities beyond the city limits as they could to downtown Philadelphia, or to the urban neighborhoods south and east of Chestnut Hill.

Chestnut Hill consequently found itself in the midst of a regional complex, partly residential and partly commercial, that was both inside and outside the city limits. Chestnut Hill thus became more and more difficult to classify demographically. As the twentieth century came to an end, residents of the Hill not only had to face the dual identity of being a suburb in the city, but also had to try to define their place in a demographic region that comprised the northwest section of Philadelphia and the newer suburban communities beyond the city limits. In struggling to find its place within this wider area, some Chestnut Hill residents urged secession from the city of Philadelphia in order to seek annexation by Montgomery County. Although the issue of secession had died down by the time of this writing, the question of where Chestnut Hill belonged in the regional complex would remain.

Exacerbating these doubts about Chestnut Hill's identity was a decline in Philadelphia's municipal government. The excitement over the reform administration of Joseph Clark and Richardson Dilworth that had inspired Chestnut Hillers in the 1950s was now dead. The Democrats had built and maintained a machine that seemed as implacable to some as the Republican organization that Clark and Dilworth had overthrown a generation earlier.

Meanwhile, the great shift of businesses and population from the northeastern United States to the sunbelt states of the South and Southwest had helped to erode Philadelphia's economy. So did greater competition from manufactured goods from abroad. As a consequence, Philadelphia's once mighty industries began to collapse. With fewer jobs available, the city's population declined further — from a high of about 2.1 million in 1950 to just under 1.6 million in 1990; and from the nation's third largest city to its fifth. Even the population of Philadelphia's Standard Metropolitan Statistical Area (SMSA) declined. Defined as the city and its suburbs, the SMSA included Philadelphia itself, the four surrounding counties in Pennsylvania (Bucks, Montgomery, Delaware, and Chester), and the three counties across the Delaware River in New Jersey (Burlington, Camden, and Gloucester). This area declined in population by 3 percent between 1970 and 1980.[3] Between 1980 and 1990 it grew by about 3 percent, leaving it at nearly 4,850,000, approximately the same number as in 1970.[4]

As Philadelphia lost jobs and population, its problems grew. According to some accounts, the number of people on public assistance rose from 200,000 in 1970 to 340,000 in 1980. Streets, bridges, and other parts of the city's infrastructure decayed for lack of funds to repair them. Public school buildings and their instructional programs likewise declined because of money shortages, and teachers struck every two or three years to protest what they considered to be low pay and bad working conditions. Public transportation also barely staggered along. In order to recoup its dwindling tax base, the city constantly raised wage taxes, property taxes, and other levies, making its overall tax rate the highest of any major city in the country by 1990. But in many cases all this did was encourage more businesses and residents to leave for the suburbs. In July 1990 the city's fiscal crisis was so desperate that it received the lowest municipal bond rating of any large city in the nation, and there were some who feared that bankruptcy was not far away.[5]

During this period, Chestnut Hill underwent a series of demographic changes. In the 1960s its population was about 9,000, little more than what it had been thirty years before. By 1970 it had risen to a precise 10,617, according to the new census tracts, which now made it possible to calculate neighborhood populations with great accuracy. This was a growth of approximately 18 percent over a decade, nearly all of it resulting from the apartments that had been built on the Morgan Tract. This apartment development was officially named Chestnut Hill Village, and the shopping center next to it went by the name of Market Square. Sharing the tract was the high-rise Morgan House. There was a total of about 800 living units and over 2,000 residents in the new complex.

By 1980 the Hill's population had fallen slightly to 10,186, with most of the decline taking place on the more prosperous West Side, in part because of its aging population and the concomitant disappearance of children and servants from their households. During these ten years, however, the nonwhite (i.e., non-European) population of Chestnut Hill rose from 97 in 1970 to 504 in 1980, for an increase of 407 (or 420 percent). Of these, 356 were black.[6] The 1990 census showed a further slight decrease in Chestnut Hill's total pop-

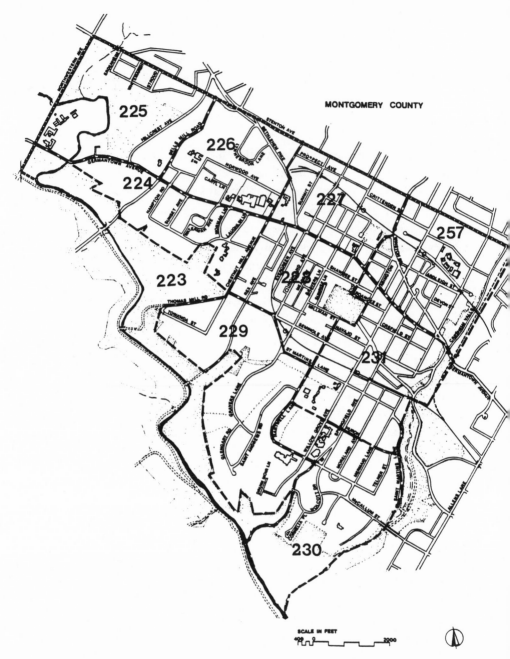

Census tracts, Chestnut Hill. ERG.

ulation, to 10,052. In 1990, however, the black population on the Hill increased to 1,188, about three times the number in 1980. Most of these black residents (951 of them) lived in the Market Square/Chestnut Hill Village area.[7] The figures for 1990 thus revealed that 11.8 percent of Chestnut Hill's residents were black, roughly equivalent to the percentage of black citizens (12 percent) in the total U.S. population. However, the percentage of blacks in Chestnut Hill was far less than in Philadelphia as a whole, where about 40 percent of the inhabitants were black.

East and West Mount Airy, located just south of Chestnut Hill, lost considerable population between 1970 and 1980. In both the Mount Airys the numbers of black residents had risen, while the white population had dropped precipitously. In West Mount Airy, which bordered directly on Chestnut Hill's West Side and in many ways resembled it, the population had fallen from 16,540 to 14,864. Nonwhite residents of the area had risen by almost 500, and the number of white residents had dropped by nearly 3,000. In East Mount Airy, which, like the East Side of Chestnut Hill, contained many row houses and semidetached dwellings, "white flight" was far greater. There the total population decline was about 2,800: just under 5,000 whites had left, while some 1,900 nonwhites had arrived during the same period.[8] It appears that many of the whites who left had settled in suburban Montgomery County.

Less evident was the fact that Chestnut Hill was home to fewer upper-class men and women than it had been a half century earlier, on the eve of the Great Depression. Although the *Social Register* was even less reliable as a guide to prominent families, it was still the only list of its kind that might be used for comparative purposes. There had been approximately 550 Hill residents in the *Social Register* in the late 1920s. By the late 1980s their number had dropped to around 330, for a decline of 220 persons (or 40 percent). Bryn Mawr and Haverford had experienced slightly smaller declines, from a total for the two of 360 or so in 1930 to about 236 in 1987, a drop of 114 individuals (or 32 percent). Chestnut Hill had thus held its own with these two prestigious Main Line suburban communities. It remained the most frequently listed Delaware Valley address in the *Social Reg-*

ister, which by the 1980s was published as a single directory for the entire United States.[9]

In the case of Chestnut Hill, this decline in listings would seem to result from two principal factors. One was the growth of the post-war suburbs to the north and east of the Hill. Thus the 1987 *Social Register* carried a significant number of entries from Lafayette Hill, Plymouth Meeting, Flourtown, Fort Washington, and Gwynedd Valley — communities that did not exist at all in the late 1920s or that were sparsely populated at the time. A cursory examination of recent editions of the *Social Register* shows that the descendants of some upper-class Chestnut Hill families had moved to these newer suburbs.[10]

The second factor was probably the increased geographic mobility of all Americans during the postwar period. In order to take advantage of better job opportunities, some upper-class Chestnut Hillers, particularly the younger ones, had left for other parts of the country (and the world). Furthermore, well-to-do sons could no longer count on automatic acceptance by their fathers' Ivy League colleges, and might find themselves on a campus hundreds or even thousands of miles away from Chestnut Hill, where there was a good chance of meeting and marrying a young woman who had no ties to the Hill and who had no intention of living there. Reinforcing this trend was the fact that young women in Chestnut Hill started going to college in large numbers after World War II. Like their brothers, some married out-of-towners and settled elsewhere.[11]

On the Hill itself, women's lives were beginning to reflect the nationwide drive for greater equality of the sexes. Although there were no figures on the number of women who worked outside the home, a decline in the amount of time that women had to devote to volunteer activities suggested that more and more of them were working at full-time jobs. St. Martin-in-the-Fields Church, for example, was forced to hold many women's meetings in the evening instead of during the day, as had been the custom. The Community Center, founded just after World War I and staffed by women ever since, also experienced a decline in volunteers. Yet in other areas of civic life women were taking on leadership roles that had been dominated by men in the past. In 1990, for example, just over 50 percent of the board members of the Chestnut Hill Community Association who actually lived on the Hill were women. This compared to only 16 percent of board members who were women in 1961.[12] The Community Association also elected its first woman president in 1974, and since 1980 four of the six presidents have been women.

Besides including more women in leadership positions, the Community Association also showed greater diversity in other demographic areas. Only one of its six presidents since 1980 was listed in the *Social Register*. Two of its presidents were Roman Catholics. (Of the other four, two were Episcopalians, one was a Presbyterian, and one was a Lutheran.) The occupations of these recent presidents were also more varied than in the past, although all of them were in business or the professions. Among the four women there was a journalist, a certified public accountant, a teacher, and an insurance manager. The two men were a market consultant and a city planner. During this period, the association had more board members who resided on the East Side than ever before. Whereas only one board member (4 percent of the total) hailed from the East Side in 1961, there were eight (20 percent) from the East Side in 1990. There were no black board members as of 1990, despite the fact that nearly 12 percent of the local population was African-American.[13]

In the school populations, however, there were few changes from sixty years earlier: prosperous Protestants still sent their children to one of the community's private schools, such as Springside for girls and Chestnut Hill Academy for boys. There were those who continued to prefer Quaker schools, such as Germantown Friends. A decision by the William Penn Charter School, located in nearby Germantown, to go coeducational in the early 1980s made it increasingly popular with the private school group in Chestnut Hill. Catholics continued to send their children to one of the private Catholic academies or to the parish school at OMC. Chestnut Hill's public Jenks School attracted fewer local students than ever by the early 1970s, in part because of continuing financial and personnel crises in the Philadelphia school system. Consequently, the majority of the students at Jenks were black children who were bused in from outlying areas. Thus in spite of efforts by Lloyd Wells and his supporters in the Community Association, Chestnut Hill's youngsters continued to be divided by both school and neighborhood. Among East Side children, the old epithet "half-cut" continued to be alive and well as a disparaging term for their counterparts on the West Side and in North Chestnut Hill. As a result, there was almost as little likelihood of marrying across neighborhood and class lines on the Hill as there had been two or three generations earlier.

When it came to educational attainment and income level, there also remained considerable division on the Hill. The 1980 census tracts revealed that the most highly educated residents lived on the socially prestigious West Side (tract 229), where 96.5 percent had graduated from high school and 68.1 percent had finished at least four years of college. At the other end of the educational scale was the lower southeast quadrant of Chestnut Hill (tract 257), which included Market Square/Chestnut Hill Village. There 73.7 percent had finished high school and 30.7 percent had graduated from college. The local extremes of income likewise fell into these two tracts. In tract 229 (the West Side), median family income was $75,000, whereas in tract 257 (the lower southeast quadrant) it was $21,000.[14] Although these local differences appear great, even the lower ranges of education and income in Chestnut Hill were higher than averages for Philadelphia. In Philadelphia only 11 percent had completed college in 1980, and the median household income was just over $13,000.[15] Comparable figures for 1990 were not yet available at the time of this writing.

There appeared to be little change in Chestnut Hill from the religious patterns of the past. The Protestant denominations, especially the Episcopalians and Presbyterians, continued to represent 50 percent or more of local residents. But impressionistic evidence suggests that the Hill's Jewish population had been increasing modestly for about two decades. A large proportion of these Jewish residents appeared to be retired couples who lived in the various apartments next to Market Square/Chestnut Hill Village. Some Jewish families had also purchased houses on the West Side and in North Chestnut Hill, and several of them had joined the Philadelphia Cricket Club, for

Councilman W. Thacher Longstreth (center), flanked by Community Association president Virginia Duke and Philadelphia Mayor Wilson Good in May 1990. *Local.*

decades a bastion of the WASP upper class. Both Chestnut Hill Academy and the Springside School also had significant numbers of Jewish students in 1990. It was difficult to know whether or not the greater presence of Jews on the Hill reflected a decline in local anti-Semitism. According to City Councilman Thacher Longstreth and other local residents, anti-Semitism had declined greatly on the Hill since the 1930s.[16]

Longstreth also believed that it was only a matter of time before prosperous black families began to move into North Chestnut Hill and the West Side. He believed that they would be generally well received, if only because their wealthy, successful, and socially secure white neighbors would not feel as threatened by blacks as would the less wealthy and less successful white residents of Chestnut Hill's East Side.[17]

The census tracts for 1980 suggested that the ethnic distribution
of Chestnut Hill residents had shifted somewhat over the past fifty
years. Of those who answered questions about ancestry, 30 percent
reported that they were Irish, 28 percent were British, 25 percent
were German, 6 percent were Italian, 6 percent were French, 3 percent were Eastern European, and 3 percent were African-American.
The German percentage was noticeably larger than the estimate for
1930, which may be accounted for by much intermarriage among this
group. The larger number of Irish can be explained by their unavoidable undercount in the 1930 *City Directory* at a time when many were
live-in servants.

The overwhelming number (83 percent) of Chestnut Hill's residents in 1980 still traced their ancestors to northern and western Europe. Preliminary figures from the 1990 census suggest, however,
that the percentage from northwestern Europe has declined over the
past ten years as the black population, in particular, has increased.

Yet another reason for changes in ethnic composition since 1930
was the presence of many newcomers on the Hill. Virtually all of
the 1,000 or more inhabitants of the Chestnut Hill Village/Morgan
House complex were relatively new to the community. At the same
time, Chestnut Hill was attracting better paid employees of Philadelphia's city government, who were required by law to live within
municipal boundaries. Others who wanted to vote in Philadelphia
elections or to run for elective office in the city also found the Hill an
attractive place to live. In the early 1970s, for instance, Mayor Frank
Rizzo settled on Chestnut Hill's West Side. His successor, Mayor
William J. Green, likewise moved to Chestnut Hill for a time. Some
bankers, lawyers, and businessmen moving to Philadelphia also settled in Chestnut Hill.

Such demographic changes appeared to have political ramifica-
tions for the community. Although even the Great Depression had
not been enough to detach most Chestnut Hillers from their alle-
giance to the Republican party, the solid wall of Republicanism had
begun to crack during the 1930s and 1940s, particularly among residents of the East Side of the Hill, who had suffered the most from
unemployment. Some upper-class residents, disgusted with years of

Chestnut Hill resident and former mayor Frank Rizzo
speaks at a local candidates' forum in October 1987.
Local.

corrupt Republican rule, had become Democrats over the years, and
most of the Jewish and black voters moving to Chestnut Hill were
already Democrats.[18] Yet there were still not enough Democrats to
compensate for continued loyalty to the GOP. The result was that in
the postwar period residents of Chestnut Hill still cast the majority
of their votes for Republican presidential candidates. But Democrats
seeking local office did start to make inroads on the Hill during the
1950s. Patrician Democrat Joseph S. Clark, Jr. (who, along with
Richardson Dilworth, had been a Republican in his early years) carried Chestnut Hill in his victorious mayoral campaign in 1951.
Shortly after that, Democrat Constance Dallas of Chestnut Hill won
a seat in city council. By the 1980s it was not unusual for Chestnut
Hillers to split their tickets in local elections.[19]

Even more significant than a growing independence in local contests was the division in 1958 of the old 22nd Ward, after more than a half century of resistance to such a change by voters in the area. As late as 1937, community leaders had seen the proposal as just one more attempt by the corrupt city machine to dilute the power of Independent Republicans in the ward. Sentimental attachment to the old German Township, whose boundaries largely coincided with those of the 22nd Ward, also had been a powerful factor in local opposition to ward division. But by 1958, when the question was placed on the ballot as a local referendum, the ward had already been torn wide open by partisan politics, with the Democrats holding an increasing lead in Germantown proper, where serious unemployment and a growing black population had taken the community out of the Republican column. Meanwhile, a growing fear in Chestnut Hill that Germantown pointed the way to its own future did much to undermine emotional ties to the old township. As a result, the referendum passed easily, separating the old ward into two new ones that split Chestnut Hill along Germantown Avenue, with the 59th Ward to the west and the 22nd Ward to the east of the avenue. A further ward division in the 1970s placed the whole of Chestnut Hill and upper Mount Airy into a much smaller district, the 9th Ward.

Because of its makeup, the present 9th Ward was divided politically. The precincts in Mount Airy, for example, were largely Democratic. The precinct around Chestnut Hill Village and Market Square was also a stronghold for the Democrats, in part because of its Jewish and minority population. Thus in 1980 that precinct (then the 2nd) favored Democrat Jimmy Carter over Republican Ronald Reagan by a vote of 283 to 186. In the 11th precinct, which ran through the heart of Chestnut Hill's wealthy West Side, Reagan won 483 votes to Carter's 192.[20] In this sense, Chestnut Hill Village seemed to belong to Philadelphia politically, while the Republican West Side was more in step with suburban Montgomery County, where the Republicans commanded large majorities.

Chestnut Hill thus remained a divided community in the 1980s. An initiative that sought to bridge one of these divisions was the opening of Jenks Academy in 1980. The aim of the Philadelphia public school system was to make Jenks into a "magnet school," with superior programs that would attract additional white students at a time when Jenks was 85 percent black. If successful, the plan would bring about voluntary integration at Jenks while creating something of a community school in Chestnut Hill that cut across social and residential divisions. Although a prolonged teachers strike in 1981 (the sixth in little more than a decade) threatened to kill the program before it really got started, Jenks Academy did meet with moderate success. The children of some prosperous and socially prominent families on the Hill were enrolled at Jenks, although most remained only until the fourth or fifth grade, at which time their parents transferred them to one of the private schools.[21]

The idea for such a community school, however limited, had been proposed in the early 1970s by the Community Association's Education Committee, but there was little evidence that the association had much to do with the establishment of Jenks Academy a decade later. Nor did the association take any action on a case of racism on the Hill in 1980. According to articles in both the Philadelphia *Evening Bulletin* and the *Chestnut Hill Local,* an interracial couple who moved into the 8100 block of Ardleigh Street on the East Side had been harassed by neighbors into leaving. Their cars were vandalized repeatedly and neighbors refused to speak to their small child. The fact that the couple were well-educated did not seem to make any difference to the neighbors. Although the *Local* deplored this case of racism, not one word about it appeared in the Community Association's board minutes, despite the fact that the association was supposed to concern itself with every question relating to the welfare of Chestnut Hill.[22]

In nonsocial areas, too, it appeared that the Community Association and allied organizations were less responsive than in the past. The most serious indication of this decline was the collapse of the Realty Trust. It had become less and less active after completing the Top of the Hill project, and finally dissolved in 1983, when several large investors wished to retrieve their money from it. In the process of liquidating its assets, the trust had to sell the old Joslin Hall (8434 Germantown Avenue), which it had purchased in 1969 for the offices

Chestnut Hill's unofficial town hall, on the second floor of 8434 Germantown Ave. Built in 1899, the structure originally was a dance hall known as Joslin Hall. The lower story was "colonialized" in 1961. *Local.*

of both the Community Association and the *Chestnut Hill Local.* Faced with the prospect of losing its "town hall," the association voted to use the Chestnut Hill Community Fund as a vehicle for raising the $250,000 to purchase the building. Several Realty Trust investors contributed their shares in the building to the campaign, and others in the community supplied the rest. Although the town hall had been saved, the Community Association remained concerned over the collapse of the Realty Trust and encouraged the formation of a successor group. Established in 1984, the replacement was called the Chestnut Hill Preservation and Development Fund. As of 1990 it had accomplished very little.[23]

Without any effective way to obtain control over properties as they came onto the market, the Community Association found itself seriously handicapped in controlling land development during the 1980s. A good example of this was the Chestnut Hill Plaza site at

7630 Germantown Avenue, near the boundary with Mount Airy. In 1980 the owner of an Exxon station on the property retired and put the parcel up for sale. The Realty Trust declined to purchase it, as did its successor, the Preservation and Development Fund. A developer from Denver, Colorado, bought the land and built a small strip shopping center. Although it is far more attractive than the abandoned gas station and weed-infested lot that it replaced, many residents found it ugly and inappropriate for Chestnut Hill.[24]

As the Community Association, Realty Trust, and Preservation and Development Fund remained relatively quiescent, the *Local* tried to renew interest in quasi government. An editorial in October 1980 complained that the Community Association just "shuffles along." Another editorial in April 1984 was far more explicit:

> A review of the CHCA files has reminded us that at one time the Community Association considered every sphere of activity, every community institution within its purview, at least to some extent. Health, education, aging people, community relations, drug and alcohol abuse, recreation — all fell within the CHCA's bailiwick. Cooperation among and between the institutions and the CHCA, although far from perfect, was at least significant.[25]

Early in 1985, yet another editorial focused on the need to work for Chestnut Hill's future, noting that past planning had been central to the maintenance of the community's suburban atmosphere: "The ambience of a country village within a major metropolis area did not just happen."[26]

In an address before the Community Association in April 1983, a visiting Ellen (Mrs. Lloyd) Wells minced few words in expressing her disappointment over the organization's record during the past half dozen years:

> It appears to me that the well-oiled machine that the Community Association is today fell into place and started rolling when it abandoned the concept of quasi-government, under which banner the Greene party marched for eight or so exhilarating years. . . . I detect a peace-at-any-price attitude. Don't rock the boat.

Then, quoting Thomas Jefferson, she added, "A little revolution, now and then, is a good thing, and as necessary in the political world as storms in the physical."[27] This, of course, was the stance toward civic life in Chestnut Hill that her husband had taken and that had led to such animosity toward him by residents who preferred a less controversial approach to community affairs.

Although no revolution was forthcoming, a struggle to control the community's newspaper, the *Chestnut Hill Local,* brought about a dramatic change of leadership in 1989 that seemed to point to reinvigoration of the Hill's quasi government. This struggle became entangled with a larger debate over the communal identity of Chestnut Hill.

From the beginning (1958), the *Local* had belonged to the Community Association, but as it replaced the *Herald* and became an increasingly powerful voice in the community, some residents began to object to the thrust of certain editorials, as well as to its news coverage. The first big confrontation came in 1967, when a furor erupted over an editorial that criticized then Police Commissioner Frank Rizzo. In response, the president of the Community Association, Bernard V. Lentz, appointed a committee to make recommendations on editorial policy for the *Local.* Out of its meetings came the so-called Lentz policy, which directed that all letters and editorials be signed so "that the views expressed on the editorial page are clearly and immediately identifiable as the views of the individual writer. . . ."[28] This Lentz policy was reviewed and reaffirmed by the Community Association on several occasions thereafter.

It was clear by the mid-1980s that some Chestnut Hillers continued to be displeased with the *Local,* as well as with the Lentz policy. Although it was often unclear what the critics disliked about the newspaper, it appears that more conservative residents thought that the newspaper was too "left-leaning" in its political opinions and was unfairly critical of President Ronald Reagan, even though the newspaper carefully lived up to its pledge to print articles and letters representing all points of view. It may also have been that critics of the *Local* simply objected to the philosophy of its editor, Marie Jones, who believed that it was better to disseminate all the facts about a given situation, even if they were unpleasant and might lead to further contention.[29]

Whatever the objections may have been, a movement to curb the *Local* began to emerge in about 1985 among some directors of the Community Association. Critical board members requested guidelines for the *Local.* Some of them wanted to forbid the newspaper from commenting on issues before the board until they had been resolved. Others wanted to force the newspaper to confine itself solely to local subjects and to refrain from commenting on national and international affairs.[30]

In defense of the *Local,* a group of residents organized the Committee to Preserve a Free Press in early October 1988, with hundreds more joining them over the next several weeks. The committee's adoption of the name "Free Press" was a public relations coup, because it implied that those who wanted any restrictions on the *Local* opposed a sacred tenet of American democracy. The strategy worked well: letters to the *Local*'s weekly "Forum" section ran overwhelmingly against the idea of restraining the newspaper in any way.[31] At a packed meeting of the Community Association and its board on 27 October, the directors voted 33 to 14, with 3 abstentions, to uphold the Lentz policy. The board also ordered the president of the Community Association, its executive committee, and its committee on the *Local* to "take no further action with regard to this matter."[32]

In order to consolidate its position, the Free Press Committee decided to choose its own slate of candidates for election to the Community Association's board in April 1989. The result was an overwhelming victory for all sixteen of the Free Press candidates. In addition to campaigning for an unencumbered *Local,* many of the Free Press candidates and their supporters had objected to other positions taken by the now defeated leaders of the Community Association. Among these were their stand on historic preservation, particularly as it related to the expansion of Chestnut Hill Hospital, and their proposal that Chestnut Hill secede from Philadelphia. Both of these matters, in turn, bore upon the question of change in the community, and of Chestnut Hill's dual identity as a suburb in the city.

On the matter of secession, some members of the Free Press Committee believed that prosecession members of the Community Association's board wanted to take over the *Local* in order to galvanize support for leaving the city. Whether or not this charge was true, the question of secession exploded at the Community Association's annual meeting in April 1988, when association president Willard S. Detweiler proposed that Chestnut Hill should consider seceding from Philadelphia. At the end of his "state of the community" report he asked, "What would be the benefits of leaving the City of Philadelphia and becoming part of Montgomery County? We keep paying higher taxes to Philadelphia and our services are going down. It's time to take another look at the idea."[33]

As Detweiler alluded, the idea of Chestnut Hill's seceding from the city was not new, having been proposed as early as the 1880s. At first there was much positive reaction to Detweiler's speech. But as time passed, there was more and more opposition to the idea. Because separation would require assent by both city and state, many concluded that it would be legally and politically impossible. Others worried about the costs of having to buy valuable property on the Hill that belonged to the city, such as park land and the Jenks School. Still others pointed out that secession would not remove Chestnut Hill physically from more deteriorated parts of the city to the south and east. Some, like Lloyd Wells, writing from his home in Maine, suspected that the secession movement was really part of a scheme by local Republicans, who were frustrated by Democratic control of Philadelphia and who wanted to merge the Hill with heavily Republican Montgomery County. Then there were those who saw secession as a selfish denial by Chestnut Hillers of any responsibility for the rest of Philadelphia.[34] The victory of the Free Press candidates, all of whom appeared to oppose secession, put an end to the question, at least for the time being.

The other issue of concern to the Free Press group, that of historic preservation, focused on expansion plans of Chestnut Hill Hospital and on the opposition to them by hospital neighbors and the Chestnut Hill Historical Society. In this instance, too, an indeterminate number of those on the Free Press Committee alleged that certain Community Association board members wanted to take control of the *Local* in order to use it as an instrument to support the hospital's position in the dispute.

Since its founding in 1967, the Historical Society had been much involved in the preservation of historic buildings. In recent years it had repaired and restored the Gravers Lane railroad station, designed by the famous Philadelphia architect Frank Furness. In the mid-1980s it had also waged a successful campaign to have nearly all of Chestnut Hill designated as a National Historic District. The district lines were identical to those of Chestnut Hill, with the exception of the Market Square/Chestnut Hill Village development, which was deleted from the district because of its recent construction. This designation as a National Historic District did not make Chestnut Hill a local historic district, and thus it could not claim zoning protection of its historic buildings from Philadelphia authorities. At the time of this writing, the Chestnut Hill Historical Society was considering a campaign to secure such legislation from city council, which would make Chestnut Hill a local historic district.[35]

Complementing these efforts by the Historical Society were preservation projects begun in the 1980s by other institutions on the Hill. Two of them focused on the centenary, in 1984, of Henry Howard Houston's first developments on Wissahickon Heights. In 1982 a neighborhood committee raised $100,000 to restore the St. Martin's railroad station (originally the Wissahickon Heights station). In 1984 Chestnut Hill Academy began a limited restoration of its building on West Willow Grove Avenue, which had once housed Houston's Wissahickon Inn.[36]

None of these efforts proved controversial. However, a lengthy conflict between the Historical Society and Chestnut Hill Hospital began in 1980, when the hospital announced that it would soon demolish three mid-nineteenth-century houses that it owned on the west side of Norwood Avenue. These were known as Norwood (8810), Disston House (8840), and Stevens House (8860). Preservationists opposed the plan, maintaining that Norwood Avenue was of great importance to understanding the architectural and suburban development of Chestnut Hill. For along with Summit Street, Chestnut Hill Avenue, and several other nearby streets, Norwood Avenue was, they argued, an integral part of the community's first railroad suburb in North Chestnut Hill.

Norwood, at 8810 Norwood Ave., during its demolition
in 1980. *Local.*

Actually, Norwood Avenue had undergone serious destruction
even before the hospital made its announcement; the houses on both
corners of Norwood and Chestnut Hill avenues had already been torn
down. The large dwelling on the northeast corner, which had once
housed the Springside School, had been demolished and replaced by
a parking lot for a medical office building. The house on the opposite
corner had been razed by Our Mother of Consolation Church and
likewise made into a parking lot.[37] In the opinion of preservationists,

the hospital's plan to tear down three more houses on Norwood Avenue would complete the destruction of a historic residential street.

In its own behalf, the hospital argued that the three houses cost thousands of dollars each year to maintain for their present usages — one as a private residence, one as a senior citizens center, and one as a convalescent home. Despite protests from the Historical Society, the hospital demolished Norwood (8810) in the summer of 1980. Then, bowing to intense community pressure, the hospital agreed in late 1980 to sell Stevens House (8860) to the Historical Society for one dollar, with the right to repurchase the property in ten years. In 1982 the hospital likewise agreed to sell Disston House (8840) to the society under identical terms.[38]

The dispute between the hospital and preservationists cooled during the mid-1980s, only to reemerge in 1988, when the hospital announced that it planned to build a new parking garage for 210 cars, later reduced to 188 cars. The hospital explained that larger outpatient facilities, as well as service to a wider area that included much of northwest Philadelphia and eastern Montgomery County, made the garage imperative. In order to obtain the necessary zoning variances, the hospital needed to regain ownership of the "green spaces" around Stevens House and Disston House and would probably repurchase them when the agreements with the Historical Society expired in 1990 and 1992. Despite opposition from the Historical Society and the North Chestnut Hill Council, an outspoken neighborhood group, the Community Association endorsed the garage proposal. Philadelphia's Zoning Board of Adjustment awarded the hospital its variance, provided that it worked with the Community Association, the Historical Society, and the North Chestnut Hill Council (which represented the hospital's neighbors) to develop a mutually satisfactory long-range plan for the hospital campus.[39] At the time of this writing, the fate of the two remaining Norwood Avenue houses and the question of hospital expansion had not been resolved. There was reason to believe that a mutually satisfactory agreement would be forged.

Although the dispute with the hospital was about historic preservation on one level, it, like the question of secession, also involved community definition. The suggestion that Chestnut Hill should secede from Philadelphia demonstrated that the old identification with both suburb and city, perhaps best realized during the first decades of the twentieth century, had been eroded. As to the hospital issue, many of the arguments about its expansion centered on whether it should be primarily a community facility that catered to the 10,000 or so residents of Chestnut Hill, or should serve a wider region that included northwest Philadelphia and parts of Montgomery County.

As the 1990s began, several other issues reflected Chestnut Hill's problem of self-identity. Among these were crime and land use. Facing these issues was a Community Association pledged to greater activism in the wake of the Free Press candidates' victory in early 1989. The board elected a new president, Virginia Duke, long a community leader as well as a former protégé and continuing admirer of Lloyd Wells. Because some leaders of the Free Press Committee had opposed both the Greene party and Lloyd Wells in the past, it would not be correct to say that Duke's election and subsequent reelection in 1990 represented a clear-cut vindication of Wells and his supporters. Yet it appeared that much of the energy and activism of the Greene party years had returned.[40]

The crime issue surfaced as incidents began to escalate in Chestnut Hill during the 1980s. In 1980 the daylight abduction and rape of a teenaged girl who had been walking along St. Martin's Lane horrified the community and led residents of the West Side to organize Chestnut Hill's first sustained town watch. A rash of crimes on the East Side also resulted in the creation of a town watch in that section, and in the spring of 1982 the two watches combined their activities.[41]

By 1988 local crime statistics had grown to new and alarming proportions. According to the *Chestnut Hill Local,* whose data were based on the police records, the crime rate on the Hill was three times higher in the summer of 1988 than it had been just a year before. These records also showed that the largest proportion of these crimes was occurring in the Chestnut Hill Village/Market Square area, the part of Chestnut Hill that was closest to East Mount Airy. At the end of the year, the newspaper reported that in 1988 there had been 157 burglaries, 106 car thefts, 39 purse snatchings, 3 rapes, and 1 murder on the Hill. In early January of 1989 the Germantown Savings Bank at 8601 Germantown Avenue was held up. Yet the overburdened police responded very slowly and sometimes not at all to calls from Chestnut Hill. Short-staffed and located two to four miles from the Hill at Germantown and Haines streets, police from the 14th district were simply unable to respond to the increasing flood of crimes in the area, much of it related to Philadelphia's epidemic of illegal drugs. This lack of police protection infuriated local residents and doubtless gave fuel to those who wanted to secede from a city that did not seem able to protect them.[42]

Although the crime figures for Chestnut Hill were low in comparison to most other parts of Philadelphia, the Community Association was determined to combat crime. With the cooperation of the *Local,* it campaigned successfully to have a foot patrolman assigned in early 1990 to the commercial district along Germantown Avenue. This action, in addition to increased activity by town watches and cooperation from the community in seeing that cases were prosecuted, led to one-third fewer crimes in the spring of 1990 than in the spring of 1989. Despite this success, Chestnut Hill was coming to seem more like a part of the city than ever before, and no longer was insulated from most urban problems by its distant location at the edge of Philadelphia.

Controversies over land use demonstrated that many residents of the Hill worried that their community would become so heavily developed and clogged with traffic that it would resemble the densely built-up city below. Most of the concern focused on Germantown Avenue, where rising property values led to more intense development of commercial lots. One such lot, occupied by a Gulf service station, stood in the forks of Germantown Avenue and Bethlehem Pike, where the old Maple Lawn Inn had once stood. The lot's owner sold the property to a developer who proposed to build a cluster of shops that would complement neighboring stores in the Top of the Hill development. Despite the fact that the developer agreed to leave an open area at the forks, in part because of intense community pres-

Officer Mike Hogan, Chestnut Hill's new foot patrolman, is welcomed in April 1990 by Vivian White, administrative assistant to the
Community Association's board of directors. *Local.*

sure, many residents were outraged at the thought of more shops,
traffic, and parking problems.[43] Because of financial difficulties, the
project has not yet been carried through.

The question of open land in residential areas also became a concern, as many residents believed that increasing land values would
tempt institutions as well as private owners to make money by subdividing some of their property. There was also concern that one of
the large institutions in the far northern part of Chestnut Hill might
some day fail and sell its land to developers. In reaction, the Chestnut
Hill Historical Society inaugurated a program that encouraged owners to limit the development of their property by ceding development
rights, in perpetuity, to the society through a land easement. In return, owners would receive tax deductions for the value of their easement donation to the society. The Historical Society's program also
provided for facade easements, which would restrict alterations to the
exteriors of local buildings placed into the program.[44]

Although actions to combat crime, limit overbuilding in the commercial area, and thwart the development of open land were all pos-

The new Cresheim Valley bridge of the Chestnut Hill-West (formerly Pennsylvania) rail line as it appeared in December 1989. *Local.*

itive, some residents detected an unrealistic and unhealthy desire in Chestnut Hill to arrest any kind of change. Such an attitude had led some inhabitants to oppose any new building, even if it meant the replacement of an ugly or bland-looking gasoline station with an attractive and well-landscaped group of new shops. The same mentality had caused residents to complain about the many unfamiliar faces that they see on Germantown Avenue — shoppers from other communities who have come to patronize the "extraordinary shops" of Chestnut Hill. Still others objected to the fact that the regional transit system, SEPTA, uses Chestnut Hill as a transfer point for buses, trains, and trolleys, bringing still more strangers into the community, if only for a few minutes at a time. For the residents of truly deprived parts of Philadelphia, such complaints have seemed both trivial and selfish. News that Chestnut Hill had also obtained a new railroad bridge, at a cost of $7.5 million, for its West Side line also angered residents in less wealthy sections of the city, who concluded that Chestnut Hillers had once more used their social and political power to obtain funds that might be put to better use elsewhere in the city.[45] Outsiders might also be angered, if they were not amused, at the energy and columns of newsprint that residents of Chestnut Hill spent on such inconsequential issues as whether a boxwood hedge, described in several letters to the *Local* as a "modesty screen" for female musicians, should be removed from the outdoor amphitheater in Pastorius Park.[46] Several years earlier, a *cause célèbre* on the Hill had involved demands to remove foul-smelling female ginkgo trees from the shopping district along Germantown Avenue.

Beyond such petty issues, Chestnut Hill would have to work hard to survive as an attractive suburb in the city. Its various civic organizations would have to make more of an effort to represent all segments of the community. Although progress had been made among women and East Side residents, it was essential to include the Hill's growing nonwhite population in the local quasi government. At the same time, these organizations would have to realize that a policy of isolation would not assist Chestnut Hill as the twentieth century came to an end. Nor would an automatic opposition to change help the community to prosper. Surrounded as it was by tens of thousands of people living in dozens of different communities, Chestnut Hill could not hold back the tides of change or chart its own independent course. For the Hill was no longer an isolated village, surrounded by thousands of acres of farmland, at the end of a commuter train line, a fact that local residents would have to accept whether they wanted to or not. Under the circumstances, only close cooperation with other communities, including the city of Philadelphia, would allow Chestnut Hill to face and solve its most outstanding problems. In the process, Chestnut Hill residents would have to redefine who they were and where they lived. Beginning as a gateway village outside the city, Chestnut Hill had become a suburb in the city, and finally a regional community. Contrary to the beliefs of some in the community, Chestnut Hill had never been a "timeless village," in which the forces of change were arrested.

One solution to Chestnut Hill's identity problem might be municipal mergers or annexations that would provide Philadelphia and its four surrounding counties in Pennsylvania with some sort of re-

gional government.[47] Given the anti-urban bias of the outlying suburbs, there was virtually no chance that this would occur. The only
alternative was for Chestnut Hill to cooperate as closely a possible
with its neighbors in finding common solutions for common problems.[48] Here the Community Association and the other elements of
quasi government could play a constructive role.

At the same time, Chestnut Hillers would have to face the painful
realization that it was no longer possible to enjoy all the advantages
of city life without having to take greater responsibility for its negative aspects. At the beginning of the twentieth century, some writers
on cities and suburbs had envisioned an ambitious decentralization
of the city, in which nearly all residents would live in suburbs of some
kind, no matter how modest. Instead, suburban living became a reality for the middle and upper classes, who for decades were able to
ignore the worst deprivations of urban life.

Obviously, Chestnut Hill's quasi government could not even begin to address all of Philadelphia's problems, and in many cases it had
no choice but to concentrate on local difficulties that could be managed at the local level. Nor was it likely that Chestnut Hillers and
their neighbors in suburbs outside the city would desert their homes
and move into the decaying portions of Philadelphia. The bulk of the
region's newer housing stock had already been built in suburbs. It
was also understandable that many families, from the middle of the
nineteenth century to the end of the twentieth, had decided that leaving deteriorating areas of the city was the best alternative for themselves and their families, concluding that their lonely determination
to remain behind in the city would do nothing to arrest the forces of
decay.

Because Philadelphia's municipal government was likely to face
limited funds for the foreseeable future, Chestnut Hill's quasi government would also have to provide many services and amenities that
independent suburbs had long provided for themselves. Chestnut
Hill's habit of persistence would be an asset only if it could modify
the elitist leadership patterns, which had been followed by Progressive reformers early in the twentieth century and in the decades since.
If the Hill's civic organizations could become more representative of

A summer evening band concert in Pastorius Park, a tradition for more than fifty years. Photo by Carl McGuire. *Local.*

the local population and make every effort to cooperate with other communities, both in and outside Philadelphia, the suburb in the city stood a fair chance of succeeding. In approaching these tasks, residents would need to understand the forces that had shaped their community over the past century and a half, and that gave them some indication of what the future might bring.

Appendix

The following tables are referred to in chapter 4.

TABLE 1
Upper-Class Occupations in Chestnut Hill in 1930, Ranked by Percentages of Male Heads of Households Listed in Philadelphia *Social Register*

Occupation	*Number in* Occupation	*Number in* Social Register	*Percentage in* Social Register
Elected office holder	1	1	100.00
Scientist/researcher	4	3	75.00
Architect	9	6	66.67
Real estate	9	6	66.67
Lawyer	48	28	58.33
Banker	35	20	57.14
Broker	22	12	54.55
Physician	19	10	52.63
Insurance executive	11	5	45.45
Corporate executive & substantial business owner	116	52	44.83
Manager	46	18	39.13
College professor	3	1	33.33
Statistician	3	1	33.33
Director, government bureau	7	2	28.57
Manufacturer's agent	4	1	25.00
Manufacturer	9	2	22.22
Artist	5	1	20.00
Sales manager	11	2	18.18
Salesman / Agent	46	7	15.22
Insurance agent	14	2	14.29

Engineer	28	4	14.28
Clergy	12	1	8.33

Total of Individuals = 462
Total in *Social Register* = 185
Total Percentage in *Social Register* = 40.04

Sources: *Philadelphia City Directory*, 1930, and Philadelphia *Social Register*, 1930.
Note: Several individuals are listed in two different occupations.

TABLE 2

**Middle-Class Occupations in Chestnut Hill in 1930,
from Male Heads of Households Who Did Not Appear in
the *Social Register***

Occupation	Number in Occupation
Middle-middle class	
Officer, eleemosynary institution	3
Foreign consul	2
Dentist	6
Patent agent	1
Purchasing agent	2
Advertising	3
Accountant	3
Metallurgist	1
Editor	1
Teacher	5
Buyer	2
Publicity man	1
Supervisor	1
Draftsman	2
Technician	1
Physical therapist	1
Appraiser	1
Notary	1
Sea captain	1
Contractor / Builder	24
Dairy farmer	1
Nursery owner	1
Druggist	4
Jeweler	2
Antique dealer	2
Florist	3
Tailor	5
Undertaker	3
Local shopkeeper	45

Lower-middle class

Bookkeeper	5
Secretary (male)	5
Clerk	48
Inspector	3
Investigator	3
Auctioneer	1
Teller	2
Telegraph operator	3
Landscape gardener	2
Golf professional	1
Apartment superintendent	2
Total Number = 203	

Source: Philadelphia *City Directory,* 1930.

TABLE 3
Working-Class Occupations in Chestnut Hill in 1930, Male Heads of Households

Occupation	*Number in Occupation*
Printer	5
Electrician	3
Millwright	1
Policeman	3
Weaver	1
Tile setter	11
Mason	17
Carpenter	14
Plumber	9
Roofer	2
Tinsmith	2
Marble cutter	1
Stone cutter / Quarrier	5
Floor layer	1
Upholsterer	2
Decorator	2
Machinist	5
Barber	5
Baker	2
Plasterer	1
Paper hanger	5
Painter	5
Garage / Service station worker	6
Mechanic	10
Auto painter	1
Blacksmith	3

Horseshoer	1
Meat cutter	1
Carpet cleaner	1
Railroad worker	12
Mail carrier	1
Foreman	7
Timekeeper	1
Watchman / Guard	11
Truck driver	12
Trolley car motorman	3
Waiter	1
Taxi driver	1
Expressman	1
Shipper	1
Packer	1
Messenger	3
Meterman	1
Meter reader	1
Sexton	1
Janitor	6
Laborer	45
Total Number = 234	

Source: *Philadelphia City Directory,* 1930.

TABLE 4
Male Domestic Servants Who Maintained Their Own Households in Chestnut Hill in 1930

Occupation	*Number in Occupation*
Butler	2
Valet	3
Steward	2
Houseman	2
Chef / Cook	3
Chauffeur	57
Gardener	70
Total Number = 139	

Source: *Philadelphia City Directory,* 1930.
Note: There were hundreds of other domestic servants in Chestnut Hill in 1930 who lived in their employers' homes and therefore did not maintain their own households or appear in the *City Directory.* A large number of these live-in servants clearly were single women.

TABLE 5
Selected Occupations and Zones of Residence in Chestnut Hill in 1930, Male Heads of Households

Occupation	Number in Occupation	North no.	North %	West no.	West %	East no.	East %	Commercial no.	Commercial %
Lawyer	49	17	34.69	29	59.18	3	6.12	—	—
Banker	35	14	40.00	19	54.29	2	5.71	—	—
Physician	19	14	73.68	3	15.79	2	10.53	—	—
Corporate executive and Business proprietor	117	43	26.75	61	52.13	13	11.11	—	—
Engineer	28	8	28.57	8	28.57	12	42.86	—	—
Contractor & builder	24	1	4.17	2	8.33	21	87.50	—	—
Local shopkeeper	44	4	9.09	3	6.82	15	34.09	22	50
Clerk	48	4	8.33	12	25.00	29	60.42	3	6
Mason	17	—	—	—	—	17	100.00	—	—
Mechanic	10	—	—	—	—	10	100.00	—	—
Truck driver	12	—	—	—	—	12	100.00	—	—
Laborer	45	—	—	—	—	45	100.00	—	—
Chauffeur	57	7	12.28	—	—	50	87.72	—	—
Gardener	70	5	7.14	3	4.29	62	88.87	—	—

Source: *Philadelphia City Directory,* 1930.

Note: For a definition of residential boundaries, see text on pages 129 and 131–132 and map on page 130.

TABLE 6
Ethnic Distribution of All Male Heads of Households in Chestnut Hill in 1930 Whose Occupations Were Listed in the *City Directory*, Based on Approximate Ethnicity of Surnames

Ethnic Group	Number of Households	Percent of Households
British	677	64.41
Irish	128	12.18
Germanic	124	11.80
Italian	94	8.94
French	20	1.90
Other	8	0.76
Total Number = 1051		

Sources: *Philadelphia City Directory*, 1930; Patrick Hanks and Flavia Hodges, *A Dictionary of Surnames* (Oxford: Oxford University Press, 1988).

Note: The British category includes English, Welsh, Scottish, and Scotch-Irish surnames. The Germanic category includes surnames of German, Austrian, Swiss, and Scandinavian origins. Because numerous Irish residents of Chestnut Hill worked as domestic servants and lived in their employers' households, the Irish figures in this table do not accurately reflect the total Irish population of the community. It is also clear that a number of Italian workers boarded with various Italian families in the community and thus do not appear in these figures.

TABLE 7
Approximate Ethnic Backgrounds of Employees in Selected Occupations in Chestnut Hill in 1930, Male Heads of Households

		Ethnicity of Surname										
Occupation	Number in Occupation	British no.	%	Germanic no.	%	Irish no.	%	Italian no.	%	French no.	%	Other no.	%
Lawyer	48	44	91.67	4	8.33	–	–	–	–	–	–	–	–
Banker	35	29	82.86	3	8.57	–	–	–	–	3	8.57	–	–
Physician	19	15	78.94	2	10.53	1	5.26	–	–	1	5.26	–	–
Corporate executive and Business proprietor	116	89	76.72	19	16.38	5	4.31	1	0.86	2	1.72	–	–
Engineer	28	24	85.71	–	–	2	7.14	–	–	1	3.57	1	3.57
Contractor & builder	24	10	41.67	5	20.83	3	12.50	5	20.83	–	–	1	4.17
Local shopkeeper	44	22	50.00	7	15.91	6	13.64	9	20.45	–	–	–	–
Clerk	48	31	64.58	12	25.00	4	8.33	–	–	–	–	–	–
Tile setter	11	–	–	–	–	–	–	11	100.00	–	–	–	–
Mason	17	2	11.76	3	17.65	–	–	12	70.59	–	–	–	–
Stone cutter/Quarrier	5	–	–	–	–	–	–	5	100.00	–	–	–	–
Mechanic	10	6	60.00	1	10.00	1	10.00	2	20.00	–	–	–	–
Railroad worker	12	6	50.00	2	16.67	4	33.33	–	–	1	8.33	–	–
Truck driver	12	6	50.00	2	16.67	1	8.33	3	25.00	–	–	–	–
Laborer	45	12	26.67	2	4.44	4	8.88	27	60.00	–	–	–	–

Sources: *Philadelphia City Directory*, 1930; Patrick Hanks and Flavia Hodges, *A Dictionary of Surnames* (Oxford: Oxford University Press, 1988).

TABLE 8

Ethnic Distribution of Male Heads of Households on Selected Streets in Chestnut Hill in 1930, Based on Approximate Ethnicity of Surnames

Street	Number on Street	Ethnicity of Surname									
		British		Germanic		Irish		Italian		Other	
		no.	%	no.	%	no.	%	no.	%	no.	%
Summit St.	16	13	81.25	3	18.75	–	–	–	–	–	–
Seminole Ave.	23	17	73.39	6	26.09	–	–	–	–	–	–
St. Martin's Lane	24	21	87.50	2	8.33	–	–	–	–	1	4.17
Benezet St. (nos. 15–43)	18	16	88.89	2	11.11	–	–	–	–	–	–
Benezet St. (nos. 103–236)	30	13	43.33	1	3.33	8	26.67	8	26.67	–	–
W. Highland Ave. (nos. 14–40)	19	5	26.32	2	10.53	11	57.89	1	5.26	–	–
W. Highland Ave. (nos. 100–212)	46	39	84.78	5	10.87	1	2.17	–	–	1	2.17
W. Highland Ave. (nos. 221–237)	7	2	28.57	–	–	–	–	3	42.86	2	28.57
Devon St. (nos. 7728–39)	6	1	16.67	–	–	–	–	5	83.33	–	–
Shawnee St. (nos. 8115–43)	18	4	22.22	–	–	2	11.11	12	66.67	–	–
Roanoke St. (nos. 8008–40)	19	10	52.63	1	5.26	1	5.26	6	31.57	1	5.26

Sources: *Philadelphia City Directory*, 1930; Patrick Hanks and Flavia Hodges, *A Dictionary of Surnames* (Oxford: Oxford University Press, 1988).

Abbreviations

These abbreviations are used in the captions for the illustrations and maps and in the notes and bibliographic essay.

AAUP	Architectural Archives, University of Pennsylvania
AR	Alumni Records in Archives of University of Pennsylvania
Beehive	*The* [Germantown] *Beehive*
CH&MA Herald	*Chestnut Hill and Mt. Airy Herald*
CHCA	Chestnut Hill Community Association
CHCC	Chestnut Hill Community Center
CHHS	Chestnut Hill Historical Society
Crier	*Germantown Crier*
EHS	Eleanor Houston Smith
ERG	Environmental Research Group
Evening Bulletin	*Philadelphia Evening Bulletin*
G&CHIA	Germantown and Chestnut Hill Improvement Association
Courier	*Germantown Courier*
FJD	Francis James Dallett
GHS	Germantown Historical Society
Guide	*Germantown Guide*
Herald	*The Herald*
HHH	Henry Howard Houston
JPS	Joseph Pennington Straus
Independent-Gazette	*Germantown Independent-Gazette*
Inquirer	*Philadelphia Inquirer*
LCP	Library Company of Philadelphia
LUPC	Land Use Planning Committee

Local	*Chestnut Hill Local*
MFL	Mark Frazier Lloyd
MWPB	Mary Wickham Porcher Bond
NCHA	North Chestnut Hill Association
PH	*Pennsylvania History*
PMHB	*Pennsylvania Magazine of History and Biography*
Public Ledger	*Philadelphia Public Ledger*
LPW	Lloyd P. Wells
PRR	Pennsylvania Railroad
PSA	Pennsylvania State Archives
SMF	St. Martin-in-the-Fields
Telegraph	*Germantown Telegraph*
TUL	Temple University Library
UPA	University of Pennsylvania Archives (general files)

Notes

CHAPTER 1

1. Horace Mather Lippincott, *Chestnut Hill, Springfield, Whitemarsh, Cheltenham* (Jenkintown, PA, 1948), p. 8.

2. John J. Macfarlane, *Early Chestnut Hill* (Philadelphia, 1927), pp. 18–21; Nomination Form, National Register of Historic Places Inventory, Chestnut Hill Historic District, Chestnut Hill Historical Society (CHHS).

3. The author will make occasional exceptions in order to discuss individuals or events in Wyndmoor, the rest of Springfield Township, Mount Airy, and other regions directly bordering on Chestnut Hill, especially when these matters have affected Chestnut Hill or help to illuminate local conditions.

4. Macfarlane, *Early Chestnut Hill*, p. 21.

5. Hannah Benner Roach, "The Back Part of Germantown," *The Pennsylvania Genealogical Magazine* (1956), p. 77.

6. Lippincott, *Chestnut Hill*, p. 11.

7. Accurate population figures for Chestnut Hill are difficult to discover for the early period and must be gathered through indirect sources. See Roach, "Back Part of Germantown," pp. 77, 78, 148; Stephanie Grauman Wolf, *Urban Village: Population, Community, and Family Structure in Germantown, Pennsylvania, 1683–1800* (Princeton, NJ, 1976), p. 42; Harry Tinkcom et al., *Historic Germantown: From the Founding to the Early Part of the Nineteenth Century* (Philadelphia, 1955), p. 1. Figures for 1850 are extrapolated from Gopsill's *City Directory* for 1855 and property tax lists for Chestnut Hill in 1854. The latter were published in the *Germantown Crier* (*Crier*) (Spring 1986), pp. 36–43 and (Summer 1986), pp. 59–65.

8. For an excellent description and analysis of this phenomenon, see Wolf, *Urban Village*, pp. 58–65. See also Edward J. Hocker, *Germantown,*

1683–1933 (Philadelphia, 1933), pp. 21–23; Macfarlane, *Early Chestnut Hill,* pp. 22–29; Roach, "Back Part of Germantown," pp. 126–127.

9. Macfarlane, *Early Chestnut Hill,* pp. 30, 38; John T. Faris, *Old Roads Out of Philadelphia* (Philadelphia, 1917), p. 204; *Chestnut Hill Local (Local),* 12 December 1962; 5 May 1977; 26 October 1978.

10. On gateway villages, see Henry C. Binford, *The First Suburbs: Residential Communities on the Boston Periphery, 1815–1860* (Chicago, 1985).

11. On the economic importance of Philadelphia during this period, see Thomas C. Cochran, "Philadelphia, The American Industrial Center, 1750–1850," *Pennsylvania Magazine of History and Biography (PMHB)* (July 1981), pp. 324–340. For a brief but excellent discussion of the pre-nineteenth-century suburb, see Robert Fishman, *Bourgeois Utopias: The Rise and Fall of Suburbia* (New York, 1987), pp. 6–9.

12. Macfarlane, *Early Chestnut Hill,* pp. 53, 55.

13. Ibid., pp. 47, 51; Lippincott, *Chestnut Hill,* p. 17; Roach, "Back Part of Germantown," pp. 147–148.

14. See Eve Kornfeld, "Crisis in the Capital: The Cultural Significance of Philadelphia's Great Yellow Fever Epidemic," *Pennsylvania History (PH)* (July 1984), pp. 189–205; Hocker, *Germantown,* pp. 126–131; Macfarlane, *Early Chestnut Hill,* p. 49.

15. The yellow fever epidemic of 1793, and of subsequent years, also brought many prosperous Philadelphians to Germantown for the first time and likewise made that community into a summer resort. See Wolf, *Urban Village,* pp. 98–99; Hocker, *Germantown,* pp. 131–162; Lippincott, *Chestnut Hill,* pp. 15–16; Macfarlane, *Early Chestnut Hill,* pp. 47–50.

16. On the origins and naming of Chestnut Hill streets and roads, see Jefferson Moak, "Street Names of Chestnut Hill," *The Chestnut Hill Almanac,* No. 1 (Philadelphia, 1986).

17. Macfarlane, *Early Chestnut Hill,* p. 46.

18. Ibid., pp. 40–46; Hocker, *Germantown,* pp. 42–45; John McArthur Harris, Jr., *Local,* 29 March 1973. For a good account of the Wissahickon mills as part of Philadelphia's industrial archaeology, see Jane Mork Gibson, "Chestnut Hill," chapt. 10 of *Workshop of the World: A Selective Guide to the Industrial Archaeology of Philadelphia* (Wallingford, PA, 1990).

19. For an unsentimental account of Chestnut Hill's experience in the Revolution, see Roach, "Back Part of Germantown," pp. 124–134. A more romantic view may be found in Lippincott, *Chestnut Hill,* pp. 56–69; and Macfarlane, *Early Chestnut Hill,* pp. 79–86. Macfarlane also provides a list of local residents who served in the militia during that period.

20. Wolf, *Urban Village,* pp. 127–153. Roach's account of early Chest-

nut Hill families and their properties in the "Back Part of Germantown" also demonstrates the heterogeneous quality of Chestnut Hill's early population.

21. Wolf, *Urban Village*, pp. 215–216.

22. Macfarlane, *Early Chestnut Hill*, pp. 56–59.

23. Ibid., p. 63.

24. Ibid., pp. 64–66.

25. In *Urban Village*, pp. 229–230, Stephanie Wolf writes, "The Germantown churches, in fact, seem to have played a very small role in the overall life of the community, even after they were organized and running in a fairly smooth and continuous way. By and large they had little influence on neighborhood development throughout the township. Unlike Germany, where the parishioners clustered around the village church and turned out at the sound of the bells, in Germantown the church bells were heard more frequently by members of another congregation."

26. Wolf, *Urban Village*, pp. 58–125; Roach, "Back Part of Germantown," passim.

27. The source for this information is Gopsill's *City Directory* for 1855. The Chestnut Hill names are listed separately — for the first and last times — at the end of the volume.

28. For figures on occupations in Germantown during an earlier though somewhat parallel period in its development, see Wolf, *Urban Village*, pp. 106–107.

29. Macfarlane, *Early Chestnut Hill*, p. 142; S. F. Hotchkin, *Ancient and Modern Germantown, Mount Airy, and Chestnut Hill* (Philadelphia, 1889), pp. 456–457; The Rev. Thomas Middleton, O.S.A., "Some Memoirs of Our Lady's Shrine at Chestnut Hill, Pa.," *Records of the American Catholic Historical Society of Philadelphia* (1901), pp. 23–24.

30. *Germantown Telegraph (Telegraph)*, 2 July 1845, 6 September 1854.

31. For a discussion of how this phenomenon applied to Germantown and the other settlements in German Township, see Wolf, *Urban Village*, pp. 155–159.

32. Alexis de Tocqueville, *Democracy in America* (New York, 1956 [1835]), p. 198.

33. See E. Digby Baltzell, *Puritan Boston and Quaker Philadelphia* (New York, 1979), pp. 109–175.

34. On Germantown's early government, see Wolf, *Urban Village*, pp. 160–176; Hocker, *Germantown*, pp. 31–42.

35. Macfarlane, *Early Chestnut Hill*, pp. 72–73.

36. Ibid., pp. 72–74; Lippincott, *Chestnut Hill*, pp. 33–34.

37. *Germantown Independent* (*Independent*), 10 August 1906; Macfarlane, *Early Chestnut Hill*, pp. 70–71.

38. Ibid., pp. 75, 112, 118; the [Germantown] *Beehive* (September 1922), p. 20; Edward W. Hocker, abstracts of news and advertisements in the *Germantown Telegraph*, 1830–1868 and *Germantown Chronicle*, 1869–1872, p. 114, Germantown Historical Society (GHS).

CHAPTER 2

1. One of the earliest writers to remark upon the dual identities of suburban commuters was Paul Harlan Douglass in *The Suburban Trend* (New York, 1925), pp. 3–4, 84–85. However, this sense of duality has not received much scholarly attention in recent decades.

2. On the division of Philadelphia into various neighborhoods and sections, see William W. Cutler and Howard Gillette, Jr. (eds.), *The Divided Metropolis: Social and Spatial Dimensions of Philadelphia, 1800–1975* (Westport, CT, 1980).

3. Cochran, "Philadelphia: The American Industrial Center," *PMHB*, pp. 323–340; Marion V. Brewington, "Maritime Philadelphia, 1609–1837," *PMHB* (January 1939), pp. 116–117; Barbara Fisher, "Maritime History of the Reading," *PMHB* (April 1962), pp. 161–165; William S. Hastings, "Philadelphia in Microcosm," *PMHB* (April 1967), pp. 164–180; Nicholas B. Wainwright, "The Age of Nicholas Biddle, 1825–1841," in Russell F. Weigley (ed.), *Philadelphia: A 300-Year History* (New York, 1982), pp. 236–239.

4. On the early history of the Pennsylvania Railroad, see James A. Ward, *J. Edgar Thomson, Master of the Pennsylvania* (Westport, CT, 1980); and George H. Burgess and Miles C. Kennedy, *Centennial History of the Pennsylvania Railroad Company, 1846–1946* (Philadelphia, 1949).

5. Sam Bass Warner, *The Private City: Philadelphia in Three Periods of Its Growth* (Philadelphia, 1968); and Elizabeth Geffen, "Industrial Development and Social Crisis," *Philadelphia: A 300-Year History*, pp. 309, 326–327.

6. Ibid., pp. 325–336.

7. Ibid., p. 318; and Elizabeth Geffen, "Violence in Philadelphia in the late 1840s and 1850s," *PH* (October 1969), pp. 381–410.

8. Michael McCarthy, "The Philadelphia Consolidation Act of 1854: A Reappraisal," *PMHB* (October 1986), pp. 531–584; Eli K. Price, *The History of the Consolidation of the City of Philadelphia* (Philadelphia, 1873); and Russell R. Weigley, "The Border City in the Civil War, 1854–1965," *Philadelphia: A 300-Year History*, p. 361.

9. *Telegraph,* 12 February 1851. See also 4 January, 19 February, and 24 September 1851.

10. Hocker, *Germantown,* pp. 220–221. On the subject of living in Chestnut Hill for political reasons, see E. Digby Baltzell, *Philadelphia Gentlemen: The Making of a National Upper Class* (Philadelphia, 1979), p. 207.

11. One of the best works on romanticism, which explains the differences between it and the principal movements before and after, remains Jacques Barzun's *Classic, Romantic, and Modern* (Chicago, 1961). On romantic suburbs and homes, see Colleen McDannell, *The Christian Home in Victorian America* (Bloomington, IN, 1986). A contemporary view of the suburban home may be found in Andrew Jackson Downing, *The Architecture of Country Houses* (New York, 1969 [1850]), pp. 257–270; and in Catherine Beecher and Harriet Beecher Stowe, *The American Woman's Home* (New York, 1869). Also enlightening on this subject are Fishman, *Bourgeois Utopias,* pp. 18–72; Kenneth Jackson, *Crabgrass Frontier: The Suburbanization of the United States* (New York, 1985), pp. 45–103; and Gwendolyn Wright, *Building the American Dream* (New York, 1981), pp. 96–113.

12. *Telegraph,* 4 February 1852.

13. Ibid., 2 April 1851.

14. Hotchkin, *Ancient and Modern,* p. 451.

15. Quoted in Francis Burke Brandt, *The Wissahickon Valley Within the City of Philadelphia* (Philadelphia, 1927), p. 49.

16. *Local,* 5 April 1984.

17. Edgar Allan Poe, "Morning on the Wissahickon," in *The Unabridged Edgar Allan Poe* (Philadelphia, 1983), p. 849.

18. Hocker, *Germantown,* pp. 126–131.

19. Ibid., pp. 163–173; Wainwright, "Age of Nicholas Biddle," p. 272.

20. Hocker, Abstracts, pp. 8, 13.

21. Ibid., p. 58; *Telegraph,* 29 January 1851.

22. *Telegraph,* 12 May, 4 August 1858; 29 June 1859; 9 August 1865; *Germantown Guide (Guide),* 4 November 1893. On the development of the horsecar, or street railway as it was often called, and its impact on suburbanization, see Sam Bass Warner, Jr., *Streetcar Suburbs: The Process of Growth in Boston 1870–1900* (Cambridge, MA, 1962), pp. 21–29, 49–66, 74–75. See also Jackson, *Crabgrass Frontier,* pp. 105–107.

23. "Centennial History of St. Paul's Church, Chestnut Hill" (Philadelphia, 1956), p. 1; Gopsill's *City Directory,* 1882. According to Macfarlane's *Early Chestnut Hill,* pp. 141–142, others who may have commuted from Chestnut Hill down to the train station at Germantown included Ambrose White, Cephas G. Childs, William Platt and his brother Clayton Platt, Francis Buck, Thomas Earp, Joseph Thompson, Hiram Hartwell, Samuel Austin, Charles Taylor, J. E. Mitchell, and John Bohlen.

24. Hocker, *Germantown*, p. 171; Hocker, Abstracts, pp. 52, 60, 61, 62.

25. *Telegraph*, 23 April 1851.

26. Ibid., 14 April 1852.

27. McElroy's *City Directory*, 1851, 1855; *Appleton's Cyclopedia of American Biography*, vol. 5, p. 335; *Dictionary of American Biography* (*DAB*) (New York, 1930), vol. 4, pp. 69–70. I am indebted to Francis James Dallett (FJD) for bringing this, and much other information on the early suburban residents of Chestnut Hill, to my attention.

28. *Telegraph*, 20 August 1851; 14 January, 25 February, 5 May, 23 June, 1 December 1852; 6 April, 15 September 1853; 26 April 1854; *Local*, 29 April 1964; Hotchkin, *Ancient and Modern*, p. 496.

29. *Telegraph*, 10 January 1855; 5 March 1856.

30. Hotchkin, *Ancient and Modern*, p. 495; Lippincott, *Chestnut Hill*, pp. 19–20; "Lease and Contract Between the Chestnut Hill Railroad Company and The Philadelphia and Reading Company," GHS.

31. See John Stilgoe, *Metropolitan Corridor: Railroads and the American Scene* (New Haven, CT, 1983), pp. 263–282; and John Stilgoe, *Borderland: Origins of the American Suburb, 1820–1939* (New Haven, CT, 1988), pp. 127–150.

32. Hotchkin, *Ancient and Modern*, p. 508; "Summit Street in Chestnut Hill," pamphlet published by the Chestnut Hill Historical Society (CHHS) (Philadelphia, 1974).

33. I am indebted to Mark Frazier Lloyd (MFL) for this insight.

34. "Summit Street," p. 3. See also G. M. Hopkins and Company, *City Atlas of Philadelphia*, vol. 1, 22nd Ward (Philadelphia, 1876), pp. 18–19.

35. I am thankful to James Duffin for this information about property development in the mid-nineteenth century.

36. Marian Willis Martin Rivinus, *A Full Life*, privately printed, pp. 21–22; Interview with Philip Price, Sr., 16 July 1985.

37. Hotchkin, *Ancient and Modern*, pp. 437–438; "Summit Street," pp. 6–30; Willard S. Detweiler, Jr., *Chestnut Hill: An Architectural History* (Philadelphia, 1969), pp. 48–59.

38. See Robert A. M. Stern, *Pride of Place* (Boston, 1986), pp. 125–167; and Kristine Ottensen Garrigan, *Ruskin on Architecture* (Madison, WI, 1973), pp. 29–61.

39. "Summit Street," pp. 21, 29; Jefferson Moak, Chestnut Hill Historic District Inventory, CHHS, pp. 333, 335.

40. "Summit Street," pp. 19–20; Moak, Inventory, p. 333.

41. Hotchkin, *Ancient and Modern*, pp. 466–467; Gopsill's *City Directory*, 1870.

42. Hotchkin, *Ancient and Modern*, pp. 507–508; Baltzell, *Philadelphia Gentlemen*, p. 74; Gopsill's *City Directory*, 1870, 1875; Frederick A. God-

charles, *A Pennsylvania Political, Governmental, Military, and Civil Biographical Volume* (New York, n.d.), pp. 8–9.

43. Hotchkin, *Ancient and Modern*, pp. 473–478.

44. Detweiler, *Architectural History*, p. 71; Moak, Inventory, p. 95.

45. Hotchkin, *Ancient and Modern*, pp. 444, 445; *Telegraph*, 19 October 1887.

46. Detweiler, *Architectural History*, p. 67; Moak, Inventory, p. 152.

47. For more precise data about these properties, see Moak, Inventory, pp. 135, 139, 140, 142.

48. Hotchkin, *Ancient and Modern*, pp. 473–474; Godcharles, *Pennsylvania Biographical*, pp. 8–9; *Minutes of the Farmers' Club of Pennsylvania . . . , 1849–1919*; *DAB*, vol. 4, pp. 69–70.

49. Hotchkin, *Ancient and Modern*, pp. 509–510; Lippincott, *Chestnut Hill*, pp. 18–19; Moak, Inventory, p. 42.

50. *Telegraph*, 29 January 1856; Hocker, Abstracts, p. 180.

51. Jefferson Moak, "The Dustpan," *Local*, 8 February 1990, pp. 1, 19, 21, 22.

52. Lippincott, *Chestnut Hill*, pp. 18–19; Edwin C. Jellett, Scrapbooks on the Wissahickon Creek, 9 vols., GHS, vol. 5, p. 72; *Local*, 12 August 1982.

53. Brandt, *The Wissahickon*, p. 39.

54. Martha J. King, "The Mower United States Army General Hospital," *Chestnut Hill Historical Society Newsletter* (Winter 1984); *Local*, 3 July 1969; Jane Campbell, Scrapbooks, 49 vols., GHS, vol. 17, pp. 63–64; Hocker, Abstracts, p. 105.

55. *Telegraph*, 4 May and 19 October 1887; *Germantown Independent-Gazette* (*Independent-Gazette*), 2 September 1910; 15 July 1920; *Beehive* (July 1928), pp. 1–3, 16–17; *Local*, 30 September 1971; 15 September 1977.

56. Hocker, Abstracts, p. 99; *Guide*, 28 December 1895; *Germantown Courier* (*Courier*), 26 January 1939; *Local*, 5 March 1970; Conversation with MWPB, 3 August 1990.

57. *Crier* (Spring 1986), p. 40.

58. Hocker, Abstracts, p. 83; *Telegraph*, 29 November 1865; *Local*, 17 August 1978.

59. *Telegraph*, 30 November 1853.

60. There is some difference of opinion about the opening date, with some sources stating 1871 and others 1872.

61. Macfarlane, *Early Chestnut Hill*, pp. 188–199; Hotchkin, *Ancient and Modern*, pp. 427–428; Hocker, Abstracts, p. 119; *Guide*, 30 January 1909; *Local*, 27 September 1973.

62. Macfarlane, *Early Chestnut Hill*, p. 66.

63. Hotchkin, *Ancient and Modern*, pp. 426–427; Macfarlane, *Early*

Chestnut Hill, pp. 66–68; Hocker, p. 66; "One Hundredth Anniversary, Presbyterian Church of Chestnut Hill" (1952); *Local*, 12 May 1977; Moak, Inventory, p. 131.

64. Hotchkin, *Ancient and Modern*, pp. 445–447; Macfarlane, *Early Chestnut Hill*, p. 68; "Centennial History of St. Paul's Church"; *Telegraph*, 20 September 1854; Moak, Inventory, p. 31; Baltzell, *Philadelphia Gentlemen*, pp. 205–206.

65. Macfarlane, *Early Chestnut Hill*, pp. 68–69; The Rev. T. W. Kretschmann, "Historical Sketch of the Evangelical Lutheran Christ Church" (1896); "Evangelical Lutheran Christ Church of Chestnut Hill, 1860–1960" (1960); Moak, Inventory, p. 117.

66. Macfarlane, *Early Chestnut Hill*, p. 69; Hotchkin, *Ancient and Modern*, pp. 455–456; *The Parish of Our Mother of Consolation* (1955).

67. The college was originally known as Mount St. Joseph's College, the name being changed to The College of Chestnut Hill in the 1930s. Through popular usage over the years, it has come to be known simply as Chestnut Hill College.

68. Sister Maria Kostka Logue, S.S.J., *Sisters of St. Joseph of Philadelphia—A Century of Growth and Development, 1847–1947* (Westminster, MD, 1950); John Lukacs, *A Sketch of the History of Chestnut Hill College, 1924–1974* (Philadelphia, 1975); *Local*, 26 August 1976; 11 May 1983.

69. Macfarlane, *Early Chestnut Hill*, pp. 77–78; Hocker, Abstracts, p. 61; Hotchkin, *Ancient and Modern*, pp. 426–427; Lippincott, *Chestnut Hill*, p. 27; *Biographical and Historical Catalogue of Washington and Jefferson College . . . , 1802–1902*, p. 99.

70. *Springside School, 1879–1979: One Hundred Years of Tradition and Change* (Philadelphia, 1979), pp. 7–11.

71. Ibid., p. 11.

72. *Telegraph*, 29 May 1857.

73. Ibid.

CHAPTER 3

1. For a biography of Henry Howard Houston, see David R. Contosta, *A Philadelphia Family: The Houstons and Woodwards of Chestnut Hill* (Philadelphia, 1988).

2. Baltzell, *Philadelphia Gentlemen*, pp. 12–13.

3. Contosta, *Philadelphia Family*, pp. 1–11, 129.

4. *Case of Christ Church, Germantown* (Philadelphia, 1872), pp. 5–20; "Christ Church, Germantown," *The Church Standard*, 4 March 1899; "St. Peter's Germantown," *The Church Standard*, 18 March 1899; Theodore S.

Rumney and Charles Bullock, *History of St. Peter's, Germantown* (Philadelphia, 1897).

5. Contosta, *Philadelphia Family,* p. 8; Baltzell, *Philadelphia Gentlemen,* pp. 223–261.

6. Interview with Eleanor Houston Smith (EHS), 11 December 1984.

7. *Philadelphia Evening Bulletin* (*Evening Bulletin*), 18 March 1950; Interview with MFL, 15 September 1986.

8. Pennsylvania Railroad (PRR) Board file no. 8; PRR Board Minutes, 6 August 1879; 8 September 1880; 16 December 1882; *Evening Bulletin,* 30 August 1879; Hotchkin, *Ancient and Modern,* p. 417.

9. I am indebted to a letter from Robert Fishman for this possible explanation of Houston's behavior. In Fishman's words, "One might look to the Venetian nobility in the time of Palladio[,] who increasingly abandoned the risks of trade to invest their capital in villas on the Venetian terrafirma. Certainly there is a parallel retreat from direct involvement in risky enterprises and the same kind of attempt to build a counter-world based on beauty, stability, and anti-urban values." Robert Fishman to author, 9 November 1989.

10. Lippincott, *Chestnut Hill,* p. 18.

11. Sandra L. Tatman and Roger W. Moss, *Biographical Dictionary of Philadelphia Architects: 1700–1930* (Boston, 1985), pp. 367–368, 375–376.

12. Contosta, *Philadelphia Family,* p. 27; Lippincott, *Chestnut Hill,* p. 18; Hotchkin, *Ancient and Modern,* p. 401.

13. *Telegraph,* 20 July 1887.

14. Henry Howard Houston (HHH) Rent Book, Alumni Records (AR), University of Pennsylvania Archives (UPA).

15. Contosta, *Philadelphia Family,* pp. 27–28.

16. *Guide,* 30 April 1902.

17. Horace Mather Lippincott, *A History of the Philadelphia Cricket Club* (Philadelphia, 1954), p. 16.

18. *Guide,* 23 May 1896; 28 May 1898; 27 May 1899; 4 May 1901.

19. Ibid., 16 May 1903; 1 June 1907; 30 May 1908.

20. Lippincott, *Cricket Club,* pp. 11–16, 29.

21. E. Digby Baltzell, *The Protestant Establishment* (New York, 1964), pp. 4, 66–68, 113, 197–224.

22. David R. Contosta, *The Church of St. Martin-in-the-Fields, Chestnut Hill, 1889–1989* (Philadelphia, 1988), pp. 15–16, 36–38, 72; Contosta, *Philadelphia Family,* p. 35.

23. The Rev. Jacob LeRoy, quoted in *The Parish News of St. Martin-in-the-Fields* (May 1890).

24. *Telegraph,* 1 June 1887.

25. Interviews with EHS, 11 December 1984, 14 November 1986.

26. Baltzell, *Protestant Establishment*, p. 161.

27. Contosta, *St. Martin*, pp. 22–24, 34, 74, 78.

28. *Guide*, 9 August 1890; 25 April and 8 August 1891; 11 June 1892; 1 June 1895; 30 May 1896; Jellett, Wissahickon, vol. 6, p. 128; "Buttercup Cottage, A Summer Home for Working Girls," pamphlet file, GHS; Contosta, *St. Martin*, pp. 22–23.

29. *Philadelphia Public Ledger*, 1 April 1884.

30. Moak, "Street Names."

31. Wissahickon Heights Plan, EHS collection.

32. Stern, *Pride of Place*, pp. 127–135; *Parish News* (November 1961), p. 5; Moak, "Street Names."

33. Hotchkin, *Ancient and Modern*, p. 417.

34. HHH, Rent Book.

35. Ibid.

36. *New York Times*, 31 December 1927; Philadelphia *Record*, 31 December 1927; Charleston *News and Courier*, 7 April 1944; Concise autobiography of Samuel Porcher, in *Book of Old Boys*, Episcopal High School of Virginia, Centennial Celebration, 1939.

37. Mary Wickham (Porcher) Bond (MWPB), *Ninety Years at Home in Philadelphia* (Bryn Mawr, PA, 1988), pp. 1–2.

38. Hotchkin, *Ancient and Modern*, pp. 422–423; *Local*, 15 May 1986; memorandum from FJD to author (n.d.).

39. George William Sheldon, *Country Seats* (New York, 1887), p. 71.

40. Hotchkin, *Ancient and Modern*, pp. 422–424; *Philadelphia Press*, 25 September 1885; *Local*, 15 May 1986.

41. Interview with Joseph Galante, 25 February 1985.

42. McCallum Street Bridge Contract, EHS collection.

43. PRR Minutes, 9 March, 22 June, 14 December 1892.

44. Contosta, *Philadelphia Family*, pp. 135–136.

45. Ibid., pp. 38, 41, 117–118.

46. Interview with Stanley Woodward, 21 June 1985.

47. Contosta, *Philadelphia Family*, pp. 50, 68, 75.

48. See George Woodward, *Memoirs of a Mediocre Man* (Philadelphia, 1935), pp. 1–88; Contosta, *Philadelphia Family*, pp. 45–52.

49. For characteristics of the Progressive reformers, see Robert M. Crunden, *Ministers of Reform* (New York, 1982), pp. 3–15.

50. David R. Contosta, "George Woodward, Philadelphia Progressive," *PMHB* (July 1987), pp. 341–370; Contosta, *Philadelphia Family*, pp. 53–62.

51. For example, see George Woodward, *The Pennsylvania Legislator*, vol. 5 (Philadelphia, 1941), pp. 231–234.

52. On the Arts and Crafts Movement in the United States, see Eileen

Boris, *Art and Labor: Ruskin, Morris, and the Craftsman Ideal in America* (Philadelphia, 1986); R. J. Clark (ed.), *The Arts and Crafts Movement in America, 1876–1916* (Princeton, 1972); and Wendy Kaplan (ed.), *"The Art That Is Life": The Arts and Crafts Movement in America, 1876–1920* (Boston, 1987).

53. *Arts and Crafts Essays by Members of the Arts and Crafts Exhibition Society*, with a preface by William Morris (London, 1903); Cynthia Ann McLoed, "Arts and Crafts Architecture in Suburban Philadelphia Sponsored by Dr. George Woodward" (University of Virginia master's thesis, 1979), pp. 16–21.

54. Ebenezer Howard, *Garden Cities of Tomorrow* (London, 1902).

55. On the English Garden City movement, see Robert Fishman, *Urban Utopias in the Twentieth Century: Ebenezer Howard, Frank Lloyd Wright, and Le Corbusier* (New York, 1977), pp. 23–88.

56. On the Garden City movement in the United States, see Carol A. Christensen, *The American Garden City and the New Towns Movement* (Ann Arbor, MI, 1986); and Daniel Schaffer, *Garden Cities for America* (Philadelphia, 1982).

57. McLeod, "Arts and Crafts Architecture," pp. 16–19.

58. William H. Wilson, *The City Beautiful Movement* (Baltimore, 1989), pp. 99–146.

59. Woodward, *Memoirs*, pp. 155–157.

60. Ibid., pp. 105–106.

61. Ibid., p. 106.

62. Ibid.

63. Robert H. Wiebe, *The Search for Order, 1877–1920* (New York, 1967), p. 139.

64. See Patricia Mooney Melvin, *The Organic City: Definition and Community Organization, 1880–1920* (Lexington, KY, 1987).

65. For example, Adna Ferrin Weber, *The Growth of Cities in the Nineteenth Century* (New York, 1963 [1899]), pp. 446–475.

66. See Alan Axelrod (ed.), *The Colonial Revival in America* (New York, 1985), especially pp. 1–14 and 71–90; and Karal Ann Marling, *George Washington Slept Here: Colonial Revivals and America Culture* (Cambridge, MA, 1988). See also Walter C. Kidney, *The Architecture of Choice* (New York, 1974).

67. Tatman and Moss, *Philadelphia Architects*, p. 221.

68. George Woodward, "Another Aspect of the Quadruple House," *The Architectural Record* (July 1913), pp. 51–55. See also Matlack Price, "Architecture and the Housing Problem: Recent Work of Duhring, Okie, and Ziegler," *The Architectural Record* (September 1913), pp. 241–247; Moak, Inventory, pp. 29–31.

69. Woodward, "Another Aspect," p. 51.

70. Ibid., p. 52.

71. Minutes of the Vestry of the Church of St. Martin-in-the-Fields, 5 January, 26 April 1916, vol. 2, pp. 49, 55.

72. Woodward, *Memoirs,* p. 103.

73. Ibid., pp. 103–104.

74. Ibid., p. 66; Moak, Inventory, p. 321.

75. For a more extensive discussion of Woodward's Pastorius Park project, see Mary Corbin Sies, "American Country House Architecture in Context: The Suburban Ideal of Living in the East and Midwest, 1877–1917" (University of Michigan, doctoral diss., 1987), pp. 272–353; Contosta, *Philadelphia Family,* pp. 69–70.

76. Harold D. Eberlein, "Pastorius Park and Its Residential Development," *The Architectural Record* (January 1916), p. 25.

77. Contosta, *Philadelphia Family,* pp. 68–69.

78. Plans and correspondence relating to the creation of Pastorius Park may be found in the Houston Estate file, Architectural Archives, University of Pennsylvania (AAUP).

79. Tatman and Moss, *Philadelphia Architects,* pp. 304, 514–515; McLeod, "Arts and Crafts Architecture," pp. 52–58.

80. Woodward, *Memoirs,* p. 109.

81. Moak, Inventory, pp. 200, 250–251, 365.

82. See Christopher Gray, "The French Village," *House and Garden* (December 1983), pp. 82, 84, 86, 88.

83. I am indebted for these insights to a lecture by Carol Franklin, delivered 18 June 1989 at Springside School and entitled "The Wissahickon Style." Franklin's ideas are also presented in the *Local,* 30 August 1990.

84. George Woodward, "Landlord and Tenant," *The Survey* (11 December 1920), p. 391.

85. In the *Pennsylvania Legislator* he asked, "What adequate punishment is there for the men who stripped a little Jewish girl of her clothing, . . . threw her into a closed chamber filled with cyanide gas and cremated her body[?]" He agreed with Secretary of State Henry Morgenthau that Germany should be turned into a land of subsistence farmers after the war. He added, "Dr. Goebbels would be forced [every year] to announce in Yiddish the observance of Yom Kippur in Berlin." See Woodward, *Pennsylvania Legislator,* vol. 7, p. 79.

86. This kind of selective or partial anti-Semitism is discussed in David A. Gerber (ed.), *Anti-Semitism in American History* (Chicago, 1986), pp. 3–7.

87. See Nathaniel Burt, *The Perennial Philadelphians* (Boston, 1963), p. 11.

88. Woodward, "Landlord and Tenant," p. 39.

89. Contosta, *Philadelphia Family*, p. 71.

90. Actually, the school took both boys and girls until about third grade. In the upper grades, it was wholly a girls school.

91. See, for example, Michael H. Ebner, *Creating Chicago's North Shore* (Chicago, 1988); Jackson, *Crabgrass Frontier*, pp. 73–86; Fishman, *Bourgeois Utopias*, pp. 134–154; Stern, *Pride of Place*, pp. 125–146; Sies, "The Suburban Ideal," pp. 206–362.

92. Woodward, "Landlord and Tenant," pp. 389–390.

93. Ibid., p. 389.

CHAPTER 4

1. This association between nineteenth-century suburbs and the social insecurity of recently wealthy or successful individuals is explored in Fishman, *Bourgeois Utopias*, pp. 142–154.

2. Baltzell, *Philadelphia Gentlemen*, p. 205.

3. Baltzell uses the *Social Register* as a guide to upper-class membership in his *Philadelphia Gentlemen*, as does Burt in *The Perennial Philadelphians*.

4. Baltzell, pp. 71–77.

5. These names and occupations were found in the *City Directory* for 1930.

6. Ibid.

7. Ibid.

8. *Who's Who in America, 1930–1931.*

9. The author counted only male heads of household, because very few of the already small number of women listed in the *City Directory* for Chestnut Hill designated an occupation.

10. The disparity between these 185 *Social Register* listings and the 550 or so listings for Chestnut Hill as a whole can be explained in several ways. There were some individuals living just outside the city of Philadelphia, such as in Wyndmoor, or in the upper reaches of West Mount Airy, who were designated as having Chestnut Hill addresses by the *Social Register*. Then there were those men in the *Social Register* who were retired or not gainfully employed; consequently, they were not given occupational designations in the *City Directory*. It also seems that some men simply did not report their occupations to the *Directory* or, if they did, gave their business rather than their residential addresses. Finally, there were a number of single or widowed women in the *Social Register* who were not employed and thus were not carried in the *City Directory*.

11. For the purposes of creating such a list, the author has adapted the occupational stratifications used by Irving Krauss in *Stratification, Class, and Conflict* (New York, 1976), pp. 83–85.

12. Eleanor Ward Altemus, *Chestnut Hill's Main Street Shopping, 1930–1935* (Bryn Mawr, PA, 1984), pp. 17, 60–62.

13. Interview with William E. Gillies, 1 July 1985.

14. Interview with Henry T. O'Donnell, 26 May 1988.

15. One might also arrive at this figure by multiplying the 1,051 male heads of household listed in the *City Directory* by 4.11, the average family size in the United States in 1930. This would give a population of 4,319 — far less than the number who actually lived in the community at the time. There is, of course, no accurate count for Chestnut Hill itself in 1930, given the unavailability of census manuscripts for that year, but estimates put the population at between 7,500 and 8,000 in 1920. By 1960 approximately 9,000 resided there. Because there was considerable residential construction on the Hill in the 1920s, and comparatively little between 1930 and 1960, a population of 8,500 for 1930 seems reasonable. This would then leave more than 4,000 people unaccounted for by the *City Directory* (i.e., male heads of household multiplied by the average family size for that time.) Some male heads of household simply did not give their occupations to the *Directory*, and widows (some of whom had children) and single women were not listed unless they were employed outside their homes. Live-in servants may well have accounted for many of the rest. See *Independent-Gazette*, 8 July 1920; *Herald*, 13 February 1958, 1 June 1961.

16. Edward Pessen, *The Log Cabin Myth* (New Haven, CT, 1984), p. 63.

17. Studies of social mobility in the twentieth century have indeed found that opening a small retail business is a means that has been employed by working-class individuals who aspired to enter the lower-middle class by becoming self-employed. See, for example, Seymour M. Lipset and Reinhard Bendix, "Intragenerational Occupational Mobility in Oakland [California]," in Edward Pessen (ed.), *Three Centuries of Social Mobility in America* (Lexington, MA, 1974), pp. 260–283.

18. Interview with the Rev. John F. Casey, O.S.A., 26 February 1985.

19. Articles in the *Local* state that the Methodist and Lutheran congregations have ranged between 100 and 150 members each in the twentieth century, and that the Baptist church claimed only forty members in 1984. These figures appear to have been given to the newspaper by the churches themselves. See *Local*, 6 November 1980, 16 June 1983, 6 September 1984.

CHAPTER 5

1. Baltzell, *Philadelphia Gentlemen*, pp. 205–206. Baltzell's claim for St. Paul's greater prominence is generally admitted, however politely, by members of the two churches.

2. Contosta, *St. Martin*, pp. 47–51.

3. Interview with John McArthur Harris, Jr., 18 February 1985.

4. Interviews with Anna N. Mastroni, 1 June 1985; Josephine and Francis Vecchione, 11 June 1985; and Alma Lorenzon, 25 February 1986.

5. Interview with Margaret Why Kimes, 20 May 1985.

6. Anonymous interview, 7 March 1985.

7. Interview with Joseph McLaughlin, 17 September 1985.

8. Anonymous interview, 7 March 1985.

9. Interview with Henry Disston II, 29 May 1985.

10. Interview with John Lukacs, 8 May 1985.

11. Interview with Sister Mary Julia (Mary Theresa) Daley, S.S.J., 16 May 1985.

12. Interview with Charles Landreth, 1 March 1985.

13. Ibid.

14. Baltzell, *Philadelphia Gentlemen*, pp. 292–334.

15. Ibid.

16. Baltzell, *Puritan Boston and Quaker Philadelphia*, pp. 426–428; Interview with Mary Jo Concannon, 17 May 1985.

17. Interview with Margaret Harris Dale, 9 July 1985.

18. FJD to author, 27 September 1989; Interview with Margaret Harris Dale, 9 July 1985.

19. Interview with Mary ("Polly") Lear Randall (who assisted Mrs. Dale at the dancing classes for a number of years), 18 March 1985.

20. Interview with MWPB, 5 March 1985.

21. On the Philadelphia debut and the City Troop, see Burt, *The Perennial Philadelphians*, pp. 93–95, 274–277; Baltzell, *Philadelphia Gentlemen*, pp. 12, 60.

22. Interview with Emilie Rivinus Bregy, 10 May 1985; FJD to author, 27 September 1989.

23. Interview with MWPB, 5 March 1985.

24. Interview with Joseph Galante, 25 February 1985.

25. Interview with Sante Romano, 25 June 1985.

26. Interview with Joseph McLaughlin, 17 September 1985.

27. Interview with George L. ("Ted") Helmetag, 22 February 1985.

28. Walter E. Houghton, *The Victorian Frame of Mind* (New Haven, CT, 1957), pp. 202–204.

29. *Guide*, 15 September 1906; *Herald*, 3 February 1955; Sports File, GHS; Campbell, vol. 44, p. 72; Lippincott, *Cricket Club*, pp. 75–85.

30. Lippincott, *Cricket Club*, pp. 55–74; *Telegraph*, 2 June, 5 May 1886; 31 May 1890; *Chestnut Hill and Mount Airy Herald* (*CH&MA Herald*), 3 September 1926; *Local*, 15 August 1960. Note: The *Chestnut Hill and Mount Airy Herald*, published in the 1920s, should not be confused with the later *Herald*, published from 1946 to 1962.

31. *Guide*, 14 March, 18 July, 14 October 1891; 17 September 1892; 9 November 1895.

32. *CHe3MA Herald*, 23 October 1925. Among those present that day, according to the newspapers, were Mr. and Mrs. P. A. B. Widener, 2nd; Mr. and Mrs. George Widener; Mr. and Mrs. Robert Strawbridge; Mr. and Mrs. J. Willis Martin; Mr. and Mrs. E. Florens Rivinus; Mrs. William J. Clothier; Mr. and Mrs. E. T. Stotesbury; Mrs. Randal Morgan; Mr. and Mrs. J. Wilmer Biddle; Mrs. Jay Cooke, 2nd; Mrs. Charles Ingersoll; Mr. and Mrs. Orville H. Bullitt; Henry F. Baltzell, Jr.; and Mr. Robert McLean.

33. *Telegraph*, 11 July 1930.

34. Baltzell, *Philadelphia Gentlemen*, pp. 169, 220.

35. Interview with Stanley Woodward, 18–19 July 1986.

36. Interview with EHS, 11 December 1984.

37. *Telegraph*, 1 June, 27 July 1887.

38. Ibid., 28 February 1912.

39. Ibid., 9 August 1907; Campbell, vol. 18, pp. 65, 140; vol. 19, p. 168; vol. 46, p. 118.

40. *CHe3MA Herald*, 10 November 1924.

41. *Local*, 15 July and 21 July 1971; 29 May 1980.

42. *Guide*, 11 May 1889; 2 August 1890.

43. *Telegraph*, 2 May 1930; *Local*, 7 February 1974; Interview with Joseph Galante, 25 February 1985.

CHAPTER 6

1. The use of such civic organizations to create and maintain a privileged way of life in suburbs is also explored with great insight in Carol A. O'Connor, *A Sort of Utopia: Scarsdale, 1891–1981* (Albany, NY, 1983). See also Mary C. Sies, "Paradise Retained: An Analysis of Persistence in Planned Exclusive Suburbs, 1880–1980," *Proceedings of the Third National Conference on American Planning History* (1990); and William Worley, *J. C. Nichols and the Shaping of Kansas City* (Columbia, MO, 1990).

2. See Wiebe, *Search for Order*, pp. 111–163.

3. Warner, *The Private City*, passim; Baltzell, *Puritan Boston and Quaker Philadelphia*, pp. 1–15, passim.

4. Wiebe, *Search for Order*, pp. 164–195.

5. Crunden, *Ministers of Reform*, pp. 3–15.

6. See John D. Buenker, *Urban Liberalism and Progressive Reform* (New York, 1967); Martin J. Schiesl, *The Politics of Efficiency: Municipal Reform in the Progressive Era, 1880–1920* (Berkeley, CA, 1977); Bruce M. Stave (ed.), *Urban Bosses, Machines, and Progressive Reformers* (Lexington, MA, 1971); Kenneth Fox, *Better City Government: Innovation in American Urban Politics, 1850–1937* (Philadelphia, 1977); and Howard Gillette, Jr., and

Zane L. Miller, *American Urbanism: A Historiographical Review* (New York, 1987). An excellent overview of cities in the United States during the twentieth century is Jon C. Teaford, *The Twentieth-Century American City* (Baltimore, 1986). For an overview of Philadelphia during this period, see Lloyd Abernethy, "Progressivism, 1905–1919," *Philadelphia: A 300-Year History*, pp. 524–565 and Michael P. McCarthy, "The Unprogressive City: Philadelphia at the Turn of the Century," *PH* (October 1987), pp. 263–281.

7. On the continuation of Progressive impulses after World War I, see Ronald Feinman, *Twilight of Progressivism and the New Deal* (Baltimore, 1981) and Otis L. Graham, Jr., *An Encore for Reform: The Old Progressives and the New Deal* (New York, 1973).

8. *Guide*, 7 October 1882.

9. These included George E. Waring, Jr., *Village Improvement and Farm Villages* (Boston, 1877); Warren E. Manning, "The History of Village Improvement in the United States," *Craftsman* (February 1904), pp. 423–435; Frederick Law Olmsted, Jr., "Village Improvement," *Atlantic* (June 1905), pp. 798–803.

10. On these early improvement associations, see David P. Handlin, *The American Home: Architecture and Society, 1815–1915* (Boston, 1979), pp. 141–148; Stilgoe, *Borderland*, pp. 207–220; Wilson, *City Beautiful*, pp. 41–46.

11. *Guide*, 7 October 1882.

12. Ibid.

13. Campbell, vol. 35, p. 150; *Guide*, 24 July 1891; 16 September 1893; Obituary file, GHS.

14. Campbell, vol. 22, p. 141; *Guide*, 30 September 1893.

15. *Telegraph*, 5 May 1886; 2 February, 19 October 1887; 22 October 1892.

16. *Telegraph*, 25 May 1887.

17. *Guide*, 3 June 1893.

18. Ibid., 2 April 1898.

19. Ibid., 1 June 1889.

20. Ibid., 3 October 1891.

21. Campbell, vol. 25, p. 150.

22. Lincoln Steffens, *The Shame of the Cities* (New York, 1904), p. 195.

23. Abernethy, "Progressivism," pp. 526–532; Allen F. Davis and Mark H. Haller (eds.), *The Peoples of Philadelphia: A History of Ethnic Groups and Lower-Class Life, 1740–1940* (Philadelphia, 1973), pp. 175–201.

24. For a discussion of corruption in Philadelphia during this time, see Arthur P. Dudden, "Lincoln Steffens' Philadelphia," *PH* (October 1964), pp. 449–458.

25. Campbell, vol. 1, p. 79.

322 *Notes to Chapter 6*

26. Community Improvement Associations file, GHS.

27. Ibid.

28. Community Improvement Associations file, GHS; Campbell, vol. 2, pp. 36, 42, 46; *Beehive* (June 1923), pp. 1–2; *Guide,* 19 February 1910.

29. Community Associations file, GHS; Campbell, vol. 3, p. 173.

30. *Courier,* 29 September 1937; 15 March 1945; *Evening Bulletin,* 23 September, 16 November 1951.

31. A Germantown Who's Who, Compiled by I. Pearson Willits, GHS; *Beehive* (June 1923), pp. 6–7; *Evening Bulletin,* 5 April 1940.

32. *Beehive* (June 1923), pp. 2–23.

33. Ibid.; Minutes, Auxiliary Committee, G&CH Improvement Association, Appendix, GHS; G&CH Improvement Association file, GHS; Campbell, vol. 2, p. 87; vol. 9, p. 201; *Philadelphia Inquirer,* 16 April 1939; Obituary file, GHS.

34. Constitution and By-Laws, G&CH Improvement Association, Community Improvement Associations file, GHS.

35. *Guide,* 13 June 1908; 30 January, 27 February, 22 May, 9 October, 20 November 1909; 8 January, 12 February 1910; 10 June 1911; 20 June 1914; 22 April, 12 August 1916; 3 February, 4 July 1917; 19 October 1918; 19 March 1921; *Independent-Gazette,* 23 September 1920; *CH&MA Herald,* 12 March 1926; 13 May 1927; 14 December 1928; *Beehive* (July 1924), p. 17; (August 1928), pp. 16–17; (May 1931), pp. 2, 17; Campbell, vol. 3, p. 15; Minutes, Auxiliary Committee, G&CH Improvement Association, GHS, 16 November 1920; 14 February 1921; 15 March 1926.

36. Campbell, vol. 22, pp. 91, 125; Obituary of James McCrea, released by the Chestnut Hill Businessmen's Association; *Evening Bulletin,* 30 December 1948.

37. *Guide,* 5 July 1913; 6 February, 6 March, 30 October 1915; 30 December 1916.

38. *Guide,* 6 December 1913; 6 February 1915.

39. Ibid., 6 February 1915.

40. Water file, GHS.

41. *Guide,* 12 July 1913; *CH&MA Herald,* 26 June 1915.

42. *Guide,* 28 June 1913.

43. Ibid., 28 April, 12 May 1917; 2 March, 23 March, 30 March 1918.

44. Ibid., 30 June, 4 August, 6 October 1917; 16 March, 20 April, 25 August, 19 October 1918; *Letters of Lydia Jane Clark* (Boston, 1939), pp. 133–134.

45. For perspective on the settlement house movement and the sorts of activities being carried on by the Chestnut Hill Community Center, see Alan F. Davis, *Spearheads of Reform: The Social Settlements and the Progressive Movement, 1890–1914* (New York, 1967); Gwendolyn Wright, *Building the Dream: Moralism and the Model Home* (Chicago, 1980).

46. *Local,* 3 October 1974.

47. Ibid.

48. See Jill Conway, "Women Reformers and American Culture, 1890–1930," in *Our American Sisters: Women in American Life and Thought,* (ed.) Jean E. Friedman and William G. Slade (Boston, 1976), pp. 301–312; Allen F. Davis, "Welfare, Reform, and World War I," *American Quarterly* (Fall 1967), pp. 516–533; and Gwendolyn Wright, *Moralism and the Model Home.*

49. Contosta, *St. Martin,* pp. 20–21, 34, 45, 56.

50. *Guide,* 6 January 1906; 25 May 1907; *Independent-Gazette,* 11 December 1919; *CH&MA Herald,* 3 September 1926; *Local,* 27 December 1979.

51. Dorothy Gondos Beers, "The Centennial City, 1865–1876." *Philadelphia: A 300-Year History,* p. 427; *Local,* 11 August 1977.

52. Hotchkin, *Ancient and Modern,* pp. 457–458. For a full account of the dedication ceremonies, including a list of the dignitaries who attended, see the *Guide,* 21 June 1902.

53. Ibid., 20 April 1901; Jellett, vol. 7, pp. 62, 67.

54. *Local,* 29 July 1971; Jellett, vol. 7, p. 67.

55. Jellette, vol. 7, p. 63. Several photographs of the unrestored inn may be seen at the Germantown Historical Society.

56. Campbell, vol. 19, p. 106; Jellett, vol. 6, pp. 24, 26, 27, 60; *Telegraph,* 12 October 1934.

57. Campbell, vol. 1, p. 87; vol. 2, p. 47; vol. 12, p. 126; vol. 26, p. 14; Jellett, vol. 6, p. 185; *Independent-Gazette,* 15 April 1920; *CH&MA Herald,* 23 October 1928; 15 February, 5 April 1929.

58. Campbell, vol. 28, p. 49; vol. 29, pp. 159, 202, 204; *Guide,* 4 December 1915.

59. Campbell, vol. 30, p. 159.

60. *Beehive* (June 1926), pp. 2–3, 20; *Independent-Gazette,* 28 October 1920; 19 May 1921; *CH&MA Herald,* 29 May 1925; *Guide,* 27 February 1926.

61. *Guide,* 14 January 1906; 13 July 1907; *Independent-Gazette,* 10 February 1912.

62. Campbell, vol. 48, p. 3; *Beehive* (April 1931), pp. 1–20; *Telegraph,* 30 August 1935.

63. *Independent-Gazette,* 28 August 1919.

64. *Guide,* 1 January 1898.

65. Ibid., 26 August 1899.

66. On the campaign against typhoid fever in Philadelphia, see Gretchen A. Condran et al., "The Decline of Mortality in Philadelphia from 1870 to 1930: The Role of Municipal Services," *PMHB* (April 1984), pp. 165–168. Newspaper accounts of Woodward's crusade for filtered

water appeared in the *Public Ledger,* 8 October 1897 and the *North American,* 13, 15, 16, 20, 22, and 25 March 1899.

67. See Lloyd M. Abernethy, "Insurgency in Philadelphia, 1905," *PMHB* (January 1963), pp. 3–20; Philip S. Benjamin, "Gentlemen Reformers in the Quaker City, 1870–1912," *Political Science Quarterly* (March 1970), pp. 61–79; Robert L. Bloom, "Edwin A. Van Valkenburg and the Philadelphia North American, 1899–1924," *PMHB* (April 1954), pp. 109–127; Dale Phalen, *Samuel Fels of Philadelphia* (Philadelphia, 1969).

68. George Woodward, "A Triumph of the People: The Story of the Downfall of the Political Oligarchy in Philadelphia," *Outlook* (December 2, 1905), p. 815; Contosta, "George Woodward," *PMHB* (July 1987), pp. 345–349.

69. *Guide,* 27 October 1906; 8 February 1908.

70. On these subsequent reform movements in Philadelphia, see Donald W. Disbrow, "Reform in Philadelphia Under Mayor Blankenburg, 1912–1916," *PH* (October 1960), pp. 379–396; Clinton Rogers Woodruff, "Progress in Philadelphia," *The American Journal of Sociology* (November 1920), pp. 318, 330–332.

71. *Independent-Gazette,* 6 March 1919; 28 July 1921.

72. 22nd Ward file, GHS.

73. *Guide,* 27 January, 10 February 1906; 4 April, 18 April, 6 June 1914.

74. 22nd Ward file, GHS; see also *Independent-Gazette,* 16 June, 23 June, 14 July, 28 July, 4 August 1921.

75. 22nd Ward file, GHS.

76. *Guide,* 28 August, 4 September, 23 October 1926; *Courier,* 17 March, 9 June 1937; 22nd Ward file, GHS.

77. *Telegraph,* 19 December, 25 December 1930.

78. Ibid., 11 December 1930.

79. On such private relief efforts in Philadelphia, see Bonnie R. Fox, "Unemployment Relief in Philadelphia, 1930–1932: A Study of the Depression's Impact on Voluntarism," *PMHB* (January 1969), pp. 86–107.

80. Margaret B. Tinkcom, "Depression and War," *Philadelphia: A 300-Year History,* p. 609; Contosta, *Philadelphia Family,* pp. 97–98.

81. Interview with Jane Jordan O'Neill, 20 March 1985.

82. *Courier,* 24 March 1937; *Local,* 3 October 1974.

83. Contosta, *St. Martin,* p. 59; *Courier,* 17 April, 8 May 1941; *Herald,* 9 March 1961.

84. MWPB, *Ninety Years,* pp. 38–47; *Courier,* 26 February, 26 March, 27 August 1942; 24 February 1944.

85. *Telegraph,* 28 July, 4 August, 1 September 1933.

86. Interviews with Stanley Woodward, 18–19 July 1986; Quita Woodward Horan, 20 June 1985.

87. On the relationship between the Progressives and the New Deal, see Feinman, *Twilight of Progressivism and the New Deal* and Graham, *An Encore for Reform: The Old Progressives and the New Deal.*

CHAPTER 7

1. John F. Maher to author, 30 May 1985.
2. Interview with Henry T. O'Donnell, 26 May 1988.
3. Anonymous interview, 19 April 1985.
4. Interview with Henry T. O'Donnell, 26 May 1988.
5. Samuel F. Houston to EHS, 11 March 1942.
6. Contosta, *Philadelphia Family,* p. 161.
7. Ibid., pp. 115–117.
8. Gertrude Houston Woodward to Donald Davidson Dodge, 23 March 1950. Cornelia Dodge Fraley collection.
9. Donald Davidson Dodge to Gertrude Houston Woodward, 30 March 1950. Cornelia Dodge Fraley collection.
10. Contosta, *Philadelphia Family,* pp. 135, 138.
11. Joseph Pennington Straus (JPS) to Lloyd P. Wells (LPW), 19 June 1989; Interview with JPS, 29 March 1985.
12. Thomas A. Bell, Negotiations Concerning the Development of the Morgan Tract, unpublished manuscript, Chestnut Hill Historical Society (CHHS).
13. *Evening Bulletin,* 26 October 1973.
14. Sidney B. Dexter, "Community Association: A History," *Local,* 23 October 1958.
15. *Social Register,* 1950, 1965, 1970, 1975, 1980; Lists of CHCA board members, CHCA office. The author is indebted to several former heads of the Community Association for information on the occupations and religious affiliations of these individuals.
16. Dexter, "Community Association."
17. Interview with JPS, 29 March 1985; Bell, Morgan Tract; *The Herald (Herald),* 17 February 1955.
18. JPS to Robert L. Johnson and Mayer I. Blum, 21 May 1954; JPS to Mayer I. Blum, 16 July 1954; Bell, Morgan Tract.
19. *Herald,* 31 March 1955.
20. For an account of these negotiations, see *Herald,* 26 May, 21 July 1955; 19 January, 26 April, 14 June, 26 July, 2 August, 23 August 1956; 25 April, 2 May, 25 July 1957; 9 January, 20 March, 17 April, 24 April, 1 May, 8 May, 4 December 1958.
21. Ibid., 1 May 1958.
22. Interview with JPS, 29 March 1985.

23. For an excellent analysis of this phenomenon in the early postwar period, see G. Edward Janosik, "Suburban Balance of Power," *American Quarterly* (Spring 1955), pp. 123–141.

24. Contosta, *Philadelphia Family*, pp. 118–120; Interview with EHS, 11 December 1984; Houston Estate Papers, general correspondence, In-Ma, Pennsylvania State Archives (PSA), MG-154; Houston Estate file, AAUP; *Evening Bulletin*, 18 March 1950; *Herald*, 12 March 1953.

25. *Herald*, 26 February, 27 August, 1 October 1953.

26. Ibid., 24 September, 1 October, 23 October 1953; 3 November 1955; 3 January 1957.

27. Ibid., 4 September 1952; 5 February, 29 October 1953; 3 March, 23 June 1955.

28. Ibid., 6 August 1953; 17 February, 24 March, 18 August 1955; 9 August 1956.

29. On the municipal reforms and reformers of this period, see Joseph S. Clark, Jr., and Dennis J. Clark, "Rally and Relapse," *Philadelphia: A 300-Year History*, pp. 649–657; John F. Bauman, "Expressways, Public Housing and Renewal: A Blueprint for Postwar Philadelphia, 1945–1960," *PH* (January 1990), pp. 44–65; E. Haveman, "Rebirth of Philadelphia," *National Civic Review* (November 1962), pp. 538–542; Emily Jones (ed.), *Walter M. Phillips: Philadelphia Gentleman Activist* (Swarthmore, PA, 1987); Kirk Petshek, *The Challenge of Urban Reform: Politics and Programs in Philadelphia* (Philadelphia, 1973). For an excellent description and characterization of Philadelphia in this period, see John Lukacs, *Philadelphia: Patricians and Philistines, 1900–1950* (New York, 1980), pp. 310–344.

30. Some historians would contend that the Progressive Era ended with World War I, but it is clear that Progressive ideas and programs continued into the 1920s and later formed the basis for many reforms during the New Deal. Municipal reformers in particular carried the Progressive emphases on reason, organization, and efficiency well into the postwar years. See Feinman, *Twilight of Progressivism*; Graham, *An Encore for Reform*; and Buenker, *Urban Liberalism and Progressive Reform*.

31. See Contosta, "George Woodward," *PMHB*, p. 368.

32. *Herald*, 10 April 1952.

33. See Contosta, *Philadelphia Family*, pp. 146–150.

34. Ibid., pp. 151–160; Contosta, *St. Martin*, p. 74.

35. Interview with LPW, 8 September 1985; Interview with G. Holmes Perkins and Georgia Perkins, 17 January 1990.

36. Interview with Eli Schmidt, 25 March 1985. Schmidt was one of Wells's partners in the hardware business; the other was Joseph Sallet. Both had worked with Wells for a year at the American Pulley Company.

37. LPW, "The Witness of Chestnut Hill's Mid-Century History,

1950–1975," two lectures delivered at Chestnut Hill College, 3 November and 10 November 1987, typed manuscript, CHHS.

38. Interview with G. Holmes Perkins and Georgia Perkins, 17 January 1990.

39. *Local,* 29 January 1970.

40. *Herald,* 22 May, 18 September 1952.

41. Among the most severe of these postwar suburban critics are John Keats, *The Crack in the Picture Window* (Boston, 1956) and William H. Whyte, *The Organization Man* (New York, 1956). In defense of the postwar suburbs is Scott Donaldson, *The Suburban Myth* (New York, 1969).

42. LPW, Witness.

43. *Herald,* 13 March 1952.

44. Interview with LPW, 8 September 1985.

45. *Herald,* 30 December 1952.

46. Ibid., 30 December 1952; 26 February, 18 June 1953; 26 May 1955; *Local,* 18 November 1982; 19 January 1989; *Evening Bulletin,* 19 July 1953.

47. LPW, Witness; Interview with LPW, 8 September 1985.

48. Moak, Inventory, p. 123.

49. Ibid., p. 117.

50. Ibid., p. 125.

51. *Herald,* 20 March, 14 December 1952; 20 April 1961; *Evening Bulletin,* 16 April 1961.

52. Interview with Russell L. Medinger, 22 April 1985.

53. Ibid.

CHAPTER 8

1. On this phenomenon, see Roger S. Ahlbrandt, Jr., *Neighborhoods, People, and Community* (New York, 1984).

2. Interview with LPW, 8 September 1985.

3. *Herald,* 23 May 1957.

4. Ibid., 28 January 1960.

5. By-Laws of the CHCA, Minute Book, vol. 1.

6. Amended Certificate of Incorporation, CHCA, Minute Book, vol. 1.

7. LPW, Witness; Interview, 8 September 1985.

8. *The Chestnut Hill Cymbal,* 8 September 1955.

9. *Local,* 28 April 1988.

10. Interviews with Mary Jane Shelly, Ruth R. Russell, and Katie Worrall, associate editors, *Chestnut Hill Local,* 31 May 1991.

11. *Local*, 28 April 1988; 18 May 1978; Minutes, CHCA, 15 June, 23 July 1959; 24 May, 20 September 1962; 24 January 1963; 20 January 1966; 16 February 1968.

12. *Local*, 19 March 1970; Minutes, CHCA, 21 November 1968.

13. *Local*, 8 May 1958.

14. Ibid., 17 July 1958.

15. Ibid., 9 October 1958.

16. Minutes, CHCA, 15 April 1959; 5 April, 14 August 1960.

17. From an early period, some board members have lived outside Chestnut Hill itself. In some cases they lived just outside the Hill in Springfield Township; in other instances they served on the board because of their institutional affiliations and could thus reside almost anywhere in the region. The author culled this information from the lists of board members (1961 to the present) in the files of the Community Association.

18. *Evening Bulletin*, 23 September 1960; 10 February 1964; 1 April 1965; *Herald*, 27 August, 17 September, 24 September, 8 October, 15 October, 22 October, 19 November 1959; 11 February 1960; Minutes, CHCA, 20 June 1963.

19. *Chestnut Hill Times*, 4 June 1931.

20. Minutes, CHCA, 18 November 1963; 27 March 1969; *Local*, 20 September 1973.

21. Minutes, CHCA, 20 June, 11 July, 17 October 1963; 19 March, 16 April 1964.

22. I am indebted for this information to Wilber Borne Ruthrauff.

23. Minutes, North Chestnut Hill Association (NCHA), 15 May 1944.

24. Minutes, CHCA, 18 April 1963.

25. *Local*, 24 April 1963.

26. Minutes, CHCA, 18 May 1967.

27. *Evening Bulletin*, 25 April 1967.

28. *Ambler Gazette*, 18 March 1971; Minutes, CHCA, 17 November 1966.

29. On the establishment of the Chestnut Hill Historical Society, see Nancy Hubby, "The Evolution of an Historical Society," *Crier* (March 1967), pp. 20–21.

30. See Robert E. Newcomb, *Planning the Past* (Hamden, CT, 1979).

31. See Richard J. Webster, *Philadelphia Preserved* (Philadelphia, 1976).

32. Detweiler, *Architectural History*.

33. *Ambler Gazette*, 18 March 1971; *Local*, 8 February 1973; Minutes, CHCA, 17 November 1966.

34. A search of surviving lists of board members of the Chestnut Hill Historical Society did not reveal even one board member from what might be considered the East Side of Chestnut Hill.

35. On the impact of the automobile on American society, see John B. Rae, *The American Automobile* (Chicago, 1965) and *The Road and the Car in American Life* (Cambridge, MA, 1971); James J. Flink, *The Car Culture* (Cambridge, MA, 1975). On the automobile and American suburbs before World War II, there is Mark S. Foster, *From Streetcar to Superhighway* (Philadelphia, 1981) and John Keats, *The Insolent Chariots* (New York, 1958). See also Jackson, *Crabgrass Frontiers*, pp. 157–171, 246–271.

36. *Guide*, 14 June 1890.

37. Ibid., 8 June 1907; *CH&MA Herald*, 15 June 1926, 18 February 1927; 25 October 1929; *Evening Bulletin*, 21 February 1927; *Courier*, 28 April 1937; *Herald*, 12 May, 12 November, 22 December 1953; 3 March, 24 March, 2 June, 15 September, 3 November 1955; 26 April, 5 July 1965; 7 March 1957; 16 January 1958; 30 July 1959.

38. *Guide*, 23 May 1891; 22 June 1895; 4 December 1897; Campbell, vol. 2, p. 39; *CH&MA Herald*, 1 February 1929; Minutes, Auxiliary Committee, G&CHIA, 19 December 1938; Houston Estate file, AAUP; Contosta, *Philadelphia Family*, p. 69.

39. *Herald*, 18 September 1952.

40. Ibid., 29 January 1953; 15 November 1962.

41. *Local*, 14 November 1962.

42. *Herald*, 3 December 1953; 23 July 1959; CHCA to the City Planning Commission, 11 October 1966; "Chestnut Hill Land Use Guidelines," LUPC (1982).

43. Minutes, CHCA, 23 January, 21 May 1964; 18 October 1965; 20 January, 17 February 1966; 16 March, 19 October, 14 December 1967; 18 January, 19 September, 18 October 1968; 20 March 1969; 29 January 1970; 21 January 1971.

44. Interview with Marie Jones, 7 March 1985.

45. Interview with The Reverend John Casey, O.S.A., 26 February 1985.

46. Ibid.; *Evening Bulletin*, 29 February 1964; *Local*, 7 September 1967.

47. For example, see *Local*, 5 January, 2 March, 2 November 1967; 3 December 1970.

48. Minutes, CHCA, 16 February 1960; 18 November 1963; 19 February 1970; 22 June 1972.

49. Minutes, CHCA, 22 April, 20 May 1965.

50. Interview with Eleanor Potter, 13 June 1985; Telephone interview with Eleanor Kingsbury, 2 August 1990; *Local*, 28 June 1990.

51. *Evening Bulletin*, 26 February 1967; 11 April 1968; *Local*, 23 November 1967.

52. See, for example, editorials on 5 October and 16 November 1967.

53. LPW, Witness.

54. *Local,* 9 March 1972.

55. *Evening Bulletin,* 19 December 1971.

56. *Local,* 25 October 1973.

57. Minutes, CHCA, 19 February 1970; 18 May, 21 October 1972; 16 October 1975.

58. *Local,* 13 January 1972; 11 November 1976; 25 November 1982; 10 November, 15 December 1988; Minutes, CHCA, 18 May, 21 October 1972; 16 October 1975.

59. Minutes, CHCA, 19 February 1970; *Local,* 26 May 1977.

60. *Local,* 29 June 1972.

61. Ibid., 12 April, 26 April, 24 May, 31 May, 5 July, 26 July, 27 September, 11 October 1973; 21 January 1974; 6 February, 12 June 1975; Minutes, CHCA, 22 June, 21 September 1972; 18 January 1973.

62. Ibid., 19 March 1970; 15 March 1973; 7 March, 12 September, 3 October 1974; 6 March 1975; 29 April 1976; Minutes, CHCA, 20 November 1969; 17 September 1970; 18 May 1972; 16 June, 19 December 1974.

63. Interview with Russell L. Medinger, 22 April 1985.

64. *Local,* 8 May 1975.

65. Ibid., 2 February 1976.

66. *Local,* 18 March 1976; Interview with LPW, 8 September 1985.

CHAPTER 9

1. 1980 Federal Census Tracts.

2. *Philadelphia Inquirer (Inquirer),* 16 September 1990.

3. 1980 Federal Census Tracts.

4. *Inquirer,* 25 January 1991.

5. Stephanie Grauman Wolf, "The Bicentennial City," *Philadelphia: A 300-Year History,* pp. 704–734; Michael DeCourcy Hinds, "After Renaissance of the 70's and 80's Philadelphia is Struggling to Survive," *New York Times,* 21 June 1990.

6. According to 1980 census tract figures for Chestnut Hill, the nonwhite population broke down as follows: black, 364; Hispanic, 122; Asian/ Pacific, 71; other, 40.

7. *Local,* 7 March 1991.

8. For a complete list and analysis of these numbers on Chestnut Hill and Mount Airy, see the *Local,* 27 January, 4 August 1983.

9. In counting Chestnut Hill names in the 1987 *Social Register,* the author went by the 19118 zip code, even though it includes a thin strip of adjacent Springfield Township. Because the *Social Register*s of the 1920s also considered this area as part of Chestnut Hill, it seemed appropriate,

for comparative purposes, to count all names in the 19118 zip code area from the 1987 edition. However, the author did not include the score or more of elderly Chestnut Hillers who had moved to the Cathedral Village retirement home just across the Wissahickon Creek in Roxborough — although a case might be made for adding them to the Chestnut Hill total.

10. This is not to say that no one in the *Social Register* lived in these communities before World War II. Plymouth Meeting, for example, had been home to several upper-class families for decades.

11. Interviews with Jane Jordan O'Neill, 20 March 1985 and E. Digby Baltzell, 6 June 1985.

12. Lists of CHCA Board Members, 1961–1990, office of CHCA.

13. Ibid.; *Social Register*, 1980–1990. In figuring percentages, the author did not include those board members of the CHCA who lived outside the traditional boundaries of Chestnut Hill.

14. *Local*, 27 January 1983.

15. 1980 Federal Census Tracts.

16. Interview with W. Thacher Longstreth, 10 June 1990. Longstreth's opinion on the greater acceptability of Jews in Chestnut Hill was corroborated by interviews with Edwin Wolf, 2nd, 23 May 1985 and Jane Jordan O'Neill, 20 March 1985.

17. Interview with Thacher Longstreth, 10 June 1990.

18. Ibid.

19. For example, see the *Local*, 17 November 1988.

20. Ibid., 13 November 1980.

21. Ibid., 24 January, 10 April 1980; 9 September, 24 September, 22 October 1981; 8 July 1982; 8 September 1983.

22. *Evening Bulletin*, 7 December, 19 December 1980; *Local*, 25 September, 6 November 1980.

23. *Local*, 31 January, 14 February, 21 February, 29 May 1980; 28 January, 11 February, 18 February, 25 November 1982; Minutes, CHCA, 19 November 1981; 23 February, 10 May 1984.

24. For a history of this development, see the *Local*, 20 July 1989.

25. Ibid., 12 April 1984.

26. Ibid., 24 January 1985.

27. Ibid., 28 April 1983.

28. Ibid., 27 October 1988.

29. See, for example, Ibid., 12 March, 14 May 1981; 4 March, 11 August, 1 September 1983; 12 April, 26 July 1984; 14 March, 26 June 1985; 27 August 1987; 7 February 1988.

30. Ibid., 31 January 1985.

31. See especially issues of the *Local* for October 1988 and February through April 1989.

32. Minutes, CHCA, 27 October 1988; *Local,* 3 November 1988.

33. *Local,* 5 May 1988.

34. For examples, see the "Forum" pages of the *Local* for April through September 1988.

35. Ibid., 23 May, 17 June, 1 August 1985.

36. Ibid., 14 January, 22 January 1982; 3 May, 18 October 1984.

37. Ibid., 25 December 1980.

38. Ibid., 27 March, 3 April, 10 April, 24 April, 1 May, 3 July, 10 July, 17 July, 7 August, 21 August, 11 September, 18 September, 2 October, 25 December 1980; 14 January 1982; *Evening Bulletin,* 14 July 1980; Minutes, CHCA, 26 June 1980; Minutes, North Chestnut Hill Council (NCHC), 12 February, 16 April 1980.

39. Pemberton Hutchinson, chairman, board of trustees, Chestnut Hill Hospital Healthcare, and Ralph T. Starr, chairman, board of trustees, Chestnut Hill Hospital, to JPS, 15 July 1988; JPS to board of directors, CHHS, October 1988; Agreement between Chestnut Hill Healthcare and the CHCA, 15 November 1988. Minutes, CHCA, 28 January, 23 June 1988; Minutes, NCHC, 15 March, 20 April, 3 May 1988. See also issues of the *Local* from January through December 1988.

40. *Local,* 11 May, 1 June 1989; 17 May 1990.

41. Minutes, CHCA, 20 November 1980; *Local,* 17 July, 11 September, 9 October, 20 November 1980; 29 May 1982.

42. Ibid., 21 July, 13 October, 8 December 1988; 5 January, 12 January, 6 April 1989.

43. Ibid., 1 February, 15 February, 15 March, 29 March 1990.

44. Minutes, CHHS, 19 March, 21 May 1990.

45. Among these critics is David R. Boldt, a Chestnut Hill resident and the editor of the editorial page of the *Philadelphia Inquirer.* On 29 April 1990 Boldt wrote in an editorial "In fact just about any proposed change in Chestnut Hill is fought tooth-and-nail. You can see this literally by just leafing through the *Chestnut Hill Local,* the community's excellent newspaper."

46. For example see the *Local,* 14 and 21 June 1990.

47. Chestnut Hill's George Woodward proposed such a scheme in the 1930s while he was a Pennsylvania state senator. Even then it went nowhere. See Contosta, *Philadelphia Family,* p. 95. The inability of cities to annex outlying suburbs is discussed in Jackson, *Crabgrass Frontier,* pp. 276–278.

48. A move toward such regional cooperation was made on 3 March 1990, when leaders from Chestnut Hill, Mount Airy, and Germantown met at Chestnut Hill College to discuss their common problems and to plot strategies for solving them in the 1990s. Interestingly, they claimed that

this was the first time that leaders of the three communities had ever come together for joint action. This statement showed that no one remembered that such meetings had been commonplace among leaders of the three communities only a generation or two earlier, and shows how far the three communities had drifted apart in recent decades. See *Local*, 8 March 1990. See also David R. Contosta, "Germantown, Mount Airy, and Chestnut Hill—A Common Legacy," *Local*, 15 March 1990.

Bibliographic Essay

Much information on the early years of Chestnut Hill may be found in S. F. Hotchkin, *Ancient and Modern Germantown, Mount Airy, and Chestnut Hill* (Philadelphia, 1889); and John J. Macfarlane, *History of Early Chestnut Hill* (Philadelphia, 1927). Drawing heavily on Macfarlane but containing some additional material is Horace Mather Lippincott, *Chestnut Hill, Springfield, Whitemarsh, Cheltenham* (Jenkintown, PA, 1948). All three of these works were written by amateur historians. Nevertheless, they contain information that cannot be found elsewhere. An excellent article on landholding and genealogy in colonial Chestnut Hill is Hanna Benner Roach's "The Back Part of Germantown," *The Pennsylvania Genealogical Magazine* (1956), pp. 77–149. Some works that deal primarily with Germantown contain valuable information on Chestnut Hill, which was once part of German Township. There are also Edward J. Hocker, *Germantown, 1683–1933* (Philadelphia, 1933); Naaman H. Keyser et al., *History of Old Germantown* (Philadelphia, 1907); and Samuel J. Pennypacker, *The Settlement of Germantown, Pennsylvania* (Philadelphia, 1899). More recent writings include Harry Tinkcom et al., *Historic Germantown* (Philadelphia, 1955); and Stephanie Grauman Wolf, *Urban Village: Population, Community, and Family Structure in Germantown, Philadelphia, 1683–1800* (Princeton, 1976). The latter, by an accomplished urban historian, is helpful in understanding the population and social structure of presuburban Chestnut Hill. A good introduction to the architecture of Chestnut Hill is Willard S. Detweiler, Jr., *Chestnut Hill: An Architectural History* (Philadelphia, 1969). A complete list of extant structures in Chestnut Hill as of 1985, except for the Morgan Tract/ Market Square area, is Jefferson Moak, Inventory of Buildings Within the Chestnut Hill Historic District, compiled for the Chestnut Hill Historical Society (1985). This work contains an abundance of information about owners, dates, architects, and builders. Also by Moak is "Street

335

Names of Chestnut Hill," *The Chestnut Hill Almanac,* no. 1 (Philadelphia, 1986).

In addition to these works, the weekly newspapers published in Germantown, nearly all issues of which can be found at the Germantown Historical Society, contain much valuable material on Chestnut Hill. These are the *Germantown Telegraph* (1830–1948), the *Germantown Guide* (1871–1926), the *Germantown Independent* (1882–1896), the *Germantown Independent-Gazette* (1896–1926), and the *Germantown Courier* (1936–   ). A helpful guide to two of these newspapers, also located at the Germantown Historical Society, is Edward W. Hocker, Abstracts of News and Advertisements in the *Germantown Telegraph* (1830–1868), and *Germantown Chronicle* (1869–1872). Three other sources at the Germantown Historical Society draw heavily on these local newspapers. They are Jane Campbell, Scrapbooks, 49 vols.; and Edwin C. Jellett, Scrapbooks on the Wissahickon, 9 vols. Besides containing newspaper clippings, both sets of scrapbooks offer a rich assortment of drawings, prints, photographs, and ephemera that relate to Chestnut Hill — much of which is unavailable anywhere else. Also depending upon the newspapers is the Germantown Historical Society's excellent Obituary File, which contains many entries on Chestnut Hill residents. Two other periodicals, *The Germantown Crier,* published quarterly since 1949 by the Germantown Historical Society, and *The Beehive,* a monthly magazine published in Germantown during the 1920s and 1930s, contain articles on Chestnut Hill.

Newspapers focusing on Chestnut Hill itself are the *Chestnut Hill and Mount Airy Herald* (1925–1929) and the *Herald* (1946–1962), which despite their similar names should not be confused. Issues of the earlier newspaper are located at the Germantown Historical Society; the latter is available at the Chestnut Hill Historical Society. More recent are the *Chestnut Hill Cymbal* (1955–1957) and the *Chestnut Hill Local* (1958–   ), which may be found at the Chestnut Hill Historical Society. Chestnut Hill and its residents have also been given occasional coverage in the metropolitan dailies, including the *Philadelphia Press,* the *Public Ledger,* the *Evening Bulletin,* and the *Philadelphia Inquirer,* among others.

Two excellent general histories of American suburbs are Robert Fishman, *Bourgeois Utopias: The Rise and Fall of Suburbia* (New York, 1987); and Kenneth Jackson, *Crabgrass Frontier: The Suburbanization of the United States* (New York, 1985). The transformation of gateway villages into early suburbs is explored by Henry C. Binford, *The First Suburbs: Residential Communities on the Boston Periphery, 1815–1860* (Chicago, 1985). On railroad suburbs there are John Stilgoe, *Metropolitan Corridor: Railroads and the American Scene* (New Haven, 1983); and Michael Ebner, *Creating Chicago's North Shore* (Chicago, 1988). The impact of trolley cars on suburbs is explored in

Sam Bass Warner, *Streetcar Suburbs: The Process of Growth in Boston, 1870–1900* (Cambridge, MA, 1962). Considering the relationship between cities and suburbs in the nineteenth century are Patricia Mooney Melvin, *The Organic City: Urban Definition and Community Organization, 1880–1920* (Lexington, KY, 1987); David Schuyler, *The New Urban Landscape: The Redefinition of Urban Form in Nineteenth-century America* (Baltimore, 1986); and Adna Ferrin Weber, *The Growth of Cities in the Nineteenth Century* (New York, 1963 [1899]). Studies of early twentieth-century suburbia include Paul Harlan Douglass, *The Suburban Trend* (New York, 1925); and George Lundberg et al., *Leisure: A Suburban Study* (New York, 1934). Criticisms of post–World War II suburbs may be found in John Keats, *The Crack in the Picture Window* (Boston, 1956); and William H. Whyte, *The Organization Man* (New York, 1956). In defense of these postwar suburbs is Scott Donaldson, *The Suburban Myth* (New York, 1969). A superb bibliographic discussion of suburban histories, containing a special focus on Philadelphia's suburbs, is Margaret Marsh, "Reconsidering Suburbs," *Pennsylvania Magazine of History and Biography (PMHB)* (October 1988), pp. 576–605. Useful for comparing Chestnut Hill to upper-class suburbs outside municipal boundaries is Carol A. O'Connor, *A Sort of Utopia: Scarsdale, 1891–1981* (Albany, NY, 1983); Mary C. Sies, "Paradise Retained: An Analysis of Persistence in Planned, Exclusive Suburbs, 1880–1980," in *Proceedings of the Third Annual Conference on American Planning History*, 1990; and William Worley, *J. C. Nichols and the Shaping of Kansas City* (Columbia, MO, 1990). The historiography of American cities and suburbs is considered in Howard Gillette, Jr., and Zane L. Miller, *American Urbanism: A Historiographical Review* (New York, 1987).

The automobile and suburbs are treated in James J. Flink, *The Car Culture* (Cambridge, MA, 1975); Mark S. Foster, *From Streetcar to Superhighway* (Philadelphia, 1981); John Keats, *The Insolent Chariots* (New York, 1958); and two works by John B. Rae, *The American Auto* (Chicago, 1965) and *The Road and the Car in American Life* (Cambridge, MA, 1971).

Helpful in understanding Philadelphia in the nineteenth century are Dorothy Gondos Beers, "The Centennial City, 1865–1876," in *Philadelphia: A 300-Year History*, edited by Russell Weigley (New York, 1982), pp. 417–470; Barbara Fisher, "Maritime History of the Reading," *PMHB* (April 1962); pp. 160–184; Thomas C. Cochran, "Philadelphia: The American Industrial Center, 1750–1850," *PMHB* (July 1982), pp. 323–340; Sidney George Fisher, *A Philadelphia Perspective: The Diary of Sidney George Fisher Covering the Years 1834–1871*, edited by Nicholas B. Wainwright (Philadelphia, 1967); Elizabeth Geffin, "Industrial Development and Social Crisis, 1841–1854," in *Philadelphia: A 300-Year History*, pp. 305–362 and "Violence in Philadelphia in the Late 1840s and 1850s," *Pennsylvania History (PH)* (October 1969), pp. 381–410; William S. Hastings, "Philadelphia in Microcosm,"

PMHB (April 1967), pp. 164-180; Michael McCarthy, "The Philadelphia Consolidation of 1854: A Reappraisal," *PMHB* (October 1986), pp. 531-584; Eli Kirk Price, *The History of Consolidation of the City of Philadelphia* (Philadelphia, 1873); J. Thomas Scharf and Thompson Westcott, *History of Philadelphia, 1609-1884*, 3 vols. (Philadelphia, 1884); Nicholas B. Wainwright, "The Age of Nicholas Biddle, 1825-1841," in *Philadelphia: A 300-Year History*, pp. 258-306; Sam Bass Warner, *The Private City: Philadelphia in Three Periods of Its Growth* (Philadelphia, 1968); John F. Watson, *Annals of Philadelphia and Pennsylvania in the Olden Times*, 3 vols. (Philadelphia, 1905); and Russell Weigley, "The Border City in the Civil War, 1854-1865," in *Philadelphia: A 300-Year History*, pp. 363-416. On the powerful Pennsylvania Railroad there are George H. Burgess and Miles C. Kennedy, *Centennial History of the Pennsylvania Railroad Company, 1846-1946* (Philadelphia, 1949); and James C. Ward, *J. Edgar Thomson, Master of the Pennsylvania* (Westport, CT, 1980).

For background on romantic nineteenth-century suburbs such as North Chestnut Hill, there are Jacques Barzun, *Classic, Romantic, and Modern* (Chicago, 1961); Catherine Beecher and Harriet Beecher Stowe, *The American Woman's Home* (New York, 1869); Andrew Jackson Downing, *The Architecture of Country Houses* (New York, 1850); Walter E. Houghton, *The Victorian Frame of Mind* (New Haven, CT, 1957); Daniel Walker Howe (ed.), *Victorian America* (Philadelphia, 1976); Kristine Ottensen Garrigan, *Ruskin on Architecture* (Madison, WI, 1973); Calder Loth and Julius Trousdale Sadler, Jr., *The Only Proper Style: Gothic Architecture in America* (Boston, 1975); Colleen McDannell, *The Christian Home in Victorian America, 1840-1900* (Bloomington, IN, 1986); Robert A. M. Stern, *Pride of Place* (Boston, 1986); John Stilgoe, *Borderland: Origins of the American Suburb, 1820-1839* (New Haven, CT, 1988); Calvert Vaux, *Villas and Cottages* (New York, 1853); and Gwendolyn Wright, *Building the Dream* (New York, 1981), pp. 96-113.

Sources on the early suburban period in Chestnut Hill are Francis Burke Brandt, *The Wissahickon Valley Within the City of Philadelphia* (Philadelphia, 1927); "Centennial History of St. Paul's Church, Chestnut Hill" (Philadelphia, 1956); John T. Faris, *Old Roads Out of Philadelphia* (Philadelphia, 1917); Gopsill's *City Directory* (1855); The Reverend T. W. Kretschmann, "Historical Sketch of the Evangelical Lutheran Christ Church (Philadelphia, 1896); The Reverend Thomas Middleton, O.S.A., "Some Memories of Our Lady's Shrine at Chestnut Hill, Pa.," *Records of the American Catholic Historical Society of Philadelphia* (1901); "One Hundredth Anniversary, Presbyterian Church of Chestnut Hill" (1952); *The Parish of Our Mother of Consolation Church* (Philadelphia, 1955); *Springside School, 1879-1979: One Hundred Years of Tradition and Change* (Philadelphia, 1979); and "Summit Street in Chestnut Hill" (Philadelphia, 1974). Hotchkin and Macfarlane, cited above, also contain much material on the early suburban period in Chestnut Hill.

Manuscript collections relating to the Houston/Woodward development in Chestnut Hill include the Houston Estate Papers at the Pennsylvania State Archives in Harrisburg; the Houston Estate file at the Architectural Archives of the University of Pennsylvania; and an assortment of documents and papers in the Alumni Records collection at the University of Pennsylvania Archives. The board minutes of the Pennsylvania Railroad, which shed light on Houston and his development of Chestnut Hill, may be found at the (Hagley) Eluterian Mills Historical Library near Wilmington, Delaware.

On the Houston/Woodward development per se, there are three pertinent works by David R. Contosta: "George Woodward, Philadelphia Progressive," *PMHB* (July 1987), pp. 341–370; *The Church of St. Martin-in-the-Fields, 1889–1989* (Philadelphia, 1988); and *A Philadelphia Family: The Houstons and Woodwards of Chestnut Hill* (Philadelphia, 1988). Studies on the architecture of Woodward's development in Chestnut Hill are Cynthia Ann McLoed, "Arts and Crafts Architecture in Suburban Philadelphia Sponsored by Dr. George Woodward" (University of Virginia master's thesis, 1979); and Mary Corbin Sies, "American Country House Architecture in the East and Midwest, 1877–1917" (University of Michigan doctoral dissertation, 1987).

George Woodward himself was a prolific writer. Relevant titles include "Another Aspect of the Quadruple House," *The Architectural Record* (July 1913), pp. 51–55; "Landlord and Tenant," *The Survey* (11 December 1920), pp. 389–391; *Memoirs of a Mediocre Man* (Philadelphia, 1935); and *The Pennsylvania Legislator*, 7 vols. (Philadelphia, 1932–1945). Other treatments of the Houston/Woodward developments appear in Harold D. Eberlein, "Pastorius Park and Its Residential Development," *Architectural Record* (January 1916); Christopher Gray, "The French Village," *House and Garden* (December 1983), pp. 82, 84, 86, 88; Horace Mather Lippincott, *A History of the Philadelphia Cricket Club* (Philadelphia, 1954); Matlack Price, "Architecture and the Housing Problem: Recent Work of Duhring, Okie, and Ziegler," *The Architectural Record* (September 1913), pp. 241–247; and George W. Sheldon, *Country Seats* (New York, 1887). Biographical information on Woodward's architects, as well as on other architects who designed structures in Chestnut Hill, may be found in Sandra L. Tatman and Roger W. Moss, *Biographical Dictionary of Philadelphia Architects* (Boston, 1985).

Also helpful in understanding the architecture and planning of the Houston/Woodward developments are Eileen Boris, *Art and Labor: Ruskin, Morris, and the Craftsman Ideal in America* (Philadelphia, 1986); Carol A. Christensen, *The American Garden City and the New Towns Movement* (Ann Arbor, MI, 1986); R. J. Clark (ed.), *The Arts and Crafts Movement in America, 1876–1916* (Princeton, 1972); Robert Fishman, *Urban Utopias in the Twentieth Century* (New

York, 1977); Walter Kidney, *The Architecture of Choice* (New York, 1974); Ebenezer Howard, *Garden Cities of Tomorrow* (Cambridge, MA, 1965); Roy Lubove, *The Urban Community: Housing and Planning in the Progressive Era* (Englewood Cliffs, NJ, 1967); Daniel Schaffer, *Garden Cities for America: The Radburn Experience* (Philadelphia, 1982); and William H. Wilson, *The City Beautiful Movement* (Baltimore, 1989). On the Colonial Revival, see Alan Axelrod (ed.), *The Colonial Revival in America* (New York, 1985); and Karal Ann Marling, *George Washington Slept Here: Colonial Revivals and American Culture* (Cambridge, MA, 1988).

Essential to studying social class in Chestnut Hill during the early decades of the twentieth century are the Philadelphia *City Directory*, the Philadelphia *Social Register*, and *Who's Who in America*. Complementing this material are a number of oral histories undertaken by the author over a five-year period, the subjects of which are listed in the acknowledgments. Also revealing are several memoirs: Eleanor Ward Altemus, *Chestnut Hill's Main Street Shopping, 1930-1935* (Bryn Mawr, PA, 1984); Mary Wickham Bond, *Ninety Years at Home in Philadelphia* (Bryn Mawr, PA, 1988); W. Thacher Longstreth, *Main Line Wasp* (New York, 1990); William U. McClenahan, *G.P.* (Philadelphia, 1974); Marian Willis Martin Rivinus, *A Full Life* (privately printed); and Ellen Taussig, *Wings on My Heels: A Newspaper Woman's Story* (Portsmouth, NH, 1986).

Helpful in placing this material in a larger perspective are three works by E. Digby Baltzell: *Philadelphia Gentlemen: The Making of a National Upper Class* (Philadelphia, 1979 [1958]); *The Protestant Establishment* (New York, 1974); and *Puritan Boston and Quaker Philadelphia* (New York, 1979). Also illuminating are Nathaniel Burt, *The Perennial Philadelphians* (Boston, 1963); William Cutler III and Howard Gillette, *The Divided Metropolis: Social and Spatial Dimensions of Philadelphia, 1800-1975* (Westport, CT, 1980); Irving Krauss, *Stratification, Class, and Conflict* (New York, 1976); and two works by Edward Pessen: *The Log Cabin Myth* (New Haven, CT, 1984) and *Three Centuries of Social Mobility in America* (Lexington, MA, 1974). See also David A. Gerber, *Anti-Semitism in American History* (Chicago, 1986); Sister Maria Kostka Logue, *Sisters of Saint Joseph of Philadelphia: A Century of Growth and Development, 1847-1947* (Westminster, MD, 1950); and John Lukacs, *A Sketch of the History of Chestnut Hill College* (Philadelphia, 1975).

The best sources on Chestnut Hill's improvement organizations during the Progressive Era and slightly thereafter are at the Germantown Historical Society, in its collections on Community Improvement Associations and the Germantown and Chestnut Hill Improvement Association. The latter collection contains the minutes of the Auxiliary Committee of the G&CHIA. The Germantown weekly newspapers also contain an abundance of news and information about the improvement associations, as do the Scrapbooks

(49 vols.) compiled by Jane Campbell. The memoirs and letters of Lydia Jane Clark (Boston, 1939) are useful in understanding the origins of the Chestnut Hill Community Center. The improvement association movement as a whole is explored in David P. Handlin, *The American Home: Architecture and Society, 1815–1915* (Boston, 1979), pp. 141–148; Warren E. Manning, "The History of Village Improvement in the United States," *Craftsman* (February 1904), pp. 423–435; Frederick Law Olmsted, Jr., "Village Improvement," *Atlantic* (June 1905), pp. 798–803; George E. Waring, Jr., *Village Improvement and Farm Villages* (Boston, 1877); and the already cited Wilson, *City Beautiful.*

On Philadelpha during the Progressive Era, there are Lloyd Abernethy, "Insurgency in Philadelphia, 1905," *PMHB* (January 1963), pp. 3–20; Philip S. Benjamin, "Gentlemen Reformers in the Quaker City, 1870–1912," *Political Science Quarterly* (1970), pp. 61–79; Gretchen A. Condran et al., "The Decline of Mortality in Philadelphia from 1870 to 1930: The Role of Municipal Services," *PMHB* (April 1984), pp. 165–168; Allen F. Davis and Mark H. Haller, *The Peoples of Philadelphia: A History of Ethnic Groups and Lower-Class Life, 1700–1940* (Philadelphia, 1973), pp. 175–201; Donald W. Disbrow, "Reform in Philadelphia Under Mayor Blankenburg, 1912–1916," *PH* (October 1960), pp. 379–396; Arthur Dudden, "Lincoln Steffens' Philadelphia," *PH* (1964), pp. 449–458; Bonnie Fox, "Unemployment Relief in Philadelphia, 1930–1931: A Study of the Depression's Impact on Voluntarism," *PMHB* (January 1969), pp. 86–107; Michael P. McCarthy, "The Unprogressive City: Philadelphia at the Turn of the Century," *PH* (October 1987), pp. 263–281; Clinton Rogers Woodruff, "Progress in Philadelphia," *The American Journal of Sociology* (November 1920), pp. 318–332; and George Woodward, "A Triumph of the People: The Story of the Downfall of the Political Oligarchy in Philadelphia," *Outlook* (December 2, 1905).

Works on urban progressivism of a more general nature are John D. Buenker, *Urban Liberalism and Progressive Reform* (New York, 1967); Robert M. Crunden, *Ministers of Reform* (New York, 1982); Allen F. Davis, *Spearheads of Reform: The Social Settlements and the Progressive Movement, 1890–1914* (New York, 1967); Kenneth Fox, *Better City Government: Innovation in American Urban Politics, 1850–1937* (Philadelphia, 1977); Michael P. McCarthy, "Urban Optimism and Reform Thought in the Progressive Era," *The Historian* (February 1989), pp. 239–262; William L. O'Neill, *The Progressive Years: America Comes of Age* (New York, 1975); Bruce M. Stave (ed.), *Urban Bosses, Machines, and Progressive Reformers* (Lexington, MA, 1971); Martin J. Schiesl, *The Politics of Municipal Reform in the Progressive Era, 1880–1920* (Berkeley, CA, 1977); and Robert W. Wiebe, *The Search for Order, 1877–1920* (New York, 1967). On the connections between the Progressive Era and the New Deal, see Ronald Feinman, *Twilight of Progressivism and the New*

Deal (Baltimore, 1981); and Otis L. Graham, Jr., *An Encore for Reform: The Old Progressives and the New Deal* (New York, 1973). On women and the Progressive Era there are Jill Conway, "Women Reformers and American Culture, 1870–1930," in *Our American Sisters: Women in American Life and Thought,* edited by Jean E. Friedman and William G. Slade (Boston, 1976), pp. 301–312; Allen F. Davis, "Welfare, Reform, and World War I," *American Quarterly* (Fall 1967), pp. 516–533; and Gwendolyn Wright, *Moralism and the Model Home* (Chicago, 1980). An excellent overview of American cities in the twentieth century is Jon C. Teaford, *The Twentieth-Century American City* (Baltimore, 1986).

Any study of postwar Chestnut Hill and the creation of quasi government must rely heavily upon the local newspapers, especially the *Herald* and the *Local.* Complementing these are minutes of the following: Chestnut Hill Community Association, Chestnut Hill Historical Society, and North Chestnut Hill Association, later called North Chestnut Hill Neighbors. Many of the above-mentioned oral histories are also concerned with this period. Lloyd Wells's "The Witness of Chestnut Hill's Mid-Century History, 1950–1975," two lectures delivered on 3 November and 10 November 1987, may be found in written form at the Chestnut Hill Historical Society. A sketch of the early history of the Chestnut Hill Community Association is Sidney Dexter, "Community Association: A History," *Local,* 23 October 1958. The establishment of the Chestnut Hill Historical Society is presented in Nancy Hubby, "The Evolution of an Historical Society," *Crier* (March 1967), pp. 20–21. For a treatment of the negotiations over the Morgan Tract/Market Square area up to 1960, see Thomas A. Bell, Negotiations Concerning the Development of the Morgan Tract, unpublished manuscript, CHHS. On community organizations in general during this time, there is Roger Ahlbrandt, Jr., *Neighborhoods, People, and Community* (New York, 1984). The history of historic preservation in Philadelphia is explored in Richard J. Webster, *Philadelphia Preserved* (Philadelphia, 1976).

On Philadelphia since 1945 there are E. Digby Baltzell, "The Protestant Establishment Revisited," *The American Scholar* (Autumn 1976), pp. 499–518; Peter Binzen, *The Cop Who Would be King* (Boston, 1979); John F. Bauman, "Expressways, Public Housing and Renewal: A Blueprint for Postwar Philadelphia, 1945–1960," *PH* (January 1990), pp. 44–65; Joseph S. Clark, Jr., and Dennis J. Clark, "Rally and Relapse, 1946–1968," in *Philadelphia: A 300-Year History,* pp. 649–703; J. R. Fink, "Reform in Philadelphia, 1946–1951" (Rutgers University, doctoral dissertation, 1971); Emily Jones (ed.), *Walter M. Philips: Philadelphia Gentleman Activist* (Swarthmore, PA, 1987); E. Havemann, "Rebirth of Philadelphia," *National Civic Review* (November 1962), pp. 538–542; J. Edward Janosik, "Suburban Balance of Power," *American Quarterly* (Summer 1955), pp. 123–141; Kirk Petshek, *The Challenge of Urban Reform: Politics and Programs in Philadelphia* (Philadelphia, 1973); John Lukacs, *Philadelphia: Patricians and Philistines, 1900–1950* (New York, 1981); and Stephanie G. Wolf, "The Bicentennial City, 1968–1982," in *Philadelphia: A 300-Year History,* pp. 704–734.

Index

Ohio State University Press

———————————

Text and jacket design by Bruce Gore, Gore Studios.

Type set in Cochin

by Brevis Press, Bethany, Connecticut.

Printed by Braun-Brumfield, Inc., Ann Arbor, Michigan.

The Cochin typeface was revived at the end of the nineteenth century by Debergny & Peignot typefoundry in France. Styled after work by Charles-Nicolas Cochin (The Younger), engraver to King Louis XV of France, it was designed from one of Pierre Simon Fournier's eighteenth-century types.